ONE WEEK LOAN

Renew Books on PHONE-it: 01443 654456

Books are to be returned on or before the last date below

Public Policy and Social Welfare
A Series Edited by the European Centre

 European Centre Vienna

Volume 31

Jenny Billings, Kai Leichsenring (Eds.)

Integrating Health and Social Care Services for Older Persons

Evidence from Nine European Countries

ASHGATE

Published by

Ashgate Publishing Limited
Gower House
Croft Road
Aldershot
Hants GU11 3HR
England

Ashgate Publishing Company
Suite 420
101 Cherry Street
Burlington, VT 05401-4405
USA

This publication was co-sponsored by:

THE EUROPEAN COMMISSION
THE 5TH FRAMEWORK PROGRAMME
QUALITY OF LIFE AND
MANAGEMENT OF LIVING RESOURCES
Key Action :: The Ageing Population and Disabilities
Contract No. QLK6-CT-2002-00227

Copy-editing and DTP: Willem Stamatiou
European Centre for Social Welfare Policy and Research
Berggasse 17, 1090 Vienna, Austria

British Library Cataloguing-in-Publication Data. A catalogue record for this book is available from the British Library.

ISBN 0-7546-4473-1

Printed by Facultas Verlags- und Buchhandels AG, Vienna, Austria

Contents

List of Figures and Tables

Figures

Introduction

Methodology

Tables

Introduction

Chapter 2

Preface

This book concludes an important piece of research on integrated care for older people in Europe. It pulls together different integrated care perspectives identifying the ways of approaching this type of care provision, provides evidence from nine European countries and demonstrates that comparative social research in Europe is progressing, despite the social policy backdrop of restricted resources being witnessed in recent times.

It is clear that there is growing interest in all activities linked to improve existing structures and practices of social and health care provision, in particular when it comes to the development of a new paradigm in long-term care. While long-term care hitherto had been more or less subordinate to the acute care model, with the increasing incidence of chronic and long-term care needs we can observe a shift towards more integrated and appropriate models to face this major challenge for ageing societies in the coming decades.

When we – a small group of researchers from Austria, Finland, France, Germany, Greece, Italy and the UK – started to develop a project proposal concerning the coordination of health and social care services during a workshop near Vienna in autumn 2000, we became increasingly aware that issues around 'integrating care services' were on the agenda of most European countries. Both in policy documents and in research activities, relevant projects and initiatives could be retrieved such as, for instance, the 'International Journal for Integrated Care' (www.ijic.org), the WHO European Office for Integrated Health Care Services (www.euro.who.int/ihb), and numerous model projects in most European countries. Also in the EU 5th Framework Programme, the Key Action 'The Ageing Population and Disabilities' had triggered some research activities on long-term care. In particular, the Thematic Network 'Managing the Integration of Services for Older People' (CARMEN) focused on similar issues to our research proposal.

Within the framework of EU policies, the communications of the EU Social Protection Committee on 'Future Strategies on Health Care and Care for the Elderly: Guaranteeing Accessibility, Quality and Financial Viability' were also encouraging our efforts.

However, when we finally submitted our proposal 'Providing Integrated Health and Social Care for Older People' (PROCARE) to the European Union's 5th Framework Programme (Quality of Life and Management of Living Resources, The Ageing Population and Disabilities), we had not expected to become an integral part of a real movement towards 'integrating health and social care services in Europe'. Only in October 2004, when almost 150 participants from all over Europe, Canada, Israel and the United States attended the final conference of PROCARE in Venice, did we become aware that this project, co-financed by the European Commission's 5th Framework Programme (2002-2004), was providing a major contribution to the definition and development of a new paradigm in long-term care for older people.

In-between these two events – the first preparatory workshop and the final public conference – our group of about 30 researchers from 10 organisations in the 9 participating countries (Austria, Denmark, Finland, France, Germany, Greece, Italy, the Netherlands and the United Kingdom) experienced a busy period. This included developing the team, the methods and the contents, as well as preparing and carrying out interviews and group discussions at selected sites. In addition, teams have been analysing, exchanging and confronting ideas and results during six project meetings. By means of thousands of email messages, preliminary findings have been disseminated and presentations prepared, following up important contacts and organising the final conference.

Through this publication we now have the opportunity to thank all those who made this project work: all partners from the participating research institutes, and staff and users of the selected model ways of working. As the coordinator of this project, I would like to thank in particular Executive Director Bernd Marin and all colleagues who were involved at the European Centre for Social Welfare Policy and Research: the web site (www.euro.centre.org/procare) was built up and regularly updated thanks to Barbara Waldschütz who also designed the logo and all posters of model ways of working. Willem Stamatiou was responsible for proof-reading and DTP of all publications. Erna Riemer (Head of Administration), Heidrun

Ernst, Martina Hofer-Moreno and Judith Schreiber guaranteed the financial administration, and Margit Wolf, apart from being a member of the Austrian research team together with Charlotte Strümpel, was an indispensable resource in solving all problems that occurred (or rather: not occurred) due to her thorough support during the lifetime of this project.

On behalf of the PROCARE consortium I would like to express our gratitude to all those who dedicated their time and energy. In particular, we are grateful to the European Commission's 5th Framework Programme and those who help administrate it as without the co-financing, no European project would be possible. We hope that the combined efforts of all people involved will contribute to further innovation in integrating health and social care services.

September 2005   Kai Leichsenring

Moments of Truth.
An Overview of Pathways to Integration and Better Quality in Long-Term Care

Kai Leichsenring, Günter Roth, Margit Wolf, Aris Sissouras

1   The Starting Point

Integrated care is not for everybody. What Leutz (1999) emphasised some years ago has certainly remained an adequate starting point to approach problems and solutions concerning long-term care for older people. However, more and more older people are experiencing the need for different kinds of health and social care services, thus creating a complex situation with respective management and coordination tasks to be accomplished by different organisations, professionals and family carers. These include, for instance, older people

- who are living alone in normal houses or apartments with functional incapacities after illness and disability, needing a range of different services,
- who are discharged from hospital with long-term care needs, who suffer from geronto-psychiatric and/or diseases of old age,
- who have chronic-degenerative diseases and are at risk of losing their autonomy.

Many of these situations become visible or occur at short notice. Such emergencies are the 'moments of truth' for social and health care systems with respect to their ability to respond to the needs of older people. With this comes the realisation that the central objective is to promote community care and to prevent care in nursing homes as long as possible. Specific problems that arise can include the following:

- The hospital discharges an older person in need of long-term care on Friday afternoon without prior warning to family members or community care services.
- The community care service is taking on an older person without a multidimensional needs assessment.
- The home help provider is providing services without any individual care plan.
- The home nurse recognizes problems of hygiene at the home of one of her patients but does not inform the home help service, neither does she call the family members living in another town.
- The GP does not inform community care services about a problematic situation and/or prescribes an X-ray to an older patient living alone without informing him/her about transportation services.

A central aim of PROCARE was to search for model ways of working that are able to overcome these and similar problems at the interface between health and social care systems, thus increasing the quality of life of all people involved in these kinds of processes. As one of the interviewed (Danish) managers put it: " ... every time you do something with frail older people – shifting from one system to another – that's where all the accidents occur, like misunderstandings, loss of information and all that".

Figure 1 sketches these interfaces that, as a whole, would constitute a 'chain of care services' within the emerging system of long-term care. The health care system with its differentiated and highly professionalized provisions provides in the first place acute care in hospitals or similar settings, and care by means of general practitioners and specialists – already characterised by a hierarchical gap and difficulties with interorganisational communication. While these primary and secondary care services are mostly funded by health care insurance or National Health Systems, a number of hybrid supply structures have developed in the residential and semi-residential care sector (short-term care, day care) with mostly medicalised approaches and mixed personnel including both medically trained staff and social care professionals. In many countries these services are only slowly getting mainstreamed with regular funding. Short-term care facilities are often part of residential care facilities that, in most countries, are the main pillar of the social care system with less professionalised personnel, and discretional entitlements with local inequalities concerning availability and access. Both systems, however, have expanded also to the community, where (medical) 'home care' is provided by nurses, nursing aides and similar health care professionals, while (social) 'home help' is provided by home helpers and similar social care professionals. Cooperation or integrated working between health and social care professionals might take place horizontally, such as between home care and home help. In this case, we usually refer to this as community care, especially if other (social) services such as housing and meals-on-wheels are added. Vertically integrated working seems to be more difficult to operationalise, such as at the interfaces between hospital and community care (including the GP) or between nursing homes and community care.

Figure 1:   The Interfaces between Health and Social Care Systems

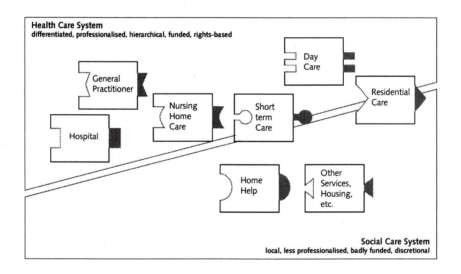

All the 18 selected model ways of working in the nine participating countries have developed with the aim of improving cooperation, integration and joint working in relation to at least one of these interfaces where conflicts and misunderstandings arise, bottlenecks and waiting-times materialise, and where dissatisfaction and frustration of users can grow.

However, not all model ways of working are focusing on the same interface, and only one model has tried to integrate the whole range of potential services, following the 'consolidated direct service model' (Zawadski, 1983; Davies, 1992; 1996). What can be observed is rather a step-wise approach to integration, based on model projects and a move towards what could be called 'pathways to integrated care'. Before presenting some more details, however, we would like to present some basic information about the background and context of PROCARE.

2   The Aims and Achievements of PROCARE

"Providing Integrated Health and Social Care for Older Persons" (PRO-CARE) was a research project co-financed by the 5th Framework Programme of the European Commission (Quality of Life and Management of Living Resources, The Ageing Population and Disabilities) carried out between April 2004 and February 2005. The aims were, above all, to explore the realm of integrated care in Europe and to find out about different approaches towards what has been described as one of the most prominent shortcomings in European health and welfare systems – the improvement of service delivery at the interface between the health system on the one hand and the system of social care for older persons on the other. In a first phase, the participants from Austria, Denmark, Finland, France, Germany, Greece, Italy, the Netherlands, and the UK had provided national overviews about the state of the art in innovative practices of integrated care, based on literature reviews and general information gathered with at least five model ways of working in each country (see Leichsenring / Alaszewski, 2004).

In a second phase, two model ways of working were selected in each country to analyse organisational features, different approaches and framework conditions of most advanced 'pioneers' of integrated care in the selected countries. These analyses were carried out by means of interviews and focus group discussions with all actors involved (for methodological details see Billings, in this book). Based on this material, transversal analysis of most prevalent issues and solutions in integrated care development were accomplished by transnational teams. Their results are gathered in this book.

3   An Overview of 18 Model Ways of Working

As already mentioned, model ways of working were considered to approach problems that arise at least at one of the interfaces between health and social care delivery in long-term care for older persons. The 'pathways to integrated care' are manifold and so are the financing and legal framework conditions of the 18 selected models in the 9 countries. For instance, in all PROCARE countries health care is a matter of national legislation under the responsibility of central government (see Table 1). While in most cases the ministries for health are also responsible for long-term care (LTC) and social care – as in Germany, France, Finland, Italy and UK – there are various or divided responsibilities in Austria, Denmark, Greece and the Netherlands. While LTC in Germany, France and the Netherlands is mainly financed by social insurance schemes, there are welfare regimes in which LTC is primarily funded by taxes like in Denmark, Finland, Italy and the UK. In Austria and Greece we find both sources and thus a mixed system of financing LTC which can also be found in Greece. While a special funding system for LTC was introduced in Austria, Germany and the Netherlands, this has not been the case in the other PROCARE countries. Social care in Europe is mainly financed by (means-tested) social assistance schemes at the regional or local level. Though a tendency to decentralisation was registered also in European health care systems (European Commission, 2003) it must be pointed out that social welfare systems remain much more decentralised than health care systems. Only the UK shows a somewhat higher degree of centralisation in health and social care systems but decentralisation efforts have been witnessed in this country since 1993. Decentralisation is also prevailing in Denmark and Finland, while in Austria, France, Germany, Greece and Italy there is a divided responsibility between the central state, regional governments and municipalities.

Table 1: Overview of Responsibilities and Ways of Financing Health Care, Long-Term Care and Social Care in PROCARE Countries

	Health Responsibilities	Ways of Financing	Social Care, LTC Responsibilities	Ways of Financing
A	Federal Ministry of Women and Health, Provinces (Länder)	Social Health Insurance, Taxes, User Contributions	Federal Ministry of Social Security, Generations and Consumer Protection, Provinces (Länder), Municipalities	Long-term care allowance, Social Assistance, Taxes
D	Federal Ministry of Health and Social Security, Provinces (Länder), Municipalities	Social Health Insurance, Taxes, User Contributions	Federal Ministry of Health and Social Security, Provinces (Länder), Municipalities	LTC Insurance, Social Assistance (means-tested), Taxes, User Contributions
DK	Ministry of Interior and Health, Counties, Municipalities	Taxes (national and regional)	Ministry of Social Affairs, Municipalities	Taxes (national and regional)
EL	Ministry of Health and Welfare, Regions	Social Health Insurance, State Subsidies, Taxes, User Contributions	Ministry of Health and Welfare, Ministry of Labour and Social Insurance, Regions	State Subsidies, Taxes, Social Assistance, Social Insurance, User Contributions, Donations etc.
F	Ministry of Health and Social Security, Provinces (Départements)	Social Health Insurance, Taxes, User contributions	Ministry of Health and Social Security, Counties	Social Assistance (means-tested), Social Insurance, National Independence Fund, Taxes, User contributions
FIN	Ministry of Social Affairs and Health, Municipalities	Taxes, State subsidies (national and regional), Social Health Insurance, User contribution	Ministry of Social Affairs and Health, Municipalities	Social Welfare: Municipal Taxation (64%), State subsidies (24%), User contributions (12%)
I	Ministry of Health, Provinces (Regions), Municipalities	NHS, State subsidies, Taxes (national, regional and local), Contributions of employers and self-employed workers, User contributions	Ministry of Health, Provinces (Regions), Municipalities	NHS, State subsidies, Taxes (national, regional and local), Contributions of employees and employers, User contributions

NL	Ministry of Health, Welfare and Sport, Municipalities	Social Health Insurance, State Subsidies, Taxes, User contributions	Ministry of Health, Welfare and Sport, Ministry of Social Affairs, Provinces, Municipalities	LTC Insurance, Regional State Subsidies, Taxes, User contributions
UK	Ministry of Health	Taxes (national), National Insurance Contributions, User Contributions	Ministry of Health	Social Assistance (means-tested), Social Services Department, Attendance Allowances, Taxes, User Contributions

As a consequence, it is important to underline that the 18 model ways of working analysed by the PROCARE national teams were financed in different ways that are summarized in Table 2. The variety of financing concepts regarding model ways of working is apparently reflecting the varied financial situation of health and social care systems in the participating EU countries (see for details Alber, 1995; Comas-Herrera/Wittenberg, 2003; Kautto, 2002; European Commission, 2001; 2003; Pacolet et al., 1999; Jacobzone, 1999; OECD, 2005).

Table 2: Fragmented Financing Responsibilities of Model Ways of Working

	National sources of funding (Social Insurance, Ministries, ...)	Regional sources of funding (provinces, ...)	Local sources of funding (municipalities, hospitals, ...)	Client fees (LTC Allowances, private funds...)
Austria	◆		◆	◆
Denmark			◆	
Finland			◆	◆
France	◆	◆	◆	◆
Germany	◆	◆		
Greece	◆		◆	
Italy			◆	
The Netherlands		◆		
United Kingdom	◆	◆	◆	◆

The basic financing and framework conditions differ in the model ways of working due to the individual basic structures of financing in the countries.

19

At the same time, these structures also influence the depth of integration, the types of coordination/integration that are being addressed and the steadiness of each single model. A short description of these models is provided in the following while some more details can be found in the Annex:

- *Austria (A1) – Integrated Social and Health Care District in Hartberg (Styria):* This model is based on horizontal integration of social and health care professionals in community care, with strong efforts towards the organisation of intermediate care (the hospital-community care interface). With a yearly budget of about 1.3 million Euros its financing depends on the Regional Hospital Financing Body for 30%, one third is funded by the 50 municipalities, 4% by the social health insurance for 'medical home care' and the remaining costs are covered by client fees (out-of-pocket contributions, mainly covered from long-term care allowances). This complicated financing model shows already that, what has been achieved – with a lot of energy by the promoting agencies – still has not been realised as a mainstream model in Austria. The two different financing systems for health care and social care do not allow for the development of 'integrated care' on a broader regional or national level.

- *Austria (A2) – Discharge management at the Hartmann Hospital (Vienna):* The model is working towards solutions at the interface between hospital and community care, focusing on discharge management (vertical integration). The discharge management takes place in different hospital wards as the heads of wards refer the patients to the discharge manager. Hospital staff delegate the responsibility for organising and coordinating the provision of home care for the patients while they are still in hospital to the discharge manager. In 2002, 389 patients were consulted concerning their discharge from the hospital, on average about 32 per month. The hospital carries the costs for the infrastructure (office, telephone, fax, computer) as well as the personnel and further organisational costs for the discharge manager. The Viennese Red Cross offers regular team meetings as well as advice when needed.

- *France – Local Information and Gerontological Coordination Centre (CLIC) in Chalûs (F1) and Phalempin (F2):* Both models' coordination efforts are focused on the link between hospital and community care. Furthermore, they represent a single point of entry to long-term care by advising, assessing needs, compiling personalised care plans, implementing, monitoring and adapting those care plans. These centres are financed through mixed funding mechanisms as they are financed by about one third from the State (Ministry), one third comes from the County Council and the remaining third from municipalities, the hospital fund or other sources. The diverse programmes for financing coordination thus remain a source of confusion for providers and beneficiaries in France.

- *Finland – Integrated home care for elderly people living at home in Helsinki (FIN1) and Espoo (FIN2):* This is horizontal integration (integrated assessment, care planning and provision/evaluation case management) with partly vertical integration (the hospital-home care interface). The first visit at the older person's home is always by a multiprofessional team, cooperation between home-help and home nursing services. If necessary, the hospital discharge nurse and a physiotherapist are involved. The model is publicly organised and financed. Municipalities in Finland finance their services with tax revenues (70%), state subsidies (20%) and client fees (10%). In this area more than 10% of older persons above 75 receive permanent home care.

- *Germany (D1) – Home Care Nürnberg – Praxisnetz Nürnberg:* The model tries to bridge the gap between different disciplines in medical and social care via case management. The highly separated and fragmented financing structure in Germany with incentives for the various providers to shift costs and benefits from one area to another makes it difficult for the model to remain viable beyond project financing.

- *Germany (D2) – Geronto-psychiatric-geriatric association in Oberspreewald-Lausitz:* A coordinator is paid by the association to improve collaboration and communication between out-patient and in-patient providers. Also this German project was mainly financed as a model project by the Federal Ministry for Family, Senior Citizens, Women and Youth. Meanwhile the promoters are trying to cover their costs in different ways, for example by means of contributions from the member organisations and the administrative district.

- *Greece (EL1) – Open Care Centres for Older People (KAPI) in Alimos, Marousi, Ilioupoli and Nea Philadelphia:* This is an example of preventative social care centres with aspects of horizontal integration. The Open Care Centres are staffed by a team comprising social workers, medical staff, visiting nurses, occupational and physical therapists and family assistants. The Centres provide a range of services to any older person, such as preventive medical care, physiotherapy, assistance (also to their

21

family), special assistance for lonely persons, organised entertainment and participation in various social activities.

- *Greece (EL2) – Help at home for elderly persons in Kifissia, Nikaia and Nea Ionia:* Horizontal integration in this model consists of social services (consulting and psychosocial support, information concerning the rights of the elderly and links to health, welfare and insurance agencies), health care services (medical and nursing care, health education and prevention, medication prescription, physiotherapy at home, accompaniment to see the physician), as well as family assistance (home and personal care, feeding, chores, accompanying, etc). The social workers, nurses and assistants who provide services operate as a coordinated team and are fully aware of the users' conditions. The model is financed and organised in the framework of a nation-wide cooperation of the Ministry of Health and Welfare, the Ministry of the Interior and the Municipalities.

- *Italy – Working Unit of Continuous Care (WUCC) in the Province of Vicenza (I1) and Single Point of Access to Home Care in Empoli, Tuscany Region (I2):* The Italian national legislation provides guidelines for integrated health and social care that have to be implemented by the regional governments in cooperation with various other stakeholders. The fragmented legal framework of health and social care as well as regional and organisational barriers reveal a strong differentiation in local supply, territorial divides and unequal service supply. The two model ways of working were only possible because health care staff took the initiative. For instance, the WUCC (I1) is totally financed by the Local Health Unit as part of the Italian National Health System.

- *The Netherlands (NL1) – Home care facility "Zijloever" in Leiden:* The facility focuses on horizontal integration of social care provision, including services for well-being, and partial coordination with GP's and hospitals. The yearly budget of about 2 million Euro for financing the project is mainly covered by the Exceptional Medical Expenses Act (AWBZ). This allows for personnel costs for concrete, tangible services to be reimbursed by the regional AWBZ agency so that the continuation of the model depends on the provision of these concrete services. Thus it will be difficult to maintain coordination activities as funding or even financial incentives for collaboration are lacking.

- *The Netherlands (NL2) – Chain of care for the elderly in Kerkrade, Landgraaf and Simpelveld:* This model consists of three components: the assessment agency (RIO), the Bureau for Care Allocation and Referral (BCAR) and the organisations that provide care (horizontal and vertical integration). Also in this case mixed funding can be found which in particular results in unclear responsibilities for funding coordination activities.

- *United Kingdom (UK1) – Limes Livingstone Integrated Care Project (LLICP), Dartford (Kent):* The model provides 'intermediate care', i.e. multidisciplinary rehabilitation care, which is geared towards assisting older people regain their independence and return to living in their own homes (vertical and horizontal integration). It has a split budget and only some jointly funded posts. Continuing problems of financial and contractual differences between the health and social care organisations involved meant that the goal of true integration (joint funding, recruitment and shared staff) had not yet been achieved. The negotiation process continues, however.

- *United Kingdom (UK2) – Shepway Community Assessment and Rehabilitation Team (CART):* This is another 'intermediate care' initiative, designed to provide rehabilitation care to older people in the community and prevent hospital admission or hasten hospital discharge. Funding for the service was uncertain, however, because of national policy changes in the structure of health care provision.

Following this short list of all selected model ways of working we would like to highlight some of the most significant interfaces between health and social care. The inconveniences that occurred at these interfaces, respectively, became the rationale for the specific focus of each single model way of working.

3.1 The Interface between Nursing Home Care and Other Social Services

A first step towards coordination and integration consists of bringing together professionals who are working in the community, visiting care-dependent people in their households. This type of integration has become relatively widespread with persistent and mainstream modes of service delivery. In fact, we can find integrated community care models like this in Finland as well as in the UK, the Netherlands, Austria, France, Germany and Greece. Usually, the merger of two separate organisations that had provided nursing care at home and home help (help in daily living, dressing, personal hygiene, eating) is the starting point for further networking with cleaning services, recreational activities and other support services (meals on wheels, transport, financial support etc). Based on a multidimensional needs assessment (see below), a shared individual care plan and common objectives, a range of different professionals works together to meet users' needs. Depending on the local infrastructure, respective models put more emphasis on rehabilitation with an integrated multi-professional team of its own (e.g. CART, UK2) or on the coordination between the organisations involved (F1 and F2).

As a classical example for this kind of horizontal integration we might consider the integrated home care model in Helsinki (FIN1, but see also FIN2), consisting of a multi-professional team of 6-10 nurses, home helpers, a home-care nurse and a chief home care officer (case manager) in a district of 350 clients. Following a first visit to assess needs at the home of the older person, with family members present if possible, the case manager sets up a care and service plan (medication, amount and frequency of home care services to be provided by the different profession, rehabilitation plan etc.). The 'good' practice of this model is in the fact that every client has his/her 'defined' carer, i.e. the team tries to respond to the user's claim for continuous care by the same providers, rather than different professionals stepping in and out of their homes.

A similar approach has been chosen to develop home care in Greece. 'Help at Home' (EL2) is a national programme with more than 280 programmes in more than 250 Greek municipalities. For instance, in the Municipality of Kifissia – a municipality in the wider Athens area with about 40,000 inhabitants almost 23% of which are above the age of 60 – one social worker, two nurses, one family helper and the GP support 43 older people in need of care and 20 family carers. They help the older people living alone feel more secure and contribute to the reduction of family carers' stress by providing home care, including medical tests and medication.

In Finland, France and Greece, legal regulations were introduced on a national level to coordinate and/or integrate home care services. It is interesting to note that this pattern can be observed in most countries – national regulations help develop regional and local service structures, presumably due to the fact that local policies are too weak to introduce this kind of innovation.

While in Finland and Denmark services are mainly provided by local public organisations, in France and Greece a mix of different providers (public, private non-profit) calls for coordination rather than integration of services, thus complicating the task:

24

"... it is important to overcome the interests of each single association or entity in order to serve together the interest of the older people. This seems to be the most difficult to achieve." (F2, key worker)

The model ways of working show, however, that these obstacles can be overcome by continuous reflection and by providing time for mutual exchange, learning and the development of common rules. This process might be time-consuming but, in the end, it serves to achieve mutually agreed objectives:

"I think we all work together – nurses, occupational therapists, physiotherapists, care manager – towards one goal, which is maintaining that client where they are and trying to progress them on to maximum independence." (UK2, key worker)

"The team has an ethos ... and because they spend so much time with each other, they are learning from each other." (EL2)

To summarise, the coordination of different professions and providers in community care (home care, home help) should be considered as an indispensable first step towards integrated care delivery. This development can be retrieved in most countries, though with different accents on country-specific requirements.

25

3.2   The Interface between Acute Care and Long-Term Care

The classical case for a bottleneck between health and social care systems becomes evident in the interface between the hospital and long-term care facilities. Different values, objectives and economic interests are the basis of a difficult relationship: while hospitals' main aim is to cure patients, long-term care facilities underline the principle of care; while hospitals are technologically most advanced and differentiated entities with superior unitary costs, long-term care facilities are much less professionalised, less differentiated and less costly. Thus hospitals have often been characterized as auto-referential systems with restricted abilities to network and cooperate. A special role at this interface is being undertaken by the GP who, professionally, is part and parcel of the health care system (also in communicating with hospitals) while, functionally, s/he might be characterized increasingly as a most important player in community (long-term) care.

In our study, at least four model ways of working (A2, DK2, I1, UK1) are particularly focusing on this interface (discharge management) in order to increase continuity between hospital and community care, to improve the process from cure to long-term care with respective rehabilitation efforts and by providing a kind of "buffer" between short-term and long-term care.

> "As an extramural (community) service, we soon saw the classical problem, that there was no interface between intra- and extramural (hospital and community) services. For example, many hospitals discharge their patients on Friday at 10 a.m. and then they do not receive appropriate support over the weekend." (A1, staff member)

In the UK, 'Community Assessment and Rehabilitation Teams' (CART) have been developed to overcome such inconveniences, with some teams having been in place for up to 20 years. These teams are usually hosted within hospitals. The teams are made up of multi-disciplinary professionals including physiotherapists, nurses, occupational therapists and rehabilitation support workers, and a social services care manager is often attached to them. CART team members visit clients in the community following referral, and provide rehabilitation input in the client's own home, usually on a short-term basis (approximately 4 weeks). Shepway CART (UK2) was established in 1999, with the aim of maximising the older person's independence at home, and of preventing hospital admission. For example, if an older person is becoming less mobile or prone to falls, then the CART team can offer rehabilitation support. The CART team also becomes involved in speeding up a discharge from hospital, helping people to feel safe and become independent at home. A parallel development in the Shepway area has been the formation of a 'Rapid Response' team. This team also attends older people at home, but is designed to offer short-term (up to 2 weeks) nursing and care support to older people who become unwell at home. The rapid response team can provide care for up to 24 hours a day, and can help older people with dementia, or who have a carer crisis. CART and Rapid Response work closely together, providing a range of specialist nursing, medical and rehabilitation care to older people in their own homes.

In Germany, a model in the Land Brandenburg (D2) shows that providers themselves can develop structures and methods to overcome barriers to collaboration. The Gerontopsychiatric-Geriatric Alliance (GPGV) in the district of Oberspreewald-Lausitz – almost 140,000 inhabitants of which 27.6% are 60 years and older – consists of two hospitals, nine out-patient services, seven residential and nursing homes and two information and counselling centres that employed one coordinator to improve the cooperation between all facilities involved in the care process. Thus, collaborative structures have been agreed upon by establishing a common knowledge-base and developing activities and innovative care provision, in particular for people suffering from dementia. The mutually agreed and developed transition form has proven to be one of the most useful methods to guarantee continuous care and cooperation between the different services/facilities. The form is used to submit basic patient information as well as special data concerning geronto-psychiatric diseases beyond the medical treatment levels.

An important feature of these efforts, also included in a number of other models (NL2, I2, D1) is the clear statement that coordination/integration is a task on its own, with respective skills and methods that have to be developed and applied. 'Coordination as a profession' is the motto of most case or care managers whom we met and interviewed during the empirical phase of this study. Their task is to intensify and improve communication between different providers, to assess the needs of clients, to share knowledge about clients, and to negotiate with health and social care services on behalf of clients – always with the aim of reducing unnecessary or 'preventable' hospital admissions. The fact that more and more often case or care managers are employed by hospitals, shows that it is in the interests of 'enlightened' hospital managers to satisfy patients' needs and expectations. A major step forward is made if the organisations and people involved succeed in defining procedures or protocols for the discharge and admission processes:

> "There is a written protocol explaining how to involve the different Hospital Units into the process. The unit to which the older person is admitted sends a form to the Geriatric Unit, asking them for the needs assessment." (I1, key worker)

> "(...) the Local Health Agency 11 of Empoli developed a protocol for 'protected discharge' from hospital. In this protocol the following aspects are defined: objectives, procedures of discharge from hospital, criteria for the activation of the home care service, target group of intervention, used resources, information instruments, criteria of check-up, etc." (I2, key worker)

The collaboration between different professional groups is a constitutional feature also of these models. Depending on the respective client's needs, medical, therapeutic, nursing, psychosocial and social care staff are involved. However, traditional hierarchies, professional prejudices and sometimes even legal regulations often impede further progress:

> "The care situation concerning the out-patient section as well as the interface with the in-patient section and between the different professions is marked by disintegration and discontinuity. In practice, the conditions for a care process

> going beyond the different sections and professions and thus towards a kind of client-centred care are not given due to a lack of legal and structural framework conditions as well as poor motivation and other barriers depending on the professional status. However, in legal terms integrated care is now being promoted [in Germany by the Long-Term Care Insurance] by means of incentives for a common budget administration, which is the basis for an effective collaboration of different professional groups in the future." (D1, key worker 1)

> "In my opinion, the collaboration was, in part, excellent, but there were also prejudices against other professional groups, competition and not enough openess." (D1, key worker 2)

To date, many users still consider it a "wonderful surprise" if, coming home from hospital, "home care has already been arranged and adaptations needed in my home have been implemented" (FIN2, users 7 and 12). In the future, many patients will take it for granted that such services exist as part of a defined quality of health and social care services. Thus, quality assurance programmes as well as accreditation mechanisms for service providers will increasingly ask for coordinated and integrated procedures at the hospital-community care interface.

3.3 The Access Problem: One-Stop-Shops, Multidimensional Assessment and Guidance

Problems can arise not only when a patient becomes long-term care dependent after a hospital stay, but also when an older person still living at home develops chronic physical or mental illness. With the increasing occurrence of dementia and related diseases, spouses, other family members and the person him/herself do not often know what services are available to them. Again, the GP would have an important role to play; this role can however be compromised through lack of knowledge or lack of time. Thus, users and their families often are referred from one service to another, which is frustrating and time-consuming for all parties involved. Therefore, model ways of working have developed in several countries to overcome these problems at the interface between health and social care. On the one hand, models such as these provide users and their families with an overview of services as well as access to those that fit best with the needs of the user. These services can also be set up as gate-keeping agencies to steer demand towards supply. Both approaches seem legitimate if sustainable service delivery is a policy objective.

In practice, solutions are represented by one-stop-windows such as the 'Single Point of Access' in Empoli (I2) where citizens are able to address their needs directly. Requests for home care are accumulated and interventions are coordinated, which helps to facilitate the integration and coordination of services between hospitals and the community. Such access points have to be based on agreements between the different stakeholders involved – in the Italian case the Local Health Agency and the regions. In addition, it has proven useful to combine the single point of access with a centralised information system, that is a database with relevant information of all clients that have been taken on. Data are available on-line for all professionals in the region to facilitate collaboration between hospital and community care. Thus, administration of long-term care clients is made easier as data about the citizen are collected and entered only once, and unnecessary communication between providers and/or professionals is reduced.

Another example of systems that reduce information and access problems is the 'Local Information and Gerontological Co-ordination Centres' (CLIC) in France. They inform, advise and support citizens by assessing their needs in multiprofessional teams. Following this procedure they compile a personalised care plan for each person and monitor its implementation with respective team members. Even those CLICs that are not providing hands-on services have shown that, with a small and dedicated team, they are able to create a 'gerontological culture' in a given area, facilitating the continuity of care services in the community and serving as mediators between clients, providers and professionals.

3.4   *Towards A Consolidated Direct Service Model*

Whether or not 'real integration' of health and social care services can be realised in a stable organisation providing for the complete range of long-term care needs of a given population is dependent upon the political, cultural and economic context. First of all, due to the existing fragmentation of health and social care systems in most countries, the different agencies and services may not be ready to accept a unique, vertically integrated decision-making authority, such as a 'Consolidated Direct Service Model' as described in the literature (Zawadski, 1983; Davies; 1992). Secondly, due to the attendant concern that social services would either lose their identity and autonomy or become enmeshed in the 'medical model', there seems to be opposition to 'real integration', especially if it occurs under the roof of a health care agency (Frossard et al., 2004). It should therefore be emphasised that the model way of working in the small Danish Municipality of Skævinge (DK1) seems to be dependent on special circumstances that include explicit long-term care policies at the national level, co-ordinated strategies on regional and district levels, and a clear determination on the local policy level. Furthermore, 'bridge builders' and 'pioneers' have been able to introduce a change process based on leadership, dialogue and communication, rather than on professional hierarchies and narrow-mindedness.

When the project was launched in 1984, it aimed to provide integrated health and social/personal care on a 24-hour basis irrespective of the housing status of the citizen – this was and still is being realised by about 136 professionals (FTE) from 13 different professional groups who are employed by the municipality. The Health Centre thus constitutes a single point of contact for potential users in the municipality. Services for those who need them are coordinated by a case manager. Staff are applying the concept of self-care and, generally, a preventative approach to care. Results of this model are definitely convincing, both in terms of quality of life and in terms of financial and economic outcomes:

- Surveys conducted in Skævinge in 1985 and again in 1997 indicate that the subjective well-being among older people has improved subsequent to the introduction of the integrated care scheme.
- Even though the number of older people has increased significantly over the past 20 years the operational expenditures have decreased over the period.
- There is no waiting time for apartments in the Health Centre or for domestic health and social care services.
- The preventative efforts have resulted in a surplus of capacity that has been used mainly to establish an intermediate care facility at the Health Centre in order to prevent unnecessary hospital admissions. Consequently, the number of days at hospitals has been reduced by 30-40% for all citizens in the municipality.
- Over the last 10 years no citizen from the municipality of Skævinge staying in a hospital had to wait for discharge after having finished treatment as the municipality has been able to take those citizens 'home' and care for them either in the intermediate care facility at the Health Centre or in the citizens' own home.
- Though costs of about 900 € per inhabitant per year are to be financed, i.e. a budget of € 5.2 million per year, the municipality's use of and

expenditure to the national health insurance is below the average of all other municipalities in the county of Frederiksborg.

The example shows that integrated care is feasible in practice if specific preconditions are fulfilled. For instance, on the political level it is useful to dispose of national, regional and local policies that are geared to the area of long-term care, and respective administrative structures. However, structures both at the political and 'shop-floor' levels are starting to emerge – with respective 'labour pains' in terms of new job descriptions, shared values and objectives, professional cultures, quality development and change processes.

In the following we would like to briefly describe the role of the European Union in tackling these issues on a political level and in terms of respective research activities.

4   Policies and Research to Promote Integrated Care in Europe

Within the relatively limited development of social policies promoted by the European Union, growing concern has been expressed during the past few years regarding health and social care services for older people. This can be seen within the social policy and social protection agendas, as well as the research agenda.

Concerning the former, the increasing problems and common challenges that the Member States are facing, from factors such as changing structures in the family and work market and the dramatic demographic changes, led the Commission to initiate the debate in 1995 on the 'Future of Social Protection' and produce the Communication *"Modernizing and Improving Social Protection in the EU"* (Com [97] 10) in March 1997 which announced four major priorities for action: employment, pensions, social inclusion and "high quality and sustainable health and social care". But the decisive political push for concrete actions on social protection came in March 2000 with the start of the well-known Lisbon Process. This process suggested new instruments to promote such policies, notably the 'Open Method of Coordination' as the driving force behind the development of European policies and cooperation between the Member States in the social policy realm.

As far as the research agenda is concerned, ageing has been one of the focal points in the Framework Programmes for Research and Development (FP). In particular FP5 (1998-2002) devoted a special Key Action of research on ageing in six distinct areas of interest, for instance on the modes of care and the management of care services. Namely, PROCARE was one of these projects in FP 5 (Quality of Life and Management of Living Resources, Key Action 'The Ageing Population and Disabilities', Contract nr. QLK6-2002-00227).

In this concluding section we will briefly summarise the developments at the European Union level, regarding the policies on ageing and long-term care for older people which have indeed reached a well-advanced stage and include:

- first, the policies designed and being promoted within the general strategy of the social policy and *social protection* model – within the Employment and Social Affairs Directorate (DG V) and,
- second, the strengthening of the *research content* and perspective on ageing – within the scope of the Research Programme (DG XII).

32

4.1   The Social Policy and Social Protection Perspective

Care for older people has been at the centre of the Lisbon process from the beginning which, as we noted, provided the momentum for the development of a European model of policies in the field of social protection. Obviously, the demography of ageing and the problems associated with this, stood out as one of the major reasons for developing such a strategy specifically for older people. Since 2000 there has been a notable series of initiatives on this subject, in which integrated types of care provision are proposed. Reflecting on the work which has been accomplished thus far on policies for older people it is stated, for example, in one of the most recent Communications of the Commission (Com 2004) that "the response to the needs of this population group will include developing a wide range of services, including care at home, which will be chosen by ever more people, and specialized institutions, as well as closer coordination between care providers often working in isolation (intensive care, primary care and social services). Thus the social protection systems need to be reformed in an integrated and coordinated way to meet the challenges. Coordination should be streamlined, contributing to strengthening the political messages in favour of the modernization of these systems of protection" (Com [2004] 304 final).

The process of building social protection policy resulted in two streams of action dealing with care for older people. On the one hand, specific action on the issue of 'Health and Social Care for Older People' has been taken forward by promoting the 'open method of coordination'. On the other hand, long-term care for older people is being examined as one of the targets considered by the development of National Action Plans for Social Inclusion (NAP/Incl).

Health and Social Care Policies for Older People

The Gothenburg European Council called on the Commission to produce a Communication and make suggestions, after examining thoroughly the issue of 'health and social care for older people'. The respective report as of May 2001 (European Commission, 2001) identified three principles which were suggested as a basis for reforms in long-term care: access to care for all, high-quality care, and financial sustainability of the care system.

This Communication raised widespread interest and was generally well received by Member States. As a corollary, during the Barcelona European Council in March 2002 the decision was taken that the Commission and the Council should "examine more thoroughly the questions of accessibility, quality and financial sustainability of the system of health care and care for older people". The Commission proceeded by initiating an intermediate stage of collecting data from Member States, through a specially designed questionnaire. The exercise was to identify policies in practice and national activities with respect to care for older people as well as the type and forms of care schemes.

The analysis and comparisons of policies and care practices amongst the Member States showed little of what we could define as integrated approaches for health and social care for older people. There are, of course, countries such as Ireland and Finland where integration of policies is more discernible. In Ireland for instance, an Integrated Services Process is in operation at the level of a Regional Board to ensure that "inter-sectoral and inter-disciplinary collaboration and integration of modes of care is promoted to achieve the highest level of health and social gain". Similar examples can be found in the Finnish Health and Social Affairs System where the integration approach is being applied and is promoting active policies and actions particularly at the local level (municipalities) where primary health care and social services are provided.

Following this exercise a synthesis report was produced in March 2003 as a Joint Report of the Commission and of the Council: 'Supporting National Strategies for the Future of Health Care and Care for Older People' (European Commission, 2003). The report strongly emphasised that certain problems are common to all systems:

- inequalities and ongoing access difficulties, despite the universal access that is guaranteed in principle;
- insufficient provision of quality services compared to the needs of the population, in some cases with excessive waiting times; and,
- growing financial imbalances.

As to proposals for further action, the report could only bring forward the general 'advice' on policies and systems of care with an integrated perspective – by noting that these policies should be 'respecting the national choices in the care system' at all times. The Communication, however, is widely stressing the use of the 'open method of communication', through which "common objectives will be identified and by respecting the diversity of the national situations and competences, explore ways of cooperation in this field via exchanges of information and good practice and the development of comparable indicators". PROCARE could be seen as a good example for revealing such activities.

The National Action Plans against Poverty and Social Exclusion

The introduction of National Action Plans is one of the most important components of EU policies to combat poverty and social exclusion of vulnerable population groups. This approach also resulted from the Lisbon Process and asked Member States to report and formulate their national plans and policies. At the same time a European approach is promoted, again using the 'open method of coordination', by referring to mutually agreed objectives and some coherence as regards the structure and content of the National Action Plans.

There have been by now, two series of National Action Plans – the first from 2001-2003 and the second from 2003-2005 – identifying relevant target groups and reporting on existing policies. The Commission produced a 'Joint Report' summarising the main findings of the submitted national plans. This report (Com (2003) 773 final) identified four major structural changes, which "can be expected to impact on current and future developments in relation to poverty and social exclusion":

- the consequences of major structural changes in the labour market,
- the effect of an ageing population and the resultant higher dependency ratios and greater demands on care services,
- the increased migration and growing ethnic diversity, and
- the continuing changes in household structures with continuing high levels of family break-ups.

It is important to underline that, when policies to combat social exclusion are considered, older people are a priority target group. In this respect, a 'greater demand on care services' is being expected, particularly when informal care services are being weakened as it the case in the (fourth) change on household and family structures. As the first National Action Plans report little on policies and actions designed and adopted for vulnerable older people, a dynamic evolution of the plans can be expected, in particular with respect to improvements in identifying and proposing policies for action including all vulnerable groups.

In summary, the area of 'social exclusion/inclusion policies' is an important approach towards tackling care for older people in European policies. Interestingly, this approach also widens the scope of looking at older people considering them as active members of the society with the right to an appropriate quality of life. This enhances in turn the scope of designing policies in which the concept of integrated forms of care becomes more significant.

4.2 The Research Perspective on Ageing

The research agenda on ageing at the European Union level had development extensively with regard to the coverage of social policy areas especially during the 5th Framework Programme for Research and Development (1998-2002). The Key Action 6 of the Programme was exclusively devoted to Research on Ageing and included five areas extending the scope of research beyond the areas of genetics and demography which the previous research programmes were usually promoting. We see that in the five areas, priority was given also to areas of health and social care for older people:

1. Age-related illnesses and health problems.
2. Basic processes of physiological ageing.
3. Demographic and social policy aspects of population ageing.
4. Coping with functional limitations in old age.
5. Health and social care services to older people.

A considerable number of projects were selected in these areas and valuable research has been developed in the areas particularly related to modes of care and care systems for older people, with PROCARE being a typical example for projects that were gathered under this key action:

- Concerning integrated health and social care for older persons, another interesting initiative was the Thematic Network CARMEN which helped to improve knowledge on the management of integrated long-term care services for older people in various European countries (see: www.ehma.org/projects/carmen).

- Within the same area, the Commission also supported a special activity in the form of a 'Forum on Population Ageing Research' (see: www.shef. ac.uk/ageingresearch). The Forum was to examine the research areas on ageing, to make policy recommendations and, most importantly, to "develop synergies between the key action on the ageing population and the national and international research programmes in the field". The Forum organised six workshops in the areas of quality of life, health and social care management, and longevity, demography and genetics.

- Other projects that were gathered in this area were dealing with family care (EUROFAMCARE, see: www.uke.uni-hamburg.de/institute/medizinsoziologie/ims2/gerontologie/eurofamcare), the role of service systems and intergenerational family solidarity (OASIS, see: www.dza.de/forschung/oasis_report.html), and multi-dimensional European policies for informal and formal care (SOCCARE, see: www.uta.fi/laitokset/sospol/soccare).

PROCARE had continuous contact with the coordinators of these projects and some PROCARE participants were even involved in respective advisory boards. Thus the final conference of PROCARE (October 2004) was also used to bring together researchers from these related projects to discuss opportunities to promote gerontological and interdisciplinary research in long-term care (see www.euro.centre.org/procare).

5   About This Book

This book intends to turn the reader's attention to the emerging new paradigm in long-term care from various perspectives based on the results of in-depth analysis of 18 model ways of working in nine EU Member States.

The relationship between coordination and integration efforts in long-term care and the search for common definitions is explored in Chapter 1 by Jenny Billings (UK) and Maili Malin (FIN). The authors illustrate our common approach by discussing various definitions of integrated care from the different stakeholders' perspectives. They emphasise that staff perceptions of policy doctrines show a positive and common understanding, "implying that staff and policy are at least in principle pulling in the same direction".

Chapter 2 by Francesca Ceruzzi (I), Klaas Gorter (NL) and Laura Maratou-Alipranti (EL) deals with a decisive 'moment of truth' in integrating health and social care – the access process. Relevant procedures should be, as the authors conclude, *comprehensive* to cover the clients' needs for health and social care, *understandable* for the clients, and *manageable* for all stakeholders involved. Again, we found that improvements are ongoing, in particular with respect to joint working and real collaboration between agencies and different professionals.

Chapter 3 by Kirstie Coxon (UK), Thomas Clausen (DK) and Dominique Argoud (F) is explicitly dedicated to solutions in this area of inter-professional collaboration. In the future, major emphasis will have to be put on staff development strategies with respect to retrieval and retention of staff in the context of an increasingly pressing labour shortage in all industrialised countries. Coordination and integration processes should play a major role in upgrading existing staff, introducing new job profiles and career patterns as well as in the promotion of generally improved job conditions in long-term care.

In Chapter 4, Natalia Alba, Giorgia Nesti (I) and Steen Bengtsson (DK) outline some of the key innovations that have been linked to the development of coordination and integration in health and care services. These instruments and methods, however, are also dependent on organisational structures that allow for coordination and integration, and on professionals who are able to implement them in integrated care processes. The chapter nevertheless shows that similar instruments are used in the different models with respect to organizational development and quality management on the one hand (e.g. team development, information exchange schemes, or mutually agreed, written procedure), and related to the care process on the other hand such as, for instance, needs assessment and individual care planning.

In all European countries, the family is taken for granted when it comes to care for an older relative, both by policies and by most existing services. The challenge for integrated care delivery will thus be to develop choices and opportunities for family and 'informal' carers, who need to be considered as partners in a complex process with different responsibilities. Cécile Chartreau, Marie-Jo Guisset and Alain Villez (F), Eftichia and Aphrodite Teperoglou (EL), Andrea Kuhlmann and Monika Reichert (D) underline in Chapter 5 that still far too often even professionals in model ways of working abstain from integrating family carers in 'their' care processes for a number of reasons (prejudices, complications, misunderstandings, for example) that need further research and development.

Chapter 6 analyses integrated care from the user's perspective. With the user perspective at the heart of the project objectives, Riitta Haverinen (FIN) and Nasrin Tabibian (NL) highlight that users and their informal carers are indispensable for improving the quality of care and service delivery. This is particularly so since the position of the user has gone through a transition in the last few years – the user has evolved from a 'patient' to a 'service user', a 'consumer' and even sometimes to a 'commissioner' of services. The life-world of the user and the systems world of services and residences are not easily reconciled, but this chapter uses an innovative conceptual framework to identify the mismatches and highlight areas for service improvement.

Last but not least the professionals working in long-term care settings will be the most decisive factor for improvements in planning, communication, delivery and outcome measurement of integrated care. In Chapter 7, Charlotte Strümpel (A), Sirpa Andersson (FIN) and Eftichia Teperoglou (EL) analysed staff's perceptions in the various model ways of working, with a focus on the multifaceted work of those professionals who are dedicated to coordination and integration: the variety of tasks reaches from straightforward administrative activities to complex coordination and management responsibilities and, of course, hands-on health and social care provision.

In the concluding Chapter 8 we summarise the most outstanding elements as factors for successful coordination and integration at the interface between health and social care delivery that we found during the research process. This list is far from being exhaustive – rather, it should be read as a 'shopping list' for further research and experimentation in different cultural and organisational settings that are facing the challenges of an ageing society.

Towards Rigour.
A Methodological Approach to Empirical Research on Model Ways of Providing Integrating Care

Jenny Billings

1   Introduction

This section provides an account of how the methodological framework for the project was developed and agreed. Following a first project phase during which national reports were produced by all participating teams (Leichsenring/Alaszewski, 2004), the project's empirical phase had to face various challenges.

The chapter will give a rationale for the research design and the plan of investigation, and provide an account of how challenges to methodological rigour were pre-empted, identified and tackled.

The Use of Qualitative Methods in European Research

Qualitative methods are increasingly being used to explore health and social issues within a European context. Commentators believe that there has been a gradual realisation among policy-makers that simply relying on statistical data sets is insufficient to understand certain health and social phenomena and develop robust policy (Fountain et al., 2000). The growth of qualitative research has been particularly evident in the field of drug use in the European Union, where the European Monitoring Centre for Drugs and Drug Addiction (EMCDDA) is increasingly focusing attention on developing comparable methodologies in qualitative methods across the EU (Greenwood/Robertson, 2000). Other areas of investigation include HIV/AIDS (Goodwin et al., 2003) and female career moves (Linehan, 2001). Not all of these projects have taken place within a European collaborative framework, however; some for example have used a team of investigators from one country and overcome the language barriers by interviewing in English (Linehan, 2001).

Without doubt there are particular challenges confronting investigators when undertaking research across European partnerships, where local investigators take responsibility for the planning and execution of an agreed research process. These include overall management and communication factors particularly when the projects are large, gaining consensus with plans of investigation, translation issues, and methodological comparability through sampling and data analysis processes. To heighten this difficulty, there appears to be little in the way of published methodological details to guide researchers, resulting in limited tried and tested examples of process for application to new projects.

Oates et al.'s (2004) study into postnatal depression does however provide some useful details about management structure, instrumentation development and data analysis. This study was concerned with developing, translating and validating research instruments that could be used in future studies of postnatal depression in different cultures and contexts. A project management team consisting of a member from each of the participating countries was convened, to encourage equal dissipation of management accountability.

All researchers received training in interviewing, and the management team developed clear data collection protocols. With data analysis, the transcripts were subjected to textual analysis in the original language, concept coding was developed and themes extracted. Then all the data were collated in one coordinating centre to ensure that final themes were not only relevant but accurately reflected the data from each centre.

Oates et al. (2004) acknowledge that, while the method appeared sound and comprehensive, there were some limitations to the study which included the small numbers of informants in the individual centres and what the authors describe as the 'perhaps controversial conflation and comparison' across centres after translation. The study does however provide some useful insight into methodological processes in European partnership research.

Following on from this, ongoing research into the treatment of drug-dependent offenders in six European countries (QCT Europe: www.kent.ac.uk/eiss/projects/qct-europe/index.htm) has tackled the issue of data analysis comparability by employing one researcher to undertake all the qualitative data analysis. While this does overcome a potential problem, it could weaken the impact of country-specific data. Constant feedback to partners to ensure correct interpretation may be a way forward.

In addition, some lessons from quantitative studies can provide some transferable management and communication tactics to help inform investigation plans. As with Oates et al.'s (2004) approach, Cook et al. (2002) agree that partnership projects are best managed by a small number of experienced professionals at a few centres. They add that electronic and other communication vehicles can be used effectively to aid study management.

So while some evidence exists to guide research plans in qualitative studies, there would appear at the present time too few accessible and detailed examples to comprehensively guide project development, particularly in the area of integrated care for older people. This project therefore provided an opportunity to build on this deficit and make the pathways to rigour in qualitative research more evident.

Project Organisation and Management

It is important at this point to explain the organisational and management structures within the present collaboration, as this had a bearing on the manner by which the project worked towards a positive outcome. The central coordination and management of the project was organised through the European Centre for Social Welfare Policy and Research based in Vienna (Austria). Each of the nine partner countries provided an academic lead and research team for the country-specific work packages. There was also a 'quality assurance' team consisting of representatives from some of the countries to monitor progress. In general, these organisational processes have promoted a sustainable 'buy-in' to the project, encouraged by a collaborative coordination style.

As with most collaborations, partners met at intervals in different European cities to discuss progress. Translation problems were largely minimised at meetings due to the verbal fluency of partners and multi-lingual skills of the lead centre team. Electronic networks were also established from the onset of the project, encouraging continuous dialogue.

2 Plan of Investigation and Rationale for Research Design

The purpose of the empirical data collection phase of PROCARE was to reveal the nature and practice of two integrated care services in each of the nine partner countries, from the organisational and user perspective. Specifically, the objectives of the investigation were to

- describe how services work to provide integrated care,
- explore the experiences of integrated care from the user and carer perspective,
- ascertain the impediments to effective working and how to overcome them,
- assess the extent to which the service was person-centred.

The development of the methods was guided by an initial theory paper generated from the National Reports (Alaszewski et al., 2004) followed by a more detailed methods discussion paper (Billings et al., 2003). An overview of the design and plan of investigation is given below, highlighting details of process and indicating where challenges were envisaged or occurred and efforts that were made to overcome them.

Research Design

Given the European scope of the PROCARE programme, it was important to ensure a valid and consistent approach across diverse contexts and environments, therefore the provision of a suitable research design was paramount.

The most fitting approach was a case-study design, which brought together different forms of data and permitted a robust study of both the objective characteristics of systems and subjective experiences across contrasting areas (Yin, 2003). Using Yin's classification, 'integrated care' became the unit of analysis. There were two case-studies per country and 18 case studies in all (multiple case-study design).

Different types of data were brought together to generate insight into integrated care from a user, carer and organisational perspective (see Figure 1 for illustration).

Most of the data sources were qualitative in order to permit the exploration of experiences, processes and perceived outcomes within the models (Pope/Mays, 2000), and the quantitative data related to the collection of some simple baseline organisational data and health profile information of the users taking part. As far as possible, these data sources were intended to be the same for each case, in order to permit meaningful comparison and 'replication logic' (Yin, 2003). This serves to strengthen developing theories across the case-studies.

The method of data analysis associated with this approach uses 'pattern-matching' that permits the blending of different types and levels of data from all the cases into an explanatory model, purported to enhance rigour (Yin, 2003). The external validity of case-study research is supported through the use of a number of tactics, in particular, the concept of analytical generalisation, which involves generalising to established theory (Yin, 2003; Keen/Packwood, 2000).

Figure 1:   Case-Study Unit of Analysis and Data Sources

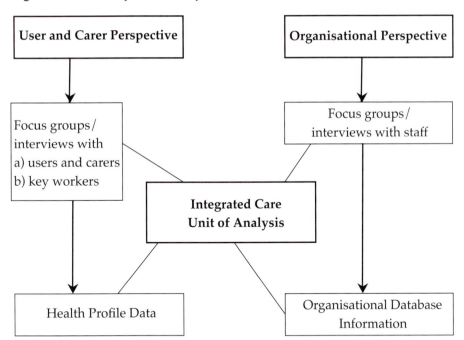

It can be seen that this design had some potential for European collaborative research in having an overall strong emphasis on blending data permitting a cross-national analysis and consequent inclusive thematic generation. In this way, it would make allowances for some natural data imprecision (such as not being able to accurately match models of integrated care across countries).

Plan of Investigation

An important feature of the planning was to ensure that common under-standing and agreement was reached regarding key terms. The establishment of criteria became an important feature of the method and considerable discussion at project meetings took place until consensus was reached. As the meetings were quite large and consisted of senior academic representa-tives with strongly-held diverse views, this was lively at times. Success was greatly enhanced by small group work of comparable membership and set-ting tasks, with timed feedback to the larger group. During this process, the value of qualitative research and the research design in particular became apparent in that it permitted the necessary degree of flexibility and allowed this diversity of integrated care delivery and context to be embraced and captured.

Selection of Sites

An initial consideration was to achieve a mutual understanding of what was meant by 'integrated care' in order to ensure some consistency of site selection. What was clear from the National Reports produced in phase 1 was that models of integrated care were very disparate, with varying or-ganisational structures, staffing levels and types, and available resources. Across the European spectrum, concepts applied to these models included seamless care (Denmark and UK), 'gerontological coordination' (France), transmural care (the Netherlands) and joint working (UK).

However, some key process features common to all were identified and were included in the selection criteria. One factor was that there had to be an organisational goal of providing integrated health and social care for older people; another that there had to be existing evidence that there was integrated / collaborative working between health and social care work-ers / professionals (i.e. at least one interface between health and social care provision). Practical criteria were also developed. The models had to be established for longer than six months, and the organisation had to be large enough to support the sampling requirements.

Sample

For both the user and carer, and organisational perspectives, the sampling framework was purposeful in order to engage those respondents who could inform the most (Pope/Mays, 2000). The number of users and carers per integrated care model was between 10-15 (n=20-30 per country) and 5 key workers were also interviewed (n=10 per country). For the organisational perspective, a focus group of between 6-12 staff were recruited per model (n=12-24 per country). The following demonstrates the actual numbers recruited across the partnerships:

- Interviews with senior managers: 29 participants across 13 projects.
- Focus groups with senior managers: 3 focus groups with 13 participants.
- Interviews with key workers: 105 interviews across 17 projects.
- Focus groups with staff or key workers: 21 focus groups with 140 participants across 17 projects (range of participants per group 2-13).
- Interviews with users and carers: 132 user participants across 17 projects, 45 carer participants across 11 projects.

There were particular problems to overcome regarding identification of staff role and achieving comparability. With the organisational perspective, there were some fundamental differences between staff types, particularly in health. Care needed to be taken when using the work 'professional' as it was not easily translated in other countries, particularly from the health perspective. Taking nurses as an example, in most countries other than the UK, there is not a professional registration requirement. Also, there is not an 'unqualified' health care assistant equivalent; in France for example health care aides have a diploma equivalent to a nursing qualification. In the UK there is a clear hierarchy relating to qualification but this is not so evident in other countries. In turn, this factor could potentially have had an impact on the focus group mix and the ensuing views expressed, and needed to be taken into consideration.

Data Collection

An important but simple factor in ensuring rigour and gaining agreement at the data collection stage was recourse to the wider methods literature for guidance about best approaches. Key data collection issues were agreed and implemented. This included interviewing carers separate from users to obtain honest and candid opinions of integrated care (Burnside et al., 1998); and providing researchers with key texts on conducting interviews and focus groups to ensure a common understanding and application of the process (Robson, 1993; Morgan, 1997). The Social Research Update website also proved useful (www.soc.surrey.ac.uk/sru/sru.htm/).

Some variations were encountered with respect to how the data were to be recorded. Whilst taping of interviews is considered the approach of choice for full data capture (Fontana/Frey, 2003), this was not deemed possible by some partners or even permitted in some countries under certain circumstances. Therefore some countries taped interviews and focus group sessions, while others took written notes. To combat the problems with data quality differences, those latter researchers were advised to ensure that notes were read back to respondents on completion of the interview to verify completeness and accuracy (Flick, 1998). In addition, the interview schedules were developed to be sufficiently detailed in order to assist in maximising data capture (see below).

Development of the Interview Schedules

The interview schedules were developed through identification of gaps and priorities highlighted within the National Reports completed in phase 1 of the research, and lengthy and intensive discussion. It was felt to be important to develop detailed easily understood questions to avoid difficulties in translating key concepts and themes between different languages and cultural contexts.

Four schedules were developed for each of the sample groups (users, carers, key workers and staff focus groups) that had common question areas but were applicable to the different configurations and organisational structures of the models. Broad sections were developed, within which the detailed questions were explored. These sections were assessment of need, evidence of person-centred care and joint working, discharge planning and experience of the integrated care service from the different perspectives.

Questions also covered every eventuality (e.g. related to home, residential centre or day care facilities and covering issues around the purchasing of care). This resulted in a series of optional questions that could be clearly navigated on the schedule. Despite efforts, piloting did not take place as it was felt to be too time-consuming and onerous to manage any additional changes and that the area had been sufficiently debated.

Data Analysis

As previously outlined, case-study design provided an analytical framework to enable the development of explanatory models in relation to integrated care for each case-study. Whilst this may seem appropriate, there were some challenges in reaching agreement about the actual data analysis process. Due to the different research backgrounds of some the partners (such as economics) ideas ranged from making abbreviated notes from the data to intense coding and thematic development. Recourse to the literature confused the issue as there are a wide spectrum of approaches to choose from ranging from simple content analysis using pre-determined themes (Flick, 1998) to in-depth familiarising, coding, categorising and conceptualising (Miles/Huberman, 1994).

A factor assisting agreement on the approach was the method of data collection, which in some instances as stated, was written notes. This, along with the added problem of time, disallowed the implementation of more depth analysis. Ultimately, an innovative two-stage approach was developed to firstly organise the data and secondly to permit the emergence and analysis of themes across the data – 'transversal' analysis.

Stage 1   In order to organise the data into a more manageable and comparable form, a content analysis approach was adopted along the lines of Flick's (1998) guidance. Four analysis protocols were developed using pre-determined themes that encompassed all the sections from the four interview schedules. Partners were required to place data within these themes justified by actual anonymised quotes, where available. While this approach signalled the way forward for the European perspective in this study, partners wishing to do more detailed analysis were encouraged to conduct this with their country-specific data for local use alongside the project requirements.

Stage 2   One of the pre-arranged meetings was used to identify early emerging ideas from the analysis protocols. Following discussion, different issues coming from the data were clustered into a number of transversal themes that appeared in general to have a European, cross-country applicability:

* Definition and perception from stakeholder's view
* Access and pathways to integrated care provision
* Professional cultures and joint working
* Key innovations
* The role of the family in integrated care
* Quality of service; outcome indicators and orientation towards clients' needs
* Working conditions
* Context and framework – financing

Partners were then organised into preferred topic areas, resulting in cross-national teams, the purpose being to explore and analyse the theme more widely within the parameters of the project aims through the collection and analysis of relevant data. These data were requested from partner countries using a specially constructed data request sheet.

The data exchange was monitored centrally to minimise overlap and repetition between themes. The themes have remained as originally constructed and are in general relevant. Some aspects of the process have been challenging and arduous. For example, partners have had to provide copious amounts of different information on the request sheets in English by scanning large amounts of raw data. In order for the teams to analyse the data in a meaningful way, partners were required to produce high-quality translations, which is time consuming but necessary to prevent data sources from losing their impact.

However, despite these difficulties this method was innovative and rewarding in terms of European research. The development of cross-national teams helped to reduce interpretive difficulties and translation errors. Furthermore, it enabled a focus to be made on the chosen issues and to concentrate on comparative views.

3   Summary and Conclusion

In summary, this project has provided the opportunity to place the process of qualitative partnership research in Europe under the microscope and to develop ways of working towards rigour in ageing research. Factors that facilitated this included the inclusive coordination and management processes, which are providing a good 'steer' to the project, the construction of universally acceptable selection criteria, detailed interview schedules, and a transversal approach to data analysis with cross-national teams. In addition, a strong feature was the research design which provided a sound underpinning and promoted an understanding of how the partner projects could be integrated and blended.

Weaknesses of the study included the lack of adequate piloting due to the complexities of managing any changes to the method, and the inconsistencies between the richness of data collected and that put forward for analysis, for which there is not an easy solution. In addition, although good electronic systems were set up swiftly, they were in general underused by all but the central management team, despite encouragement. Although not a weakness, a challenge of the project was the sometimes necessary but protracted and occasionally 'angst ridden' discussion, especially around developing definitions and criteria. This was due to the large group and the importance attached to partner involvement, and the complexity of the projects stimulating the need to capture and incorporate every eventuality.

Reflecting on this process, it could be argued that in order to combat threats to rigour, it is possible to impose too much structure. Qualitative methods are purposefully designed to encourage the emergence of ideas not previously planned for, and confining the methods in less flexible criteria and schedules could reduce this potential. This could be compounded by the use of pre-determined themes, which has a tendency to generate data within its confines with the result that more meaningful data could become disassociated from the main body of analysis. However, alternative methods of handling vast quantities of data would necessitate adding length and resources to projects, which, given European commissioning requirements, may be less acceptable.

Added to this is the fact that condensing large amounts of country-specific case-studies into a European level analysis will inevitably strip away colourful local context. However, partners are producing country-specific reports for local application to counteract this. In general it is perhaps important to strike a balance between conformity of approach and natural inconsistencies that will result from the variations. Qualitative approaches are of course ideal to absorb these anomalies and case-study design in particular, in that it promotes the blending of data and lends itself to a natural comparative element.

To conclude, people joining European research partnerships come with a diverse range of expertise, experience and expectations about what the project is there to achieve and how it should be done. It is rarely possible to do the 'textbook' approach but it is possible to work towards this. Achieving success is largely about compromise to ensure the 'greater good', with negotiation and debate being important elements to overcoming challenges.

CHAPTER 1

Definitions of Integrated Care from the Stakeholder Perspective

Jenny Billings, Maili Malin

1   Introduction

The importance of providing integrated, holistic, and cohesive primary care for older people has been increasingly emphasised in recent policy initiatives and directives (Bartlett, 1999; Johri et al., 2003). In many parts of the western world, health and social services have been organised by different organisations, provided by different professionals, and even fragmented inside sectors to smaller caregiver units. For sometime now there has been a realisation that it is more effective for all stakeholders that care is integrated into a single whole, with a smoother and more consistent coordination of the service network (Eng et al., 1997; Watt et al., 1999; Truman/Triska, 2001; Hudson/Henwood, 2002; Schwab et al., 2003).

The blending of health and social services however in this manner is problematic. Integrated care is multifaceted, requiring as it does a multi-skilled workforce to enable the seamless coming together of many different parts to meet complex needs (Stewart et al., 2003; Brown et al., 2003). A significant factor that creates disturbance is that social and health service sectors have different understandings of the direction of service provision based on professional histories and practices in each cultural context (Carpenter et al., 2003; Chevannes, 2002; King/Ross, 2003). These understandings can raise barriers to unification and integration (Hudson, 2002; Reilly et al.,

2003), resulting in staff who are not pulling in the same direction with a consequent impact on the quality of care (Glendinning, 2003; Mur-Veeman et al., 2003).

Given that an understanding of the function of integrated care is fundamental to a harmonious service, the PROCARE project provided an opportunity to examine this further at the European level. The aim of this section therefore was to identify how staff, and to a smaller extent users and carers, defined and described integrated care through a comparative analysis of the empirical data. It sought to determine if there was a collective view of what integrated care is there to achieve, or if differences exist within and between models and countries, and how this compared to definitions in policy and research. The chapter is set out in the following way:

- It will commence with a brief summary of work to date on how integrated care is defined through the National Reports.
- Ideas of how models are defined will be discussed and compared, and analysed through six conceptual frameworks, namely identification of broad concepts, pre-conditions, practical processes, expected outcomes, threats to realising integrated care and user and informal carer perspective. These frameworks will help to expand and magnify the components that constitute integrated care.
- The findings will be discussed in relation to the wider literature regarding integrated care conceptual definitions.

2   Definitions within the National Reports

A previous phase in the project consisted of each partner country writing a National Report of policy and practice in integrated care (Leichsenring/ Alaszewski, 2004). These reports were scanned for examples of existing definitions or statements about integrated care, derived from policy and research. The purpose of this was to examine the extent to which stakeholders in the PROCARE project shared a consensus view of the more established interpretations.

Once identified, there appeared to be many common links between the partner country definitions. Delnooj (2001) provides a useful classification of integrated care that was used to cluster these definitions, as follows:

- *Clinical integration* which takes place at the micro-level or the primary process, and involves 'chains of care' and transmural care.
- *Professional integration* refers to professionals within institutions working together in a mutual way.
- *Organisational integration* comes in the form of mergers, or networks forming between institutions.
- *Functional integration* refers to the cure, care and prevention aspect.

In the table below, the latter three Delnooj classifications were used, as no definitions fitting clinical integration were evident.

There are clear areas of common understanding in these definitions, relating to how an integrated service should be constructed and organised. Intrinsic is the merging of professionals and services into a single flexible unit that centres near the old person as in community-based services like in Greece, the Netherlands, Finland, France, and Denmark. In most countries the integrated care is more determined and thus promoted by the health care sector when the public health discourse is dominating. In almost all national reports the horizontal integration is the main way of integrating the social and health services. Horizontal integration is the same as organisational and functional integration of services between social and health care sector. In national reports of Austria, Germany, Italy, Finland and Denmark the vertical integration is additionally stressed, where the organisational integration between intramural and extramural care is taking place by various means. It was of interest that most definitions appeared to be evident among the Northern European reports, where perhaps integrated care has a longer history.

Cutting across these definitions were common terminology that could be categorised into three areas, emphasising further key elements of integrated care:

i.   the orientation of care was evident through the use of 'seamless', 'flexible', 'client-centred' and 'demand-led';
ii. connections were highlighted through strong use of 'collaboration', 'coordination', 'joint working' and 'networking';
iii. outcomes were articulated through 'prevention' (of deterioration) 'meeting need', 'improved quality of care' and 'cost effectiveness'.

All these characterisations of integrated care can be found in the following analysis of the data from the PROCARE country models.

Professional integration	"an organisation of professional people who pool their means and resources ... working to a common objective" (Frossard et al., 2004: 244) "Integrated health and social care is the remit of home helps, home nurses, rehabilitation and nursing home professionals" (Colmorten et al., 2004: 144)
Organisational integration	"The process of integration can aim at linking parts within a single level of care, for instance the creation of multiprofessional teams (horizontal integration) or the linking between different levels of care, i.e. primary, secondary and tertiary care (vertical integration)" (Grilz-Wolf et al., 2004: 117) "A discrete set of techniques and organisational models designed to create connectivity, alignment and collaboration within and between the care and cure sectors at the funding, administrative end/or provider level" (Ex et al., 2004: 415) "Integrated Services: a set of services made available for a single population group over a given geographical area ... by a single company or organisation, grouped together under a single decision-making authority" (Frossard et al., 2004: 244) " ... seamless service chains are defined as an operating model, where the services received by a client ... within social welfare and healthcare services ... are integrated into a flexible entity which will satisfy the client's needs regardless of which operating unit provides or implements the service" (Salonen/Haverinen, 2004: 187)
Functional integration	"Integrated care is a concept of rendering care services in which the single units act in a coordinated way and which aims at ensuring cost-effectiveness, improving the quality of care and increasing the level of satisfaction" (Grilz-Wolf et al., 2004: 117) "Demand-oriented care simultaneously means *integrated care*. After all, when the requests and needs the client may experience in various areas are met, then that constitutes integrated care" (Ex et al., 2004: 415) "Joint working brings together health and social care to promote independence and improve quality of care for older people" (Coxon et al., 2004: 465)

3   Conceptualising the Data

At the onset of each interview, staff were asked to define what they understood by integrated care from their own contextual viewpoint. This information revealed a wide descriptive narrative amenable to categorisation within themed conceptual clusters. This section of the chapter describes these clusters with the use of direct quotes referenced to the model type and country of origin. The six main conceptual clusters were identified as follows:

*   broad impressions (or definitions) were isolated, being initial ideas of how integrated care was perceived;

Once these had been expressed, the dialogue was expanded, where respondents appeared to qualify their answers. This was subsequently classified into the following concepts:

*   *pre-conditions*, being a set of conditions or circumstances conducive to the broad concepts becoming operational;
*   *practical processes*, being examples of more concrete practice-based process criteria important to operationalise the broad concepts;
*   *expected outcomes*, being actual or potential positive products of the integration;
*   *threats to realising integrated care*, where respondents identified real or envisaged challenges to the ideals of integration.

With respect to the latter, it was felt pertinent to include potential 'threats' to offer a comparative reality perspective to the sometimes idealised definitions. In addition, a further clustering of the *user and carer perspective* was attempted. The difficulties of getting 'definitions' from this group was recognised, however data that revealed how integrated care was experienced through the eyes of users and carers was used, telling something of how staffs' definitions were working in practice.

3.1   Broad Impressions

This section provides general first impressions given by respondents concerning their understanding of integrated care. Responses were varied, but could be grouped into three further categories, organisational perspective, person-centred holistic care and supporting independence.

3.1.1 Organisational Perspective

A dominant finding seemed to be that staff described integrated care through the service provision perspective and the way that care was organised and integrated horizontally and vertically. An initial example of this was in the German home care model, where staff explained that integrated care was a comprehensive care system where all services that are needed are linked by an interdisciplinary management system:

> "(Integration of services is) a comprehensive care system with the provision of services particularly for older persons in need of care, involving linking the available provisions and services in the health system by interdisciplinary quality management" (D1, key worker).

> "... Integrated care is a network of social and health services, which aims to coordinate all the provided services for older people in need of care" (EL1, key worker)

In the same vein, in the UK integrated care was often referred to as 'joint working'. Connecting of different actors was found to be one of the key concepts of integrated care in the national reports, too. A British member of staff in the hospital to care facility model put their understanding of it simply:

> "Joint working to me would be working with other agencies ... like going to district nurses ... that's what I gather ..." (UK1, key worker)

Furthermore, this was taken forward as 'team work' in the Austrian hospital to home model:

> "Integrated care is team work ... incorporating family, neighbours, nurses and doctors in the planning and service process" (A2, key worker)

In the Greek models (home care and one-stop shop), the notions of coordination and cooperation came through strongly:

> "Joint working ... is a network of services for older citizens characterised by steady cooperation" (EL2, key worker)

The benefits of vertical integration could be seen in the Danish model where having staff working in both hospital and community settings was expressed in the hospital to home model. Additionally, it was implied that the coming together of local professionals using local contexts and knowledge benefits the service and clients:

> "Well, it means you are working in the Health Centre and the community...it is of huge benefit that the care staff work 'inside' and 'outside' as the staff know the older people in the municipality" (DK2, key worker)

Also in the Danish hospital to home model, staff described integrated care in terms of a safe transmission of the citizen through the system of rehabilitation. But above all, functional rehabilitation systems based on integration of services seem to be more cost-effective than hospitalisation for the municipality:

> "It is in the interests of the municipality to ensure that citizens obtain as good
> a rehabilitation ... as possible. The alternative is ... a lot of citizens requiring
> nursing homes" (DK1, key worker)

These statements provide some comparisons with Delnooj's classification. Organisational integration comes through clearly in the German and Greek models, and professional integration is more evident in the Austrian, Danish and UK models. With reference to vertical and horizontal integration, there appears to be a predominance of horizontal integrations within the definitions, so therefore more fusion of multi-professional teams within primary care services in the models. This may be largely responsible for the perception coming through the data of the importance of professional 'know-how' as expressed in the second Danish model, also echoed in the Austrian models.

3.1.2 Person-Centred Holistic Care

For all models, the notion of person-centred care encompassing the whole person was intrinsic to integrated care and came through strongly. This was also seen in the national reports as an important orientation of the services and is a theme echoed throughout the chapters. The subsequent integration of person-centred care means that well-being, autonomy, integrity and dignity of the old person have the potential to be realised:

> "Integration is ... well being, autonomy, better quality of life for the old person
> ... it means a global approach" (I1, key worker)

> "Integrated care is ... using the citizen as the starting point. It is in the everyday
> experiences of the citizen ... insofar as we can support the users in leading their
> lives in dignity." (DK2, key worker)

> "I see integrated care as a process of creating a unified package that corresponds
> with the needs and wishes of the individual ... the challenge is to provide
> adapted services that respect the integrity of the citizens." (DK2, key worker)

This was also extended to include improved life conditions:

> "Integration is ... well being, dignity, autonomy, better quality of life." (I1,
> key worker)

The inclusion of informal carers into the integration process of services and fulfilling person-centred care was important, too:

> "[This project] represents the first attempt to take care of users and their families after discharge ... not only is the older person important, but also the carers and family." (I1, key worker)

> "[The project] advises [clients] and their carers to make a choice in an increasingly complicated and confusing world." (NL2, key worker)

Also in the German models, not only were the services delivered taking the client's point of view into account, but the importance of maintaining well-being among family caregivers was seen as crucial, especially in model 2 which was concerned with dementia care.

Client-centred care was a primary goal in the models of the Netherlands. Underpinning this primary goal were key principles relating to maintaining function and self-respect, involving people in decision-making and sustaining autonomy. In addition, this was articulated around the connection to the structure of the services in the hospital to home model:

> "Services were created in order to streamline the care process for older people from beginning to end, striving to provide a client oriented service ... the needs and when possible specific wishes of the clients are the starting point in the planning and providing the required services. Flexibility and speed in adapting to the physical and psychological changes of the client are seen as an essential pre-condition to achieve this goal." (NL2, key worker)

Further to this, the notion of 'holism' was also included in the definitions. In Finland, respondents described the purpose of the service as looking at the whole life situation of the old person, extended in Austria to include informal carers. A respondent in the Danish 24-hour community-based care summed up the view:

> "... you have to consider a holistic approach ... where you take all the traits of the individual into consideration ..." (DK2, key worker)

In this section the clear unanimous view given by staff of the central place of the client and informal carer was evident and appeared to be firmly internalised, irrespective of the model or country. Given the gradual philosophical shift to a client-centred orientation over the years, this confirms that the position of the client in health and social care has become focused in integrated care delivery. It is of interest that underpinning the notions of 'client at the centre of care' appeared to be a suggestion that what the service, and therefore the workers, are doing for clients is right, hence providing a moral and legitimate base to their work.

3.1.3 Supporting Independence

The notion of integrated care as the key to sustain independence was again strong across countries. Supporting independency of the old person is one important outcome of integrated care mentioned also in many national reports. The ideal perception is that the older person becomes as independent as possible of others. The philosophy of elderly care in Denmark and Finland for example was to support citizens to remain in their own homes as long as possible. Independent living is believed to enhance the quality of life for the individual. Similarly, in the UK, both models were developed from intermediate care policy, which again is underpinned by the aim of assisting older people to return to independent living. The following quotes illustrate these ideas:

> "It's about making the client safe, independent and able to do what they need to do to move on." (UK1, key worker)

> "One of the important goals of the care system is to provide the pre-conditions so as older people can live in their own home independently as long as possible and safe." (NL2, key worker)

Also, the aim of the programme in Greece is to promote, maximise and restore independence of older people. The KAPI one-stop shop model particularly emphasises the importance of integrated care as a mechanism by which to increase social solidarity and prevent isolation, assisting older people to remain active citizens in their own communities. This model also has a reliance upon extended partnerships. This quote highlights the benefits of this with respect to the neighbourhood network:

> "Integrated care means that older users remain at home and do not change their daily habits ... they stay near family and friends and are not isolated." (EL2, key worker)

A respondent from the Netherlands hospital-to-home model was however keen to point out not to do too much for the older person, but instead let her/him to do small daily tasks as physical exercise in their daily living:

> "One of the important issues in the care has always been the delicate balance between caring enough for people but not too much so that they do not stop caring for themselves." (NL2, key worker)

In addition, in Denmark as well as in Finland there is a political imperative to this rehabilitative way of working. It has been noted that the combination of the political ambition to enable older people to remain in their own homes for as long as possible and high labour market participation for women pinpoints the need for flexible and person-centred care in a society.

The strong presence of supporting independence in the data would suggest the internalisation of modern political thought, although as the Danish respondents infer, this ideal represents good economic sense. Comparing these last two sub-themes with Delnooj's classifications, ideas of functional integration are evident, focusing on the aspirational 'cure and care' aspect of the services.

An interesting observation of the data in this section was that, while Northern countries were able to provide encompassing notions of the concept of integrated care due perhaps to the longer establishment, ideas in Greece were also anchored to similar elements, despite the immaturity of the structural development of services.

3.2 Pre-conditions

In this section, themes were identified that appeared to relate to sets of pre-conditions that needed to be in place for the broader definitions to be realised. These themes were seamless care, roles and responsibilities, and shared goals among different professionals as well as among seniors and juniors in one profession.

3.2.1 Seamless Care

Seamless care was articulated in terms of a set of vital processes that made up the concept of integrated care and were necessary for its implementation. It was often associated with person-centred care and described as different professional groups working together to meet the needs of individual users. In the Netherlands for example professionals saw this type of care as the conduit through which they are able to achieve the goal of their work, client-centred care. In the Danish 24-hour care model, a respondent summed up this view:

> "I see integrated care as a process of creating a smooth and unified, seamless package that corresponds with the needs and wishes of the individual ... the challenge is to provide individually adapted services that respect the integrity of the citizens." (DK2, key worker)

In the UK, staff in both models recognised the relevance of a smooth passage through the system within an integrated care service:

> "I mean it's continual care isn't it? It's a nice follow-through all the way for that client which is good for them." (UK1, key worker)

> "... patients should be able to go through the system from start to finish...with relatively no hiccups at all ... so they travel through the system and come out the end maintained or better." (UK2, key worker)

In the Dutch home care model, staff recognise the importance of seamless care through the coordination of the services as a key feature of the quality of care, needing immediate rectification if failing:

> "If we notice that things are not linked, we immediately come into action to do something about it." (NL1, key worker)

Interestingly in Greece, with the inception of the 'help at home' model, agencies did not envisage or work towards a formal joint-working or seamless care process. Instead, all interviewees described their service in terms of cooperation/coordination, as outlined in the previous section. Also in the French models the coordination of the work of different care providers was stressed instead of just talking about integration. Included in this however was the pre-condition relating to the older person's wider environment, such as friends and neighbours, who would be vital to continue support once the team has withdrawn. This factor was not so evident from the professional perspective in other countries, although involving carers was evident to some extent.

In most countries the data here implied that there cannot be integrated care without some form of seamless care or joint working, and indeed is central to the functioning of the project in the Netherlands. While there are different labels attached to this form of working, the descriptions of what is meant by them in these quotes infer a common understanding. A key individual to coordinate services is an important ingredient to make the integration work in practice. In Germany and Austria, the case manager assumes this function and in Finland, the chief officer of home care.

3.2.2 Roles and Responsibilities

Having an understanding and appreciation of the different multi-skilled professional groups within the models was highlighted. It was clear that the multi-professional approach was key and it was mostly evident as a form of teamwork. There was a view that the rehabilitation process relied upon the expertise of several disciplines, with the right professionals being available at the right time. The Italian team in the hospital to home model stated eloquently:

> "Integration is not the sum of every single professional but its synthesis ... if you respect roles, you can reduce errors and the user is happy ..." (I1, key worker)

The UK respondents in the home care model attempted to elaborate on this by trying to describe how this worked in practice:

> "It's very complex, the way we work together. Part of our success is how people have learned to negotiate the way they work ... we are truly interprofessional ... because of the way we negotiate the care...that is quite hard, because people are very used to working in their own professional groupings" (UK2, key worker)

and notions of equality and respect inter- and intra-professionally were also seen as essential ingredients:

> "I think everybody's equal. This is the only team I have worked for where I've got immense respect for everybody ... the (more junior) workers do just a good a job as I do, and I don't see those boundaries so much" (UK2, key worker)

In a summary of Danish respondents' views, it was clear that the multi-professional approach was vital. There was a view that the rehabilitation process relied upon the expertise of several disciplines, with the right professionals being available at the right time.

3.2.3 Shared Goals

The importance of having common aims or goals among multiprofessional workers within the models appeared to be a key factor in many models and across countries. The Greek respondents in KAPI were in agreement that integrated care meant above all a common and shared goal. In the Finnish models multiprofessional carers felt they had gradually developed and negotiated the same aim of the work as their clients – they have a shared understanding about the holistic situation of the client. A respondent in the hospital to home model stated:

> "... services received by clients ... are integrated into a flexible smooth entity which will satisfy the clients' needs regardless of which unit provides or implements the service." (FIN1, key worker)

Quotes from other countries supported this view as well:

> "With integration it is fundamental to define effective and realistic goals ... it means having common and shared goals among professionals and users/carers with respect to each other's roles and competencies." (I1, key worker)

Again with shared goals, there was agreement that there needs to be consensus especially with users and carers. However it could be argued that there needs to be a shared understanding before there can be shared goals, and the extent to which clients share the same vision is less clear.

3.3   Practical Processes

Having provided broad impressions underpinned by a set of pre-conditions, this section highlights some of the more practical processes that needed to be evident. These practical processes qualified the respondents' interpretations and understandings of the meaning of integrated care. This section is divided into three sub-themes: structures in the organisation, communication issues and tools.

3.3.1 Structures in the Organisation

In Denmark, as well as in the Finnish model 2 the fluidity of integrated care appeared to be enhanced by the organisational structure where social and health sectors work in the same physical space or very near to each other. A Danish respondent in the 24 hour care model stated:

> "We have a very flat structure ... whoever identifies a problem ... deals with the problem ... without having to send the matter through some hierarchy for approval ... it is dealt with properly and promptly." (DK2, key worker)

Some models have resulted in the creation of new and innovative posts to ensure the delivery of the service. In Denmark model 2, coordinating nurses have been specifically employed to keep track of hospital in-patients and arrange appropriate discharge. Also in the German model for dementia, a new type of professional, a social education worker, is being established as the result of the project:

> "Their task is to promote cooperation between providers by means of newly-established committees, to advise and help in individual cases, and to fill any gaps in provision with services of appropriate quality." (D2, key worker)

63

In Austria, the hospital to home model is thought to work because it is area-based where the local workers can use their regional knowledge in planning and doing the services in a responsive manner:

> "Flexibility is my work. A lot of the time you have to completely scrap something ... because the situation has changed ... for this I need flexibility." (A2, key worker)

Also in the Finnish models the services are produced and delivered near the client where there is familiarity with the local population. As in Austria, flexibility and adaptation were seen to be intrinsic factors to respond to needs quickly in Denmark, Finland and the Netherlands. This Dutch respondent illustrated:

> "Take for instance a client who tended to receive only assistance with bathing once a day. The person falls, breaks an ankle, goes to the hospital, and returns with his ankle in plaster. At the same day we visit that client eight times per 24 hours. If it appears today that the next day different care is needed, we can provide it. That is what we call integrated care." (NL1, key worker)

In Italy, the creation of institutional agreements in the one-stop shop was important to enhance interprofessional working. This included protocols and procedures to improve differences in career patterns, training and legitimisation within the models. In the Danish 24-hour care model, Greek one-stop shop and the UK home care, having a common base was seen as a sound factor for integrated care, especially in Denmark as all the facilities as well as personnel are under one roof. The following quote from a user exemplifies this:

> "Well I had to go to the health centre for my physio and then I started to pop in at the day care facility, and then I just kept coming here. And I still think it's nice to go there and be with others – and to help others." (DK2, user)

In addition, a Greek member of staff felt that having all services available under one roof produced better outcomes:

> "A one stop shop approach ... ensures better use of available resources and improved care of older people." (EL1, key worker)

In Italy and the UK, having a pooled budget was also felt to promote service integration. Teamwork was also mentioned in the UK home care model, how the whole is stronger than individuals:

> "We can get in and get things done ... we achieve a lot more than perhaps a GP or district nurse working on their own ... we've got multi-skilled people and can provide more than just our basic skills." (UK2, key worker)

This sub-theme therefore highlights the range of structural, bureaucratic and financial/organisational factors that appear to assist staff to work towards optimal service delivery.

3.3.2 Communication

The importance of good communication between multi-skilled and multi-professional staff as a pathway to best practice is well documented (Challis et al., 1995). In our study, the components of frequent formal and informal dialogue and discussion underpinned by knowledge through regular contact were felt to be vital. The physical working arrangements made multiprofessional contacts and discussions possible where the carers were able to learn different professional language and form a common language together:

> "Integration means to put into practice communication theories; it means to exchange abilities and knowledge among different professionals on a regular basis whilst maintaining respect." (I1, key worker)

In the German home care model and in Austria, communication between different care providers and between different professionals was seen as pivotal for care:

> "The fluidity and easiness of communication ... is essential in order that the care giving will be successful." (D1, key worker)

With respect to practice, for all countries, this was through opportunistic encounters, such as residing in the same building, or more formal methods like discharge conferences or staff meetings, where staff were able to coordinate client issues speedily. In addition, there were computer-based client systems (like medical records) as well as written records of home care clients:

> "Information about clients (users) from home nurse, home care and home help is in common use. You can call and talk about clients and their situations. Our home nurses are such that they can do some shopping, if the fridge is empty. They are flexible. We have common knowledge. The home nurse phones all, if there is some changes in the well-being of the old person. Not only do they write in the note book, but they make a phone call and meet in the office." (FIN1, key worker)
>
> "It's about communication and working alongside each other, so that everybody knows what everyone else is doing." (UK2, key worker)

The staff in this UK model also viewed themselves as the central information point:

> "We are an integrated network of professional people ... we've become an epicentre for communication of information for not only ourselves as a team but for our patients" (UK2, key worker)

In the UK, the success of the communication pathways were clear in users' responses, with this client from the hospital to care facility model having a grasp of future care:

> "When I go home I shall hopefully have a carer to look after me in the mornings ... it's what they call a 'care package'. They set it up for you when you leave." (UK1, user)

Communication with users and formal carers was also viewed as important in all models:

> "... I think letting them read what you're writing, not having any secrecy, not having anything spoken that they're not party to, I think that's very important." (UK1, key worker)

> "We have regular weekly contact with her at her home, it gives security for the client. She knows that on certain days at a certain time the home carer will come to her house." (FIN2, key worker)

3.3.3 Tools

This sub-theme describes the various tools or instruments used to document the care of or assess the older client (see Chapter 4 for more detail). As with previous research in this area (see Carpenter et al., 2001), they were seen as a vital component to the practice process of realising older people's care, and in this case, integrated care. In Finnish models as well as in the Danish 24-hour care model the needs assessment of new clients was done with multiprofessional teams according to multidimensional standard procedures. All PROCARE models emphasised the relevance of written documented individualised care plans based on some standard of need assessment to realise client-centred care, and making the planning and evaluation of care possible. In the Italian hospital to home model and Denmark, respondents stressed the importance of having common validated assessment tools:

> "The WUCC realises integration using instruments and strategies ... usable by everyone ... such instruments are filled by single professionals and then discussed to define a common goal." (I1, key worker)

In addition, the Danish and Finnish models used accessible logs that provided information about day-to-day changes to caregivers.

Thus the practical processes in place illustrated by our respondents appear to be a necessary requirement, and are echoed elsewhere. Challis et al. (1995), for example in their study of multidisciplinary working in a new project, found that the various channels of communication that were established early were vital for providing the means by which problems were identified and resolved in a timely fashion.

3.4 Expected Outcomes

This section looks at how respondents articulated the potential or actual outcomes of integrated care, which worked as legitimate reasons for integration of services at all levels, from the policy level to the personal level of the older customer

3.4.1 Organisational Outcomes

In Denmark, Germany and Austria there were expectations that integrated care services made 'socio-economic sense' with cost savings being expected. This included factors such as reduction of hospital admissions and rapid discharges to home. In the Finnish models the cost savings in the forms of reduction of hospital admissions and shortening the hospital stays were a major impetus for increasing and intensifying the supply of home care for frail older people living in their homes. Overall, in many models the integrated way of organising care was felt best to support the independence of older people, while at the same time it would reduce expensive costs of residential placements.

Other positive organisational outcomes of integrated care were the expectation of better work outcomes expressed for example by the Austrian staff in the following way:

> "Better planning and better work from the client point of view ... to plan the work together with the multiprofessional team and also with family members ... if I plan alone ... it will usually fail ..." (A2, key worker)

Additionally, multiprofessional carers felt that their work satisfaction had increased, there would be better information exchange between agencies promoting better understanding of hospital and social care services and the associated working cultures. The integrated way of organising care made more sense to the work of multiprofessional carers.

3.4.2 Preventive Outcomes

According to inter-European staffs' perceptions and experiences, integrated care also prevented the deterioration of the client. The Italian team in the hospital to home model felt that this was due to increased support for other professionals such as GPs:

> "... the service helps them in solving the more complex problems, the ones that happen every year ... we are able to reduce 'social' admissions ... the hospital has understood how relevant we are to guarantee users' well being and to reduce other avoidable admissions ... and rapid discharges." (I1, key worker)

In the hospital to home Danish model, the frail older persons were not discharged without referral to rehabilitation or other relevant service. In Greece, KAPI (one stop shop) was felt to assist in the halting of disease progression, due to close follow-up of patients.

Home services also felt that integrated care services reduced the amount of formal carer stress by ensuring services were adequately in place and that the older person was well supported. In Finland one philosophy of home care was that it is rehabilitative for the older person instead of having an adverse passive effect which comes from living in institutions.

3.4.3 User/Carer-focused Outcomes

This section looked at health and social improvements as expressed by the staff. All countries articulated the importance of increasing the health and welfare of older people, both users and informal carers, and enhancing the quality of life:

> "An excepted outcome is to stabilise the quality of life in the home for those in need of assistance – the quality of life of the old person as well as the quality of care received will be increased ... it intends to benefit the totality of persons suffering from geronto-psychiatric problems." (D1, key worker)

> "... to reduce the fear and the insecurity caused by the new personal situation of older people in the need of care." (A2, key worker)

Overall, the understandings articulated in this section by respondents mirror intended benefits and outcomes specified in European National Reports (Leichsenring/Alaszewski, 2004) and other integrated care projects (Nies/Berman, 2004). Therefore the goal and purpose of integrated care would appear to be internalised, despite their arguably ambitious nature.

3.5   Threats to Realising Integrated Care

It was clear that for most groups, conceptualising their ideal of what integrated services ought to be was closely followed by caveats suggesting that ideals were in reality difficult to put into practice. This aspect of PROCARE has been analysed more deeply in Chapter 3, but the experiences were clearly intertwined with the expressed definitions of integrated care and thus worth mentioning here. There were two main themes identified: tensions between services and challenges to realising person-centred care.

3.5.1 Tensions between Services

Tensions between services within and outside of the projects had been experienced. In most countries, staff had experienced issues around territorialism, with professionals not understanding each other's roles and policies. The experiences of staff bore witness to the difficulties in communicating among professionals who were divided by status and ideology, which all had an impact on their ability to function as a team:

> "There were difficulties with integration ... because the other social workers viewed (the social worker in the hospital) as a newcomer with an unclear role." (I1, key worker)

> "I do have difficulty with social services and their policies and procedures ... everything is set in stone ... they have some very archaic policies and they are almost blocking us." (UK1, key worker)

Outside the project boundaries, there were also problems with inappropriate or inadequate referrals, due to other agencies not fully understanding their service, or pressure to discharge. This seemed to be the point at which the vertical integration of services was in jeopardy in all hospital-to-home models. The coordination either did not seem to function properly or it was not arranged at all, as in Greece. As one respondent from the home care model explains in the UK:

> "Some of the communication problems we have come from hospital discharge ... we just get a referral at the last moment with a few details ... there should be liaison between health and social care managers but that doesn't often happen, we go in and pick up the pieces." (UK2, key worker)

In Greece, there were unique problems around the 'newness' of integrated care. As the projects became established, there was the realisation that the

69

models were heavily dependent upon networks of personal relationships that required considerable effort to sustain. There were at the time of the study no formal coordinating services or proper planning, and a perception that what they were trying to achieve was not fully understood:

> "... there is no institutional cooperation between the health and social welfare sectors ... which would facilitate various allocations and other payment benefits." (EL1, key worker)

In Germany, France and Austria, there were also numerous perceived problems relating to conflict of interest and cultural clashes, especially with the medical profession. In Finland model 1 for example, there was concern that doctors were not sharing the same vision; in Germany, issues centred around the increasing challenges by the nursing profession that complicated cooperation with doctors. Status inequality and unclear work division between professionals were an issue in other countries; Austrian problems with organisational hierarchies created an imbalance in democracy between the services; and the French models were concerned with loss of professional power and autonomy. These last quotes are examples of the desire to succeed, despite these problems:

> "It is important to sacrifice the interests of each association ... for the sake of an older person." (F1, key worker)

> "It's all about championing and it's all about belief in the original vision ... we need to hold on to the vision and push it on and not give up." (UK1, key worker)

Problems between health and social services have a long history in Northern Europe (Hudson et al. 1997). Despite these problems, these last quotes are examples of the desire to succeed. What is interesting is that in the newly formed services in Greece, there is also evidence of lack of cooperation, implying that the imposition of professional boundaries remains problematic across a variety of environments.

3.5.2 Challenges to Person-centred/Seamless Care

Although on the whole many service users were satisfied with the care they received, some felt distanced from the collaborative process. When asked how the team worked together, the response from a UK home care model user was:

> "I haven't got a clue." (UK2, user)

The problem of information exchange was recognised by staff in Finland and Austria, explained as a shortage of carers who are in a constant hurry, with no time to read the records, or participate in the meetings:

> "We got the formal plan ... so that the carer will have a more comprehensive view of the client's life situation. But in the middle of this hurry when there is great turnover of the workers, we have not been able to do it ... then all this talk about comprehensive care is questionable." (FIN2, key worker)

In some cases this had undesirable consequences for the user:

> "... I'm left lying in bed for 13 or 14 hours on my back. That really doesn't do me any good." (UK2, user)

A staff respondent in the UK seemed to recognise the relationship between poor service integration and seamless care, and patient-centredness:

> "... joint working generally involves two agencies liaising but working very much to their own standards ... it's not necessarily something that is seamless or client-centred – you can still have people falling through the net." (UK1, key worker)

In most models the older customer would receive integrated health and social services for an unlimited time, as long as the person needed it. However a key issue for carers in the home care UK model was the withdrawal of the team after the stipulated period of six weeks. Many commented on the abruptness of discharge and the fact that there was a general absence of any other follow-up service than the overused voluntary sector. This informal carer stated:

> "Apparently they're not allowed to do more than six weeks ... they stopped coming in directly he'd finished ... there's no follow-up, nothing ... he's really gone downhill." (UK2, informal carer)

This section starts to inject a reality perspective into integrated care service delivery, by matching aspirational perceptions with the organisational, environmental and professional actualities of trying to make it work. What this particular theme appears to start to infer is that the consequences of these tensions and barriers seemed to paradoxically create a shortfall in the quality of care provided, and perhaps experienced. This could arguably lead to an inability to realise the most fervently articulated goal of person-centred care.

3.6   User and Carer Perspective

We knew that getting users and carers to clearly state their understanding of integrated care would be difficult and indeed it was not obvious in the data. We did find some evidence of how integrated care was experienced that at first glance seemed to tell us something about the operationalisation of the staff's conceptual understanding and ideals. The first quote seems to provide an example of seamless care or joint working in operation, the second intimates good communication between staff and the third an example of a person-centredness experience of a carer:

> "They tell one another. In fact one time they said to each other, you have the bottom half of her and I'll have the top half! They all work together." (UK1, user)

> "My carer was so efficient. I didn't have to tell him anything, he was so good." (UK2, user)

> "The services provided to my husband have him at the centre." (EL2, user's wife)

In the Greek, Danish and Finnish models, a summary of views indicated that users and carers had the impression that the teams worked well together by the fact that they all shared the same information, and communication channels were good:

> "There is a good working atmosphere, one can feel that they like their work and working together." (FIN2, user)

In addition, staff were seen to provide a useful, supportive and friendly service that generally met needs. In the Sollerod model (Denmark), users had experienced a smooth transition from the hospital to their homes or care facility, and that their rehabilitation programme had significantly helped them in this process.

In the KAPI Greek model, older people felt more a part of the community than before the inception of the project. A more formal evaluation of the 'Help at Home' service undertaken previously indicated that older people living alone felt more secure, and that the burdens of family dependency have been decreased.

The views expressed here do appear to be encouraging. However, given the methodological difficulties associated with obtaining older user views (Burnside et al., 1998), this interpretation could be challenged. The quotes could be regarded as a superficial confirmatory view; users and carers were largely still in receipt of services given by different professionals and could have felt obliged to be positive. Incongruously, despite the humour, the first quote from the UK tells us of a physical division of labour for the service benefit and not the client's, which is removed from what professionals would believe to be the ideal approach.

So this raises doubts as to whether the integrated care ethos expressed by the staff is pervasive to the level of the recipient. Whether users and carers share the same goals and ideals about what is largely a service and policy driven development is also questionable.

4   Conclusion

Within this analysis there appeared to be a complex and interrelated collective European view of integrated care that enabled common conceptual groupings to be formed.

- *Broad impressions* included organisational perspective, person-centred holistic care, and supporting independence.
- *Preconditions* included seamless care and roles and responsibilities as well as shared goals.
- *Practical processes* included organisational structures, communication and tools.
- *Expected outcomes* were concerned with organisational and economic outcomes, preventive outcomes and user outcomes.
- *Threats to realising integrated care*, where respondents identified real or envisaged challenges to the ideals of integration.
- *User and carer perspective*.

Supplementary to this, there were clear links from the perceptions of staff to the policy doctrines outlined in the National Reports, which shows a positive and common understanding, implying that staff and policy are at least in principle pulling in the same direction. The fact that a clear and simple definition was not possible testifies to the complicated and convoluted nature of integrated care service delivery, and of course reflects that the responses stem from different contexts and environments. Comparing these findings with the wider literature on definitions of integrated care, we find a number of similarities with respect to collaboration, cooperation, organisation, processes, meeting needs, supporting independence and improved outcomes. Hiscock and Pearson (1999: 151) define it as 'collaborative actions or activity, undertaken between health and social service organisations and practitioners ... with the ultimate aim of providing an improved service to the client or patient'.

Nies and Berman's (2004: 12) definition from the Carmen project states:

> "By 'integrated care' we refer to a well-planned and well-organised set of services and care processes, targeted at the multi-dimensional needs/problems of an individual client, or a category of persons with similar needs/problems ... built up by elements of acute health care, long term care, social care, housing and services such as transport and meals. It should also address empowerment of older persons, to enable them to live their lives as independently as possible."

With respect to the identified 'threats', it comes as no surprise that expectations of what the service is there to do should be in the same breath attenuated with challenges to its execution; it is ambitious. Nowhere is there an area more fertile with potential cultural friction than the health care arena (Hudson et al., 1997). Chapter 3 elaborates on these issues more. Peck et al.'s (2001) service integration research demonstrated that shared cultures were widely believed to lead to seamless services and collaboration, but that concern over protecting roles and skills told another story. From our findings, it would also appear that no country is free from this conflict. It was contradictory that the main threats to realising integrated care impacted upon a main purpose of the service of providing person-centred care, and the frustration of staff could be witnessed through their vocalised illustrations.

However, staff interviewed were confident in their perceptions and held a belief in the fundamental 'rightness' of the approach, a view that thread through much of the conceptual analysis. In between the tensions there was a single unifying desire to serve the client the best possible way. There can be no doubt that in essence, this basic formula is needed for the service to work. It was interesting that the views of countries with little policy guidance and relatively immature service development (Italy and Greece) were anchored to elements similar to those expressed with a stronger tradition of integration.

The user and informal carer position in this scenario was interesting. It was unsurprising that users and informal carers were mostly positive about the service. This concurs with other findings, such as Carpenter et al.'s (2004) study of integrated mental health services. What is less evident in the wider literature are the contradictions that appeared to exist between the staff and user understanding centring on issues such as seamless care and common goals. This is again perhaps unsurprising, given the difficulties inherent in engaging older people in their care (Tinker, 1995; Hamalainen et al., 2002) and the generational barriers older people have when it comes to questioning care decisions (Irvine, 2001).

The resulting detachment that may proceed a lack of engagement could result in professionals taking over and older people becoming reliant on workers to do their decision-making for them. This in turn results in a less than client-centred outcome. Moving on from this there is the potential for service providers to make assumptions about how the service is operating and for whom particularly in the situation where limited service resources are divided among an older population. As a result, there are different interests occurring that impact on the possibilities and full understanding and perhaps use of services by users and carers.

So while the rhetoric of integrated care is worthy, there are indications that realising the expressed ideals of integrated care is difficult, as is gaining a common understanding between staff and users. Consideration must be given to the perceived theory/practice divide here, leading to the question of how much is possible in practice. If clients are unable to internalise the same aspirations, it will ultimately be challenging to achieve a patient-centred service and goals of independence when very ill-health frail older people are in need of every possible care given to her/him. Equally, it could be argued that having working definitions that are built around legitimate and moral foundations of what seems right are commendable and motivating for workers, but could lend themselves to a form of lofty integrated care professionalism that is difficult to challenge.

Paradoxically, such a situation may render professionals unable to truly listen to the client, especially if it is dissenting. This can contribute towards a form of subtle dominance by staff over older people in the health and social care setting, recognised by authors such as Giddens (1998) and Chevannes (2002), often disguised as caring. A further perspective focusing on the gender issues can also be put forward here. Frequently the care given in the home of older people includes traditional female work tasks, such as caring and curing given by professional female workers to mostly female older customers due to their longevity. There is perhaps a stronger potential for female carers to assume responsibility over the older women due to an associated resonance with their situation. Overall, such a situation runs counter to the ethos of empowerment and practice of participatory care.

On the other hand, however, there are counter arguments that provide an alternative perspective. Some frail older clients living at home may expect to be given all their care by the same carers who know them and their habits and needs. Consequently, a 'take-over' of decision-making may be more perceived as an accepted part of total care. We must not forget the generation discrepancy between the modern day desire for people to participate in their care and the actual desire and ability of older people to become fully participative (Ham / Alberti, 2002). From the professional perspective, limited resources could also play a part in the situation. Encountering unmet psychosocial needs that professionals are unable to satisfy is demoralising and frustrating. Maintaining control in the care setting may be one way of countering this frustration. It is clear that more research is needed in this area.

Despite these arguments, it is important to consider the contribution this section of the analysis can make towards understanding best practice in integrated care. The findings have recognised the broadness of what is understood by integrated care and importantly includes the perceptions of staff, users and informal carers at the frontline. It will be important to harness and include this breadth in the development of best practice indicators. That there is a common understanding at least by staff across the nations irrespective of model type provides a good foundation upon which to develop unified and consensus quality indicators. What will be more challenging will be to include dimensions that will be sensitive and meaningful to all stakeholders, especially recipients of the service. A recommendation of this chapter will therefore be to ensure that service users and informal carers fully understand the components of the service being delivered to them, through an active participatory approach from an early stage.

The best practice indicators of integrated care based on the definitions of PROCARE models can be summed up to be:

i. Seamless functioning of organisation in terms of vertical as well as horizontal integration by means of good and working coordination.

ii. A common understanding of what integrated care is there to do. This is enhanced by forming the shared work culture multiprofessionally by constant and regular cooperation, getting known each other, sharing know-how between different multi-skilled professionals in order to construct the same concept of the client, the same concept of the aim of work and to construct the shared work culture.

iii. Having multidimensional tools to enhance, maintain and secure the good exchange of information among formal carers about the clients' situations.

iv. Having a client-centred view of work that truly involves clients.

CHAPTER 2

Access to Integrated Care Provision

Klaas Gorter, Francesca Ceruzzi, Laura Maratou-Alipranti

1   Introduction

A central theme of PROCARE was concerned with discovering users' experiences of integrated care. As was made evident in the first definitions chapter, they should experience it as continuous, seamless care that does not have gaps, waiting, overlap or conflict between different components. The care system should be a unified entity, which responds in a coherent and integrated fashion to users. Modern technology, especially information technology, can be used to create virtual organisations. That is, organisations which are formally separate but because they have full and rapid exchange of information, function as a single entity. In our data we found some "one-window models" that have features of the integrated organisation, especially with its emphasis on a single point of contact or portal entry for older people who wish access to the services. However, in most countries the service delivery is still highly fragmented (see for example Lesemann/ Martin, 1993, and Martin, 2003).

This chapter deals with the first steps in the process of service provision, starting at the moment that a person applies for a service and ending the moment that a decision about service delivery is taken. The central question is: Which pathways do older people have to follow to get to integrated care?

In the following section we present some quantitative data about the admission of clients to models. They mainly concern the number of access episodes and staff involved in access.

In section 2 the various access procedures in the models are presented. We will not describe them one by one in detail, but cluster them into a few categories according to common characteristics. The assessment of the needs of the older people receives special attention, being an important component of the access procedures.

Sharing information is one of the major components of an effective modern health and social care system. Lack of information can create impediments to integration especially when it reinforces professional or organisational boundaries. Section 3 provides data about the exchange of information when new clients access the service. Both information exchange between organisation and client and between organisations are illuminated. The chapter ends with some conclusions about the requirements access procedures have to meet and examples of good practice.

1.1   Data about the Models

In the annexed Table 1 some quantitative data about admission in each of the models are presented, for example number of access episodes and number of staff involved. The present section summarises these data by classifying the models according to the kinds of services they provide and to their number of staff in relation to their number of clients.

The models are mainly focused on home-based care, which concerns a wide range of services to dependent older people who otherwise would need institutional care. According to their mission at least four types can be distinguished:

- *Promoting coordination between service providers* (actions directed towards organisations). This is the main duty in model Germany 2 (Gerontopsychiatrisch-Geriatrischer Verbund Oberspreewald-Lausitz) and one of the tasks in model Austria 1 (Social Care and Health Districts in Hartberg).
- *(Home) care provision.* Examples are the models Finland 2 (Programmes for elderly care in Leppävaara), Greece 2 (Help at Home), Netherlands 1 (Care facility "Zijloever" in Leiden) and United Kingdom 2 (Community rehabilitation).
- *Hospital discharge management.* Examples are the models Austria 2 (Vienna discharge management) and Finland 1 (Helsinki, discharge from hospital to home care).

- *Case management*. Examples are the models Austria 1 (Social Care and Health Districts in Hartberg), France 1+2 (CLIC – Centre Local d'Information et de Coordination) and Italy 2 (Single Point of Access to Home Care).

The models vary considerably in their size. Some models have several thousands of users, others less than 100 (see annexed Table 1). An exact comparison is difficult, however, because each model has its own particularities and modalities in counting the number of staff and the number of clients and times the service is accessed. In the analysis we have tried to calculate service access per worker (ratio between clients and staff). Between the 'home care models' differences appeared. Models with a relatively low client/staff ratio (2/1 to 7/1) are Netherlands 1 (Home care facility Zijloever in Leiden), Denmark 2 (Integrated care in Skævinge) and Finland 2 (Programmes for elderly care in Leppävaara). Models with an intermediate ratio (9/1 to 19/1) are Greece 2 (Help at home, areas 2 and 3), Italy 2 (Single point of access to home care) and Austria 2 (Vienna discharge management). Models with a relatively high ratio (22/1 to 23/1) are United Kingdom 2 (Community Assessment and Rehabilitation) and Greece 2 (Help at home, area 1).

2 Ways of Accessing Services

In this part we present ways through which older people can access services and to whom they have to make their request. Analysing the models, five broad ways of access to services can be observed:
- by clients (or family),
- by a chief worker,
- through hospital discharge,
- by the structure that is acting as gatekeeper,
- through in-built or separate assessment *after* hospital discharge.

2.1 Access by Direct Request of the Client

The first type of access provides the possibility for the client him/herself (or a relative) to request the activation of the service. In Finland and in Greece (model 1 and 2) older people wishing to participate in the programmes may contact the service either directly on their own initiative or be urged by their family members or other people:

"A neighbour urged me to contact the service." (EL2, user 1)

"My decision to access this service was right." (EL1, user 2)

In order to make this kind of access work, it is necessary for the client to have a good understanding of the service and its access facilities. However, the research findings showed that most older clients have a poor understanding of the admittance process. Many of them did not remember how they arrived into home care and who took the initiative. The ones who remembered said that the initiative was taken in hospital before he/she was going back home:

> "One very ill old woman said that it was an incredible surprise to have home care since she would have never even imagined getting personal help at her home: as a woman she had always done everything by herself and never received any kind of help" (FIN2, user 13).

2.2 Access by a Chief Worker

In this method the GP or other health-social professional – mainly doctors, nurses, care managers – makes a referral or fills a form to activate the service (for example sending a fax to the office).

In UK model 1 (Limes Livingstone integrated care project) the GP is a gatekeeper for acute medical services and screens individuals according to clinical criteria before making a referral to secondary services. Secondary services are effectively accessed by GPs on the patient's behalf. In emergencies older people or their carers can bypass their GP and gain direct access to more specialist services through Accident and Emergency departments in hospitals.

In the Italian model 1 (Working Unit of Continuous Care) the process starts with the identification of older people at risk by hospital staff. The nurse of the unit fills the form and gives it to the administrative office; the administration passes the form to the geriatrician. Then the social worker examines the patient, interviews the family and the GP and makes the needs assessments.

In the Greek model 2 (Help at Home Programme) the chief social worker decides about access to the service and he/she is responsible for the assessment of needs. In the Austrian model 2 (Social Care and Health Districts in Hartberg) applicants can make a request for services directly to the manager. The manager works in the Red Cross organisation and is responsible for getting older people in need of care the help they need at home. If necessary the manager also visits the older person if they cannot visit the office.

2.3   *Access through Hospital Discharge*

In the Danish model 1 (Rehabilitation upon discharge from hospital in Søllerød) the movement of frail elderly through the care pathway is considered a delicate process, as frail older people often find themselves in a state of anxiety regarding their future situation – will they regain their previous health state, will they be able to return to their own home? Thus, in order to produce person-centred outcomes the delivered services have to continuously meet the needs of the user, which stresses the need for communication between the relevant providers in individual chains of care. Furthermore, the user needs to be continuously informed about the proceedings in order to prevent feelings of insecurity. However, the discharge procedure from hospital for people needing rehabilitation can be a complicated affair in that it consists of several points of access and exit from different providers.

A senior manager describes the process:

> "Every time a Søllerød-citizen above the age of 67 is admitted to hospital they send a fax to the coordinating nurses no matter what the condition of the citizen is. Then we're informed that our citizens are admitted to hospital and the two nurses then visit the citizens at the hospital. Then we gather information on the treatment and the time-plan for care. If the citizens need municipal services – that is rehabilitation, domestic services, aids, meals-on-wheels or whatever, then we arrange a discharge meeting midway where the citizen is present with representatives from the hospital and the municipality. We agree that it is important to take a general perspective on the issues we have to deal with prior to the discharge of the individual. We do this because every time you do something with frail elderly – shifting from one system to another – that is where all the accidents occur, like misunderstandings, loss of information and all that" (DK1, manager).

The needs of people who are discharged from hospital are assessed by the coordinating nurse. The coordinating nurse is independent from the rehabilitation facility. According to their level of frailty people from this group can either be admitted for intermediate care at the rehabilitation facility, be admitted for respite care prior to rehabilitation or be sent on to their own homes. The needs of people belonging to the latter group are assessed according to the procedures for the outpatient group.

For the outpatient group the needs assessment for rehabilitation/training is undertaken by the leading occupational therapist and the leading physiotherapist. When the rehabilitation programme is concluded, representatives from the services in question assess the needs for long-term care services at a multidisciplinary discharge conference where the citizen and relatives are present. At the discharge conference, for example needs for domestic care services, day-care facilities or aids are finally assessed and agreed upon. An assessing nurse who is independent from the actual service providers heads such assessment teams. A written care plan for the individual is produced at the discharge conference.

People who have gone through a rehabilitation programme have their functional abilities mapped through the training plans, and this assessment is the basis of the final needs assessment.

2.4   In-built Assessment or Separate Assessment

In some models the service-providing organisation itself does the needs assessment and decides about admittance. This type might be called in-built assessment. An example is the UK model Community Assessment and Rehabilitation. The CART-team itself collects information about the patients that enter the service. In other models the needs assessment is positioned outside the service-providing organisation. There the requests for services should be addressed to a specific agency that collects information about the needs of the applicants. After this assessment, the people who have been found eligible for services are referred to suitable care providers.

The latter type might be called 'separate need assessment'. An example of this type is the Single Point of Access to Home Care in Italy. The Territorial Assessment Unit decides whether integrated home care is necessary and defines the care programme for the client. The French local coordination centres (CLICs) and Dutch regional assessment agencies (RIOs) have a similar function. An overview of all models, classifying them in the two categories of in-built and separate assessment, is presented in the Annex to this chapter.

The Danish model 'Rehabilitation upon discharge from hospital in Søllerød' is a special case. The rehabilitation facility selects its clients, thus administers in-built needs assessment. But at the end of the rehabilitation period, a discharge meeting is organised to assess the care needs of the person after leaving the facility. This meeting can be regarded as a separate needs assessment, because the required care after discharge has to be supplied by others (like home care agencies and day-care facilities).

2.5 Gatekeeping Organisations

Some of the above-mentioned agencies act as gatekeepers. In the Netherlands, the RIOs act as the gatekeeper for both home care and institutional care. There are some 85 RIOs, whose functioning falls under municipal responsibility. The system was set up to divide the allocation and provision of care. People who request care have an independent needs assessment. Independent means: without being influenced by the parties involved in the financing and delivery of care. RIOs are responsible for objectively assessing care, attuned to the needs of the client. Thus, if an older and/or disabled person articulates a care need in the area of nursing, home care, or material support (e.g. transport or housing facilities), then s/he has to turn to a RIO. In mutual consultation with the client, a special trained assessment consultant determines the kind of care that is needed. To assess the care need, consultants make use of a standard and nationally used protocol (so-called 'model protocol') in which criteria for the access to specialised care are formulated. What kind of care is required, is determined on the basis of seven functions: housekeeping assistance, personal care, nursing, supporting guidance, activating/advising guidance, treatment, and accommodation.

When the RIO considers the care to be necessary, the decision is passed to the administrative care office in the region. Subsequently, the administrative care office is responsible for purchasing the required care from the available care providers.

France introduced a systematic orientation towards joint working to facilitate the access process. In 2000 the Ministry for Employment and Solidarity launched a 5-year programme for the creation of 1,000 Local Information and Gerontological Coordination Centres (CLICs) with financial support from the state. The objective was to set up a geographically-based network with three levels of competencies: Level 1 – welcoming, informing, advising and supporting; level 2 – assessing needs, compiling personalised care plans; level 3 – implementing, monitoring and adapting those care plans. A certification process allows each CLIC to be qualified for each of these levels.

In Italy, simplifying access to home care services is the specific objective of an experimental project carried out in the Val d'Arno and Empolese Valdelsa area (Tuscany). Single Points of Access, where all the requests for home care – including the protected discharge from hospital – are collected, have been made available within the area covered by the Local Health Agency. The project is promoted and coordinated by the Department of Primary Care of the Local Health Agency 11 (Empoli) and is an example of a 'friendly health service that adopts a strongly client oriented approach'.

Information about the older person is sent to the Single Point of Access by telephone (if the situation is communicated by a relative or by the family's GP) or by fax (with standard forms, at least five days before the discharge if the situation is communicated by hospital department). If the situation is communicated by phone, the administrator will fill out the personal form of the patient containing this biographical information and the needs of the patient (social, medical, and regarding rehabilitation). This information gets put onto a centralised system with a specific identification code for each patient.

The administrator makes copies of the information in the personal form and sends them to professionals involved in the case. In addition the family's GP gets informed that his patient will be discharged from hospital. This allows an immediate intervention: at least one operator and the doctor of the district will carry out a first visit at home (within 24 hours). The family's GP knows that his patient is at home and he decides independently when to carry out a visit. After that, within one week after the discharge, the Territorial Assessment Unit gets together to define the individualised interventions (new evaluation of the needs after the first intervention). Every time a member of staff carries out an intervention with the patient, he will record this and subsequent progress in the centralised information system.

The person can be discharged from home care in the following ways: if objectives have been reached (for example the patient's condition get better); if the patient has been readmitted to hospital; if he has been referred to a rehabilitation service or to another municipality; or if the patient has died.

3   Exchange of Information during the Process

This section describes which types of information are exchanged between client and organisation and between organisations. All phases of the access procedure are covered.

Access to integrated care requires the exchange of a lot of information between all involved parties: clients who request care, professionals who decide on it, relevant service providers and possible intermediaries.

Information exchange is vital, especially during needs assessment and at the outcome, when decisions about care are made. The clients have to state their needs and wishes in order to receive all the necessary care. At the same time they need to know what the services can do for them, such as ways in which they are supplied and possible costs. The assessment will end with a decision about service requirements which is shared with the older person and their families. In some models the assessment agency continues supporting the clients by getting in touch with the relevant service providers.

If we approach integrated care from a client-centred perspective, the information should cover all care needs in the life domains of the person (like health, activities of daily living and housing). Integrated care can also be approached from the perspective of the organisational interfaces, where information should be shared with the relevant health and social care providers and professional disciplines (like home helps, nurses, occupational therapists and doctors). In practice however, both approaches will yield similar results, because care in the respective life domains is usually assigned to certain disciplines.

With respect to the interviews conducted in this study, clients were asked several questions about their experiences with the process of access. Were their wishes and needs respected? Was the information provided of the right sort and easy for them to understand? Did they feel that they were involved in decisions about their case? And did they get what they wanted?

It was found that most clients do not have a clear picture of the access procedure. At the most they could only recall that 'a lady' has paid them a visit to talk about the necessary care or that a son or daughter arranged the application for them. Similar findings appeared in many other countries. In the Finnish model 'Integrated home care for older people living at home' most of the interviewed clients did not remember how they started receiving home care and who took the initiative. In some cases their daughter or some other family member organised the start of the care (FIN2, users 1 and 2). The French CLICs inform the older people about their personal allowance and existing services. However, in general the people hardly remember anything about the information. For reaching the best solution they rely upon the coordinator. Also in the Italian WUCC (Working Unit of Continuous Care) the users hardly remember the needs assessment and the way it was conducted. Similarly, most clients of the Dutch home care facility Zijloever only had a faint impression of the assessment process. In many cases they even knew nothing about it, because their children had arranged it for them. A user of the UK model 'Limes Livingston Integrated Care Project' reacted in the same vein to questions about assessment:

> "I honestly can't remember. All I know is that I'm glad I did come. My daughter has done all the arrangements". (UK1, user)

The active participation of the family members is further illustrated by a Greek example:

> "My daughter urged me and I came here to overcome the melancholy and the loneliness I felt for my husband's loss. In the beginning I had preconceived ideas and I came reluctantly". (EL1, user)

Thus in general, clients have a poor understanding of the access procedure. From this observation it follows that interviews with the service users do not teach us much about involvement in the assessment process from the clients' perspective. If older people are not aware of being involved, it can be suggested that they may not be in control or not even a partner in the process. Many of them tended to leave the initiative to the professionals or to their relatives. Moreover, they expressed little interest in the subject matter. Their primary concern was not the way decisions took place in the past, but whether they received the right care at that time.

The interviews with the key workers and managers showed that the models in this study differed how they dealt with information. We describe three aspects: informing the public about available services, information exchange during admittance of prospective clients to the services, and the use of information systems.

3.1 Informing Older People about Available Services

In order to get the most appropriate care, older people should be informed about the available services and how they can be accessed. It is not always easy to find the appropriate services in the 'jungle' of different providers, each with its different regulations for admittance.

The models in this study dealt primarily with the supply of care to people who have requested it, not with informing the public about existing types of care. Nevertheless, some data about how the public got informed were evident.

The usual way to inform the older people is through written material (leaflets etc.), describing the types of services and what they have to offer. Another common way to draw the attention to the services is through the general practitioners: if their patients are in need of care, GPs inform them about the relevant care providers or refer them to the relevant organisations. In some models and countries the GP even acts as a gatekeeper; in order to access care a GP referral is required.

In some models specific arrangements for providing information have been established. One of these is the Gerontological Coordination Centres in France. These CLICs not only have a task in supporting individual clients, they also play a role in informing the older citizens in general about available care. The system in the Netherlands has a similar function. In order to help people to find appropriate care, many municipalities have established a window where interested people may obtain information and advice about all kinds of available services and facilities and about how to access them. This window for information and advice is a central point where people can ask questions about the different health and social care agencies. An interesting approach for ascertaining the covert needs of older citizens not yet receiving any form of long- or short-term care services takes place in Denmark. The health centre conducts preventative home visits to all elderly above the age of 75 or contact visits to older people who appear to be in need, such as following the death of a spouse or after getting a hint from the GP. The preventative home visits and contact visits provide an opportunity for the health centre to uncover unmet care needs among older citizens in the municipality.

Such a system is also available in the UK through a Primary Care Visitors scheme.

3.2 Attributes of Information Supply and Exchange

The information exchange during access can vary in its extensiveness. Other important attributes of information supply and exchange systems in the models included achieving a personal approach, using tools for needs assessment, and applying a more or less advanced information system. We will examine these attributes in more detail.

3.2.1 Degree of Information Exchange

Models also differ in the amount and range of the information exchanged. In some models the procedure for admittance ends at the point when the decision for services is made. In some other models the organisation acts beyond this by offering assistance to the client in obtaining the care, e.g. contacting relevant service-providing organisations in the region. The Open Care Centres (KAPIs) in Greece are an example of a less extensive approach. A social worker of KAPI can only inform the clients about the available services and provisions. The Dutch model Bureau for Care Allocation (BCA) is an example of a more extensive procedure. BCA receives information about the client from the assessment agency, visits the client to conduct a second assessment, explains about possibilities for care, and assists the client in contacting the relevant service-providing organisations. These are just two examples. The table in the Annex classifies all the models into a dichotomy (extensive, less extensive) and gives a short description of the information exchange. On the whole, the table shows that the models with separate needs assessment (see section 2.4) have a more extensive information exchange. This outcome was to be expected, considering that in these models appropriate service-supplying organisations for the clients must be determined.

3.2.2 Personal Approach

In most models the information exchange between (prospective) clients and service providers and between the respective professionals is mediated by one person. This person thus has a very central position in the dissemination of information. An example is the Austrian model on hospital discharge in Vienna. The key person in the process of information exchange is the discharge manager. She keeps in touch with the clients and organises contacts between the various professionals who are involved in the case. Her actions include:

- collecting information about the patients from the hospital;
- participating in team meetings with different professionals in the hospital where patients are discussed;
- having informal, one-to-one communication with nurses and doctors;
- conducting interviews with the patients and/or their family members about their care needs and living conditions;
- passing information to the municipal agency that organises home care.

In the German model 'Home Care Nürnberg' (HCN) the case manager has a similar central position in information exchange. The case manager ascertains the client's needs by a detailed assessment in the course of a visit at home. Thereafter the case manager offers the client different suitable possibilities of support, which he then will organise for the client by contacting the respective services. The resultant plan is coordinated with the GP. HCN furthermore:

- informs the client about the local offer of services, legal affairs, regulations determined by law and claims for services rendered;
- informs GPs about the support/care plan, the termination of the case management and the client's retransfer to the GP;
- contacts and organises the services and facilities being involved in individual cases.

Many other models also have such a key person in the information process, as shown in the following examples.

In the Danish model 'Rehabilitation upon discharge from hospital in Søllerød' the coordinating nurse bridges the gap in the every day cooperation between hospitals and the municipality. She compiles information on the health statuses of patients at the hospital and passes it on to the rehabilitation facility.

In the Finnish model 'Programmes for elderly care in Leppävaara' the chief home care officer decides about the access, informs everybody concerned and coordinates the services. In the Greek model 'Help at home for older people' the chief home care officer (a social worker) has a similar central position by assessing the needs of potential users, deciding about access to the services, informing everybody concerned, keeping a social and medical history record of the clients and evaluating the services.

In the French CLICs the case manager has an important role. She offers information, advice, and guidance for older people and their families, and visits the older people to assess their needs. Thereafter she organises a co-ordination meeting with the professionals concerned to draft a care plan, which is proposed to the client. The role of the care coordinators in the Dutch model 'Bureau for Care Allocation and Referral' is comparable. After receiving information about the results of the needs assessment (done by a separate agency), the care coordinator conducts an access interview with the applicant for additional information. Together with the client, she explores the wishes as well as the different possibilities for care. After agreement is reached, she refers the client to a care provider.

In the Dutch model 'Care facility Zijloever' the care mediator is the central person in information exchange, both at the start and during the service provision. She arranges one of several access interviews with future clients to inform them about the way the service provision operates and she explores their needs, wishes and preferences. During the service provision she monitors clients' (dis)satisfaction with the delivered care.

In the UK-model 'Limes Livingstone Integrated Care Project' the care manager's role is pivotal. She explains about home care after discharge, and about any financial benefits or entitlements the older person may have, and she spans the acute sector (hospital), the community hospital and the Limes social rehabilitation centre.

3.2.3 Assessment Tools

Integrated care calls for a comprehensive needs assessment, covering all relevant life domains of the person who requests care. In several models specific tools for assessment are used. Standard tools promote uniform needs assessment, and the resulting information can easily be transferred to other professionals and organisations involved. Thus they are also an aid to information exchange. The following examples illustrate their set-up.

In the Danish model 'Integrated care in Skævinge' the needs of new users are assessed with the tool 'Common Language'. This tool has been developed by the Ministry of Social Affairs in cooperation with the National Association of Local Authorities. The Common Language assessment tool should facilitate quality assurance and uniform assessment of needs across the municipalities in Denmark. It focuses on the following overall dimensions of the functional abilities of the service user in performing IADLs and PADLs (Instrumental respectively Physical Activities of Daily Living):

- personal care (personal hygiene, dressing, going to the toilet, eating and drinking);
- cooking;
- mobility (balance, movement inside the house and walking, movement outside the house and transportation, handling of objects);
- housekeeping (performance of housekeeping functions, ability to help other people);
- capacity to plan the tasks of everyday living;
- social relations;
- participation in social life and fields of interest;
- mental functions;
- ability to monitor own health situation.

The tool thus clarifies the overall functional ability of the citizens and points towards specific areas where given services may be required. A multiprofessional assessment team undertakes the assessment for services upon request from a given individual.

The Italian model 'Working Unit of Continuous Care' also applies a multidimensional assessment. Different professionals are involved in it: the geriatrician for the health aspects, the social worker for the social aspects and the nurses for both of these aspects. In the multidimensional assessment a regional tool, called SVAMA, is used. It analyses the following aspects of the patient:

- autonomy profile (cognitive situation, mobility, functional situation);
- social support;
- need of health care;
- health assessment (pathologies, communication);
- housing situation;
- economic situation (income).

In the Finnish model 'Discharge from hospital to home care in Helsinki' the 'RAVA-index' is becoming more important as a tool. Coping with the tasks of every day life is an important assessment criterion.

In the Finnish model 'Programmes for elderly care in Leppävaara' the Resident Assessment Instrument (RAI) is used to determine the eligibility of the old person to home care. It takes the old person's social functional capacity into account. This Home Care Resident Assessment Instrument (HC-RAI) is also deployed in the German model 'Home Care Nürnberg' (HCN). The social assessment concerns the client's life situation in the fields of health, cognitive capabilities, body care, domestic care, the client's strengths and weaknesses, mobility, social and emotional supporting systems, dwelling situation, purchase and meals, economic situation by means of a self-assessment by the client. This social assessment is supplemented by complementary assessments (medical, auxiliary nursing, functional therapeutical, psychological assessments). So while HCN aims to undertake a multidisciplinary assessment, only some of the outpatient nursing services are actually using HC-RAI because of its time-consuming and detailed nature.

The problem of detail is handled in the UK-model 'Community Assessment and Rehabilitation' by splitting the needs assessment in a core assessment and an appendix of more in-depth assessments. The core assessment is a screening tool. It covers medical history, transfers, mobility, social situation, skin integrity, bladder and bowel function, speech, hearing, vision, home environment, cognitive, perceptual, mental state, and sleep patterns. The appendix is used if it is found from the screening tool that a more in-depth assessment would be required (such as an assessment with regard to nursing, physiotherapy, occupational therapy, care management, or speech and language assessment).

3.2.4 Information Systems

One of the organisational elements to realise integration in social and health care services concerns access to shared information that is collected during the different phases of the care process by all the involved services and staff. A suitable information system can facilitate accessibility to the data.

In the German model 'Home Care Nürnberg' a self-developed transfer sheet is used in case of a transferral or changeover between different kinds and levels of treatment (care). It provides basic information concerning the patient beyond the medical treatment levels. The sheet contains general and current information about the patient (e.g. current state of health in case of transfer to a hospital). The employee of the facility that wants to transfer the patient, fills in the transition sheet for the employee of the receiving facility.

In the Danish model 'Rehabilitation upon discharge from hospital in Søllerød' the importance of accessible information is stressed. According to the interviewed staff, the obstacles of producing an integrated care pathway for the individual primarily relate to the availability of information about rehabilitants. Problems mainly concern the difficulty of getting in touch with specific personnel who hold information that may have to be used in the assessment of needs. It is expected that the forthcoming introduction of an ICT-based record system for all users of services for older people in the municipality will eradicate the problems of the horizontal flow of information.

Among the models in this study, the Italian 'Single Point of Access to Home Care' developed the most elaborate information system. The project was conceived because of the need to monitor medical and pharmaceutical expenses in the territory, starting from the general practitioners' prescriptions. Once started, the Department of Primary Care realised that this was an opportunity to link all primary health care services, including social services. Now, all data of citizens who are treated by a general practitioner, supported by social and health services or hosted in hospitals, old-age and nursing homes, can be searched and tracked down in a single database that is continuously being updated.

This "Single Point of Access to Home Care" aims at collecting and organising all the information regarding the health and social situation of citizens who received territorial services into one single database. In this way, every citizen would have his/her own file containing complete information (biographical, social, medical, and rehabilitation needs of the person).

This system allows every operator to consult any file at any time through his company Intranet or from his personal computer at home, just as he could insert new data using a common web browser. Each patient gets a specific identification code in this centralised system, and every time a service provider carries out an intervention with the patient, he will record it and the outcome on the health of the patient. When the system is fully implemented, every older person that is being assisted by either a GP, social service, hospital, or rehabilitation facility, can be traced through one unique users' archive that is constantly updated.

Privacy is guaranteed through a password and through systems encoding the information that is running over the net. The kind of access a member of staff has, will depend on his professional profile. It will be possible for users to have access to their personal file after having been provided with a digital certificate.

Several success criteria have been formulated: the collaboration between service providers is facilitated and the information passages between the offices are reduced, the administration and bureaucracy are simplified, the data about the users are collected and entered only once, and the territory and hospital services are put online. The Italian project has also highlighted the various obstacles in introducing such an information system. They include resistance against joint working and the use of personal computers, the cultural cleavages between health and social care workers, the large number of people involved, and the geographical distance between staff members.

4   Conclusions

Needs assessment is a crucial step in the attainment of integrated care. First, the available care supply should not form the basis of the needs assessment, but the client's needs – *supply follows demand* being the primary consideration.

In general, clients seemed to be satisfied with the advice they receive, and with the manner by which their needs are provided for; this is elaborated on in Chapter 6. Nevertheless, the quality of needs assessment still requires improvement, especially with regard to integral and demand orientation. Ex et al. (2004) concur with this finding.

The assessment should cover all life domains of the person who requests services, by considering both social and medical aspects. Older people's needs for care often transcend the boundaries of the service providing disciplines, like home help, personal care, nursing, occupational therapy, physiotherapy, supply of aids, primary health care, care in the hospital, etc. Professional grouping might influence the allocation of services. This means that if needs are assessed by medical service providers, it is most probable that medical interventions are prescribed. Similarly, social care is likely to be recommended if the needs assessment is conducted by people from social professions (Leichsenring, 2004). A comprehensive, multidimensional needs assessment, covering all life domains, should prevent such disciplinary biases. It should help to involve different kinds of professions, to improve communication between them, to improve information flows.

One issue that impedes information flow is concerned with professional territorialism. For instance one tactic used is to emphasise the privileged status of the relationship that they have with their clients or users, in particular the confidentiality of this relationship. This 'restriction' in the flow of information can be reinforced by data protection legislation, which specifies that data obtained for one purpose and stored electronically should not be reused for another purpose. Such restrictions on the free and easy movement of information are increasingly seen as a major impediment for integration. This tendency reinforces the tensions between agencies and in particular restricts the flow of information as each profession claims ownership of the information it has collected and uses (Alaszewski/Leichsenring, 2004: 66). For example in England, the Department of Health has identified such problems in the following way: "Assessments are often duplicated with no coherent approach across health and social care services. This problem is exacerbated by fragmentation of information systems, which unnecessarily duplicates information held about individuals. Failure to share such information results in failure to deliver the best package of care. Care provided on the basis of assessment may not be well coordinated or follow the complex pathway that an older person might follow" (Department of Health, 2001a : 24).

Results from almost all models showed that the clients have a poor understanding of the needs assessment. They may find the assessment overwhelming. It is obvious that the clients become more dependent on professionals, and thus loose control, in that they do not understand the procedures. Lack of insight makes it difficult for them to make their needs and wishes clear in the appropriate way, and there is insufficient time for them to have any influence on their care.

Advocacy for social and health services clients is a way of protecting and asserting elderly rights: to make choices about their lives, to receive the social and health services on the basis of their needs, to be informed of their rights, to make a complaint when something goes wrong, to explore alternative sources of support, to increase communication levels between elders and others and to facilitate access procedures.

A simple and conveniently arranged access procedure will probably prevent the clients from losing their way. It can be added that clear access procedures not only have advantages for the clients, but also for the professionals. As various professionals are involved in integrated care, it can be inferred that in the access procedure a multidisciplinary needs assessment is preferable. The reports from models confirm this inclination: generally they welcome multidisciplinary needs assessment. On the other hand, it was shown that this type of assessment by its nature is rather complex. If it is too extensive or time-consuming there is the risk that it will not be applied in practice. This has for instance occurred in the Finnish models: Although a multidisciplinary assessment is aspired to, the chief home care officer conducts the assessment for the most part. In the Netherlands a similar situation exists: the assessment adviser performs the task in most instances; only in complex cases a multidisciplinary assessment team is called in. And in the German model an elaborate assessment is often avoided because it is too time-consuming.

Information technology (IT) offers promising possibilities, which are used insufficiently until now. The Italian model 'Single Point of Access to Home Care' shows how an information system can be employed. Further introduction of information systems may facilitate the exchange of information about clients between service providers, an important factor in achieving integrated care (Nesti, 2004). IT can be used to create a virtual organisation, i.e. organisations which are formally separate but because they have full and rapid exchange of information, function as a single entity (Billings et al., 2004). While the one-window model focuses primarily on the point of access, it is also important to facilitate the development of a virtual integrated organisation for older people. As stated in the Dutch Congreskrant OL2000 (2002): "The central issue is whether the so-called 'front office' manages to make effective contacts with various provisions and functions in the 'back office': (in fact) the local service providers. The better the mutual cooperation between these providers the better the chance that the 'front office' facility will succeed.

It should be noted that in the models with separate assessments (see section 2.4) we can also see front offices and back offices. The first are the organisations that conduct the assessments, the latter the ones that provide the services. To prevent tensions between them, smooth exchange of information and close cooperation must take place.

To be able to get the appropriate care people have to know about existing facilities. Services should be accessible in the first place. Well-established points for information and advice, like those in France and in the Netherlands, are useful in helping people to find and reach the required services. The Danish model 'Integrated care in Skævinge' is an interesting example of a method in detecting covert needs. The health centre conducts home visits to frail elderly in the municipality. This information is especially important for older people not yet receiving any form of long or short-term care, considering that clients of care institutions should get information and support from their service providers.

To sum up, there seems to be a certain strain between a comprehensive, multidisciplinary approach on the one hand and a simpler and easier manageable approach on the other. Access procedures should meet at least three requirements:

- They should be *comprehensive* to cover the clients needs for health and social care.

- They should be *understandable* for the clients: Simplifying the procedures of access to the services; reducing and facilitating the administration activities; offering organised and efficient information on the available services and their costs.
- They should be *manageable*. If they are very time-consuming the professionals will tend not to use them. The assessment tools should be designed in such a way that the monitoring of the client's needs can be conducted with the least effort. In addition, information about waiting lists, resources and interventions should be easily available.

Furthermore, personal traits of the client and the professional assessing should not influence the assessment decision – *objectivity* must be guaranteed. The needs assessment must be free from influence of municipalities, care agencies, care providers, professionals who refer, and patient interest groups – *independence* must be guaranteed.

Annex: Features of Access in the Models

The following table summarises some characteristics and data of the 18
models.

The entries are:
- Country and name of the model.
- Design of assessment: built in / separate (see section 2.4).
- Information exchange (see section 3.2).
- Indications of size: number of times the service is accessed and number
  of involved staff. If these specific figures about access were not avail-
  able, the number of users and staff are stated (see section 1.1).

Table 1: Data about the Models

Model	In-built/ Separate Assess-ment	Information exchange	Number of ac-cessions/users	Number of staff
Austria 1 Social Care and Health Districts in Hartberg	Separate	Extensive approach Care manager: • informs clients and makes care plan • organises meetings between providers	Clients can directly apply In 2002: 941 elderly received care services in the districts	51 people (managers, home nurses, home carers, home helpers) plus volunteers work in the district
Austria 2 Vienna discharge management	Separate	Extensive approach Discharge manager: • receives information about patients from hospital • has meetings with pro-fessionals in hospital • has interview with pa-tients and/or relatives about care needs • communicates with home care organisa-tions about necessary services	In 2002: 389 patients were consulted concerning discharge from the hospital	No evidence Staff on discharge man-agement in the hospital
Denmark 1 Rehabilitation upon discharge from hospital in Søllerød	In-built + separate	Extensive approach • Coordinating nurse in the hospital informs home care facilities about older citizens who are admitted to the hospital & passes information on the health status of the patient to the rehabili-tation facility • During treatment a multidisciplinary group exchanges information about the progress of the patient • For people returning to their home a multi-disciplinary meeting is organised, in which needs for services at home are assessed & relevant service provid-ers are informed	-------	-------

Model	In-built/ Separate Assessment	Information exchange	Number of accessions/users	Number of staff
Denmark 2 Integrated care in Skævinge	In-built	Extensive approach • Single point of entry to the health centre • Needs assessment by team, leading to a care plan • Assessment tool is deployed to promote quality and uniform assessment, focusing on PADL's and IADL's	In 2002: • 55 people were residing in the apartments in the Health Centre • 192 people received domestic care • 104 people received training and rehabilitation • 141 people were attached to the regular day care facility at the health centre • 522 people had received aids or adaptations to housing • Total clients: 1014	136 workers from 13 different professional groups are employed in the older people care sector of the Municipality (full-time and part-time).
Finland 1 Helsinki, discharge from hospital to home care	In-built	Less extensive approach • Assessment by multi-professional team (in demanding situations) or by chief home care officer (in most cases) • Chief home care officer informs the patient about available services. • Assessment tool (the RAVA-index) is used, leading to a care and service plan	No evidence	Every Teamwork comprises: 6-12 home helpers 1 home nurse 1 chief home-care officer

Model	In-built/ Separate Assessment	Information exchange	Number of accessions/users	Number of staff
Finland 2 Programmes for elderly care in Leppävaara	In-built	Less extensive approach • Chief of the home care and home nurse visit the client, make needs assessment using the RAI-instrument, and inform the client • A care and service plan should be written, but this is not always done in practice • Home care and hospital staff have assessment meetings concerning the situation of older people who are going home.	District KL: 80-100 permanent clients District KV: 80 permanent clients	KL: 18 workers KV: 12 workers
France 1 CLIC (Local Information and Gerontological Coordination Centre) in Chalûs	Separate	Extensive approach • Case manager visits the old person to assess needs; supplies the people with information about available services • Case manager organises a Coordination meeting with the concerned professionals before the start of the service delivery • During service delivery the case manager organises regular steering meetings with the professionals to evaluate the care plan.	38 old people (2002)	3 workers: intermediates (acting as coordinators)
France 2 CLIC in Phalempin	Separate	See CLIC in Chalûs	99 old people (2002)	3 workers : intermediates

Model	In-built/ Separate Assess- ment	Information exchange	Number of ac- cessions/users	Number of staff
Germany 1 HCN (Home Care Nürnberg); Praxisnetz Nürnberg	Separate	Extensive approach • HCN is informed about the client's situation by the GP or client • Case manager visits client to conduct a needs assessment. Assessment tool (Home Care-RAI) not always used, because it is time-consuming • HCN informs client about available services etc. • HCN informs GP about care plan • Case manager contacts the relevant services and facilities • In case of transfer, a transfer sheet is used, containing basic infor- mation about the client	2002: 122 2003: 89	2 workers acting as coor- dinators
Germany 2 GPGV OSL (Gerontopsy- chiatrisch-Geria- trischer Verbund Oberspreewald- Lausitz)	N.A.	Not applicable: The model comprises meet- ings with professionals to promote cooperation (clients are not directly involved).	Not applicable	1 coordinator of the associa- tion 3 representa- tives of the association
Greece 1 KAPIs (Open Care Centres for Older People) in 4 places	In-built	Less extensive approach • Social worker informs the client about the services and provisions of KAPI • Staff members have regular meetings in which information is exchanged (during provision)	KAPI of Maroussi (KM): 3,500 registered/ 500 users KAPI of Nea Philadelphia (KNP): 3,150 registered KAPI of Ilioupolis (KI): 2,500 registered users KAPI of Alimos (KA): 550 registered users	11 workers 9 workers 7 workers 5 permanent + 2 part-time

Model	In-built/ Separate Assess- ment	Information exchange	Number of ac- cessions/users	Number of staff
Greece 2 Help at home for older people	In-built	Less extensive approach • Social worker visits the potential user to assess needs and to inform about available services • A social and medical history record is kept, containing information about health, social conditions and needs of client • The social worker informs everybody involved in the care	3 Municipali- ties in Greater Athens (at the time of the study 2003): • Help-H. Nea Ionia: 70 users • Help-H. Nikaia: 55 users • Help-H. Kifis- sia: 43 users	Staff: 3 workers 6 workers 5 permanent + 2 part-time
Italy 1 WUCC (Work- ing Unit of Con- tinuous Care)	Separate	Extensive approach • WUCC conducts multidimensional as- sessment, after being signaled about the patient by the hospital • Assessment instru- ment (SVAMA) is used, focusing on disabilities, social support, housing and economic situation • WUCC activates the necessary services	2000 to 2003: 2,000 clients	Permanent members of the WUCC are 2 workers: a geriatrician and a social worker Coordination of the acces- sions

105

Model	In-built/ Separate Assess- ment	Information exchange	Number of ac- cessions/users	Number of staff
Italy 2 Single Point of Access to Home Care	Separate	Extensive approach • Information about ap- plicants is inserted into a centralised informa- tion system and passed to the TAU (Territorial Assessment Unit) • Multiprofessional as- sessment team decides whether integrated home care is neces- sary and defines the programme • All involved service pro- viders receive informa- tion about clients from the centralised informa- tion system and insert information about the clients into the system • The information is used by TAU to evaluate the interventions	Treatments at home. 703 (total users)	Empolese District: 2 district doctors 4 physio- therapists 6 nurses full- time and 2 nurses part-time 9 social assistants (operators + 3 SSO/ social- sanitary opera- tors) Valdelsa District: 1 district doctor 3 physiothera- pists 22 nurses + 2 SSO (social- health assist- ants) 6 social assistants Valdarno District: 1 district doctor 2 physio- therapists 26 nurses + 2 SSO (social- health assist- ants)
Netherlands 1 Home care facil- ity "Zijloever" in Leiden	In-built	Less extensive approach • Assessment agency (RIO) conducts the first assessment and decides on eligibility for care • Second assessment by service provider (Zijl- oever), before client is taken into care. The care manager arranges intake interviews with the future clients to inform them about the way Zijloever works and to explore their wishes and preferences	135 clients	80 staff members (24 hours care)

Model	In-built/ Separate Assess- ment	Information exchange	Number of ac- cessions/users	Number of staff
Netherlands 2 Bureau for care allocation (BCA) in Kerkrade and environs	Separate	Extensive approach • Assessment agency (RIO) conducts the first assessment and decides on eligibility for care • The second assessment by a care coordinator of BCA. In an intake interview she explores the wishes of the ap- plicant and explains about the available possibilities for care • The client is referred to the relevant care providers	-------	-------
United Kingdom 1 LLICP (Limes Livingstone Integrated Care Project)	In-built	Less extensive approach • Each discipline (reha- bilitation worker, OT, nurse etc.) does own assessment and informs the client about the treatment etc. • The care manager in- forms the client about the decision. • The care manager spans the acute sector (hospital), community hospital and the reha- bilitation centre	Approximately 500 people per year (25+38 beds)	Approximately 88 workers
United Kingdom 2 CART team (Community Assessment and Rehabilitation)	In-built	Extensive approach • Information about the condition of the patient collected by single assessment (a core as- sessment) and specialist in-depth assessments • After admission, the team informs the GP that CART is involved • CART teams act as an information 'pivot', connecting hospital medical care, commu- nity medical care and nursing care	approximately 400 clients (4 weeks care)	18 (WTE) workers

CHAPTER 3

Inter-professional Working and Integrated Care Organisations

Kirstie Coxon, Thomas Clausen, Dominique Argoud

1   Introduction

In the first stage of the PROCARE project, it was established within the national reports (www.euro.centre.org/procare) and the European overview (Leichsenring, 2004a) that 'integrated working between health and social care agencies' has risen up the political agenda of European governments, and that this represents one response to the demographic challenge of population ageing and long-term care. The emerging tension is very clear – there is often a concerted effort to achieve integration between health care and social care agencies, but the reality is that in most countries, these agencies are structurally divided and struggle to work together in an 'integrated' manner. This provides an example of how the 'real world' rarely sets the stage for ideals such as 'integrated care' to be translated into actual practice.

Organisational theory and sociological discourse suggest that differences between professionals (identity, status, knowledge base and role) are likely to impede integrated working arrangements (Hudson, 2002; Trice, 1993; Morgan, 1997). This divide appears to be particularly evident between the sectors of health and social/personal care (Bloor/Dawson, 1994; Witz, 1990; van Raak et al., 2003). Within this chapter, we present data that support this hypothesis where integration occurs across organisational boundaries, and some data that refutes this hypothesis where different staff groups come together *within the same* 'integrated care' organisation. This finding is not isolated, and adds to a small but growing literature of 'local' evaluation studies. In view of this, we consider the implications of these ideas for both policy and practice.

In spite of many good examples of successful ventures of inter-professional collaboration these problems are also mirrored in the processes of inter-professional joint working observed in the PROCARE fieldwork. The 18 model projects that have been investigated here comprise a variety of collaborative ventures towards the provision of integrated care. Some of the model projects have achieved the integration of health care and social care workers within a single care-providing organisation ('intra-organisational integration') – whereas other model projects aim at providing integrated care through inter-organisational collaboration. This latter arrangement poses an additional challenge, as the integration of health and social care provision will not only have to deal with the reconciliation of varied professional cultures but must also work across organisational barriers.

The material from the PROCARE fieldwork allows us to probe into factors that constitute both facilitators and obstacles to inter-professional collaboration *within* and *between* organisations in the provision of integrated health and social/personal care for older people. The ability of the organisations involved in the provision of integrated care services to overcome the barriers to joint working that pertain to differences in professional and organisational cultures therefore appears crucial to the implementation of integrated care services.

This chapter will focus on the issues, problems and solutions experienced within inter-professional joint working in the model projects that have been investigated for the PROCARE fieldwork. We add to the work already undertaken by our PROCARE colleagues in Chapters 1 and 7, and upon 'Working conditions within integrated care' (see Andersson et al, in this book). To achieve this we looked for common *features of integrated care models*, and *factors which staff felt made their jobs different to previous jobs (non-integrated or traditional working)*. This strategy led to grouping of the data, and the development of comparative tables, which are presented later in the chapter.

The first section of this chapter identifies the common features of the models which have emerged in the field of 'joint working' for older people, and this is drawn from the findings of the research teams and data from staff working for these projects. Specifically, we look at the kinds of *professional and organisational arrangements* that were found within integrated care projects, and we also consider whether it is possible to identify the impact of 'integrated' or 'joint' working upon staff.

For the next part of this chapter, we concentrate on data that suggested that integrated working was different from other traditional or mainstream roles in older people's care. At the end of the chapter, we summarise the implications for practice that have arisen from this research.

Existing Theoretical and Research Literature

Although the data for this chapter was considered within the context of the wider literature, the process of gathering literature for PROCARE was subject to a particular challenge. On the one hand, there was little research-based literature pertaining directly to the development of integrated health and social care for older people, although this in fact changed during the course of the project. Nevertheless, it was possible to draw on the emerging theoretical literature (e.g. Kodner and Spreeuwenberg, 2002). On the other hand, there is an extensive literature base in related areas. For the purposes of this chapter, we drew on literature from a number of fields including political and organizational theory (including the New Public Management [NPM] model), Mintzberg's (1989) work on innovative organizations, as well as specific texts such as Flynn's (2002) 'degrees of collaboration' model. In the UK, a number of authors have developed the debate on collaboration and integration, notably Hudson's (2002) reflections on the 'pessimistic tradition', which suggests that the barriers to joint working are too great or too established to be overcome, and the 'optimistic tradition', which counters that some organisations manage to develop sustainable collaborations despite the evident difficulties of achieving this. Ranade and Hudson (2003) identify the following tensions within health and social care integration:

- National government policies requiring that health and / or social care provision are contracted out to numerous service providers, and simultaneously insist that care should be seamless between providers.
- Staff may be asked to both protect client confidentiality (or organisational data, where competition between providers is an issue) and share knowledge and information about their service users. In countries where there are numerous competing providers, (for example, Germany), the need to maintain a business advantage clearly works in opposition to a data-sharing approach. The UK has also attempted to introduce a market (or 'quasi-market') culture in health and social care, and this has the effect of further care fragmentation and resistance to partnership working in competing organisations (Ranade / Hudson, 2003; Holtom, 2001).

- Organisations may be asked to share their workload or client group, and maintain accountability for the care they provide. Such tensions are an inevitable part of the 'solution' of inter-agency working, and some of the PROCARE findings regarding staff experience of joint working can be explained within this framework.
- Groups of staff in high status professions such as medicine may be asked to maintain their specialised expertise and relative exclusivity and to be available to the many care providers that their clients may encounter. Understandably, some professionals who were interviewed for the PROCARE research expressed a view that they agreed with the 'ideals' of integrated working, but were unable to fully cooperate or collaborate because the 'practicalities' had not been considered. This could lead to a stalling of the integration process, where health and social care professions mutually accepted the need for better collaboration, but equally understood that the potential extent of each others' input was, in reality, limited.

Identifying 'Success' in Integrated Working

There is a fairly extensive literature that relates to theoretical concepts such as 'success' and 'barriers' within integrated working. For example, Flynn (2002), writing from a public sector management perspective identifies a concept of 'degrees of collaboration', where the extent of collaboration is evaluated by considering how closely two organisations interact. According to this conceptual view, 'shared meetings' represent the beginning of a collaboration venture that leads eventually to 'merger' or 'acquisition'.

This corporate perspective is interesting because it suggests that 'merger or acquisition', (the outcome which individual organisations and governments steer clear of) is a natural consequence of an inexorable collaboration process. However, in the 'real world' of integrated working found within the PROCARE research data, there are few signs that integration resembles the linear or iterative idea that Flynn's model suggests – it is more likely that the conceptual ideas of collaboration are present, but actual acceptance and internalisation of these ideas lags behind and develops, moves on, stops, and changes direction according to the external demands of policy, staffing, leadership, finances and organisational survival. This 'ebb and flow' explanation represents a rival explanation to Flynn's (2002) framework of 'degrees of collaboration', and suggests that the *process* of collaboration is dependent on many factors, some of which are external and some internal, and that the pressure brought to bear by these factors can *either limit **or** facilitate* successful collaboration.

A more recognisable model of success in inter-agency working is that proposed by Rushner and Pallis (2002). These practitioners identify the following elements of effective integrated working:

- 'Soft' outcomes (e.g. a more supportive work culture)
- 'Process' outcomes (e.g. improved communication, better problem-solving)
- 'Hard' outcomes (e.g. better staff retention, responsive service development)

This model is service-based, and does not extend to improved health outcomes for service users, instead suggesting by implication that health outcomes will improve if the identified outcomes are attained. This model in fact lends itself well to the PROCARE data, partly because the study is also mainly limited to organisational and process outcomes. (Although service user data was sought, this relates to perceptions and experiences of service users rather than to concrete changes to health state resulting from the service.)

Recognising Barriers to Integrated Working

Wistow and Hardy (1991) identify five categories of barriers to collaboration. These are:

1. *Structural barriers:* These represent the main divisions between organisations. Wistow and Hardy (1991) recognised two distinct examples of structural barriers, which were fragmentation across agency boundaries (i.e. the separation of health and social care) and 'non co-terminosity' (different geographical boundaries for health care organisations and social care organisations. The 'solution' of co-terminosity (shared populations) has been proposed and debated in the UK, but discounted by government because of the costs and disruption involved (Holtom, 2001).
2. *Procedural barriers:* planning, IT solutions.
3. *Financial barriers:* cycles – collaborative vision is a pre-requisite.
4. *Professional barriers.*
5. *Status and legitimacy.*

The findings from PROCARE relating to integrated organisations suggest that structural barriers continue to represent the main challenge to service integration. Many services continue to struggle to collaborate despite the impediments that these barriers represent, but this requires a great degree of energy and resource, leading to questions about sustainability. Other organisations 'solve' this problem by creating single 'stand alone' integrated organisations, which staff regard as effective, but which ironically adds a further structural barrier between the 'new' organisation and existing 'mainstream' organisations.

Professional Cultures

> "Partnership working, while opening up opportunities for closer cooperation, also raises the potential for significant clashes of professional interests and organisational culture." (Holtom, 2001: 430).

The traditional view within the literature is that entrenched professional cultures represent an obstacle to collaborative working, because professional groups act in self-interest in order to maintain professional boundaries (e.g. Holtom, 2001; Rushmer/Pallis, 2002). Sullivan and Skelcher (2002: 211) identify 'differences in training, values and notions of good practice between professional groups' as problems that limit integration of health and social care staff, and problems of professional integration are often seen as a major barrier to joint working. Similar findings have been observed elsewhere. Cornes and Clough (1999) completed evaluations of intermediate care schemes in the UK, and found that sharing an office and client group facilitated collaboration, whilst barriers between teams and the outside environment impeded collaboration. Macneil (1985, from Ranade and Hudson, 2003: 36) suggests that such relationships form 'entangling strings or reputation, friendship and interdependence' which enhance the potential for collaboration within the organisation.

2 Professional and Organisational Arrangements for Integrated Care

2.1 *Organisational Solutions to Integration of Health and Social Care*

Table 1 breaks down the 18 models researched by PROCARE teams into 'types of integrated care provision'. It identifies that the majority of research activity was focused in three main 'types' of integrated care:

1. The provision of *integrated home care* to older people, which is prevalent in the northern European studies,
2. *Discharge management schemes*, which are found across North and South Europe, and
3. The practice of *'case management'* or 'care management', again concentrated in North Europe but also found in Italy. Organisations that provided care management often coordinated multiple care providers.

Table 1:   Types of Model and Numbers of Each Studied within PROCARE Research

Type of integration model	Number studied within PROCARE research	Country
Day-care provision	1	EL
Home care provision	7	EL, UK, DK, FIN (x2), NL, A
Discharge management (Hospital to home)	4	I, DK, UK, A
Case management and coordination, or networks (usually dual roles)	5	D, NL, F (x2), I
Network of specialists	1	D

This classification is far from firm, and there is in fact overlap between several categories of model project. For example, the Italian 'Single point of access' scheme is both a case management scheme and a method of improving discharge management, and the UK CART and LLICP models overlap between discharge management and the provision of home, or at least non-hospital, care. As long as these limitations are borne in mind when the findings are discussed, it remains useful to consider the data of similar model projects together, because this allows common contextual features to emerge, and the relevance of the findings can then be interpreted within the context of the type of model being studied.

The two 'outlying models' also indicate something about their countries of origin. The development of 'day care' in Greece is a fairly recent one (model 1, KAPI), although this type of service tends to be mainstream elsewhere in Europe. This is related to the strong culture of family-based care found in this country, and reflects the growing need amongst Greek families for respite or support, given that older people with very complex problems and high dependency are cared for at home in Greece. The network of specialists found in Germany (D2, 'Geronto-psychiatric association') is one solution to the issue of multiple providers, which was identified in that country.

The next section looks at the main groups of integrated care services from Table 1 in some more detail, and considers the kinds of organisational and professional arrangements that have emerged within these services. Common problems are identified, and solutions to the challenges of care integration are highlighted.

2.2 Home Care Teams

Table 2:   Services that Are Integrated into 'Home Care' Teams
within Model Projects

	EL 'Help at home'	UK 'CART'	DK 'Skae-vinge'	FIN2 'Home care teams'	NL 'Zijl-oever' care inte-gration	A Hartberg collabo-ration
Social care	√	√	√	√	√	√
Health care	√	√	√	√	√	√
Family support*	√					
Rehabilitation specialist (OT/ physio)		√	√			
Meal delivery			√		√	
Transport					√	

*)   'Family support' was important to other country home care teams, but was highlighted by the Greek research team, because of the current demand for respite care in Greece.

In this context, the term 'Home care teams' describes teams of staff who visit clients in their home environment on a regular basis, to deliver either personal care (help with washing, dressing and other 'activities of daily living') or help with practical tasks such as housework or shopping. The frequency of visits can range from several times a day, to once or twice a week. In most of the models studied, there is provision for both 'health' and 'social' care to be delivered to the client's home. Some go further and deliver specialist care such as rehabilitation therapy (UK, DK) and others have diversified into providing meals (NL, DK), 24-hour care (DK) or linking in with the local leisure and travel infrastructure (NL).

Shared Integration Strategies of 'Home Care' Teams

One of the clear findings from the research into professional cultures and integration was that the teams shared many common solutions to the traditional communication barriers that impede interagency care. These solutions related to the process of getting together and sharing information, and nearly every team reported that they held daily (or very regular) meetings with each other. Most had developed paperwork or documentation that was shared by all team members, and accessible to all. A further finding was that sharing a work-base or office was essential for the development of smooth interagency working.

When the above features were in place, the interagency teams reported they shared more abstract concepts of their work. This was commonly referred to as the shared 'team ethos':

> "The team has an ethos ... and because they spend so much time with each other, they are learning from each other." (EL)

> "The team has an ethos, and perhaps our joint documents have helped, and because they spend so much time with each other, they are learning from each other." (UK)

The ethos of interagency teams was expressed as sharing of values or beliefs about the work that was being undertaken, and the teams visualised themselves as working together for the holistic benefit of the client:

> "I think we all work together – nurses, occupational therapists, physiotherapists, care manager – towards one goal, which is maintaining that client where they are and trying to progress them on to maximum independence." (UK)

> "The carers communicate frankly with their team leaders and with the management. Hierarchical relations are not perceived as an obstacle to a direct communication - in interaction, equality seems to prevail." (NL)

> "In this setting there is a blurring of our roles." (UK)

Two further themes emerged from the data regarding 'home care teams'. Firstly, most teams identified that they had good management support, and that this was a key contributor towards effective team integration:

> "In this team, the management supports us in working together – (she) is a key reason for the team's success" (UK, staff respondent)

Also in the Austrian example (Hartberg) we have seen that the role and the communication work of the manager of the model way of working is very important to the success of this way of working.

The second theme was related to education and training of staff. Most models identified the importance of ongoing training, and in Denmark, this encompassed maintaining the values of the model project through making time available for workshops:

> "The values (of the model) are continuously maintained at 'future-workshops', where the staff discuss fundamental issues regarding the organisation. At these sessions the problems and solutions in inter-disciplinary or joint working are regularly dealt with. At the time the fieldwork was conducted work-shops and courses on conflict resolution were conducted for all at the Bauneparken health centre".

As might be anticipated the 'home care teams' faced common problems of interagency working, considering that they had developed on similar lines, and indeed there were similarities between the projects. The most commonly reported challenges to home care team 'interagency' working were

- A lack of time and resources, which meant that staff felt they could not always meet the true needs of the client,
- a lack of clear career structure (with consequent recruitment and retention problems), and
- difficulties working with specific sectors.

The most consistently reported example concerned the transfer of clients from hospitals to the community, where there were often difficulties engaging medical staff in the model project, or achieving transfer of client data from the hospital. The 'home care teams' tended to work in isolation in the sense that they were developed in the community setting, and had strong *internal* relationships across health and social care agencies, but this did not necessarily imply that the projects had equally strong relationships with outside agencies and providers such as councils, hospitals and general practitioners (GPs). Nevertheless, there was also evidence of solutions to these shared problems being developed. For example, the UK CART team has negotiated good access to a specialist older person's doctor ('consultant') at the hospital. However, this relationship had developed because the team is actually based within a hospital, allowing a formal and reciprocal relationship to develop naturally:

> "We have access to a consultant every day, if we need advice. We meet him once a week to discuss any issues, ... If the consultant recommends a change to the patient's medications then we write to the GP the same day". (UK2)

Other reported problems included difficulties for individual members of staff. These persons had moved from large organisations into a small team setting, and found themselves gradually excluded from their normal professional support structures, a factor noted by social services staff at both the UK model projects. Researchers in Finland also noted a tendency for some staff to lose confidence when they were working alongside other professions:

> "Maybe my working style is out-of-date: I want to have time for conversation with service users too." (FIN)

Staff could also become anxious about taking on new roles and responsibility, which were not part of their former roles:

> "I don't want to take such a big responsibility, which is now being expected – administration of medicines and injections, for instance." (FIN)

Other projects reported uncertainty about their long-term status. This was partly because only new and 'innovative' projects were chosen for the research, so most operated outside mainstream of care provision. However, the oldest example of home care team included in the study was the UK CART team, and even this was affected by wider policy changes that put the future funding of their organisation in doubt.

2.3 Discharge Management Schemes

Four model projects reported the development of discharge management schemes. These were:

1. Italy (WUCC) – Continuity of care between hospital and home (I1)
2. Austria – Vienna discharge management project (A1)
3. UK (LLICP) – Post hospital rehabilitation care (UK1)
4. Denmark (Søllerød) – Hospital to community discharge management strategy (DK1)

The first two schemes mentioned here are hospital-based discharge coordination schemes, arising from the problem of communication at the interface of hospital and community care:

> "As an extramural (community) service, we soon saw the classical problem, that there was no interface between intra- and extramural (hospital and community) services. For example, many hospitals discharge their patients on Friday at 10am and then they do not receive appropriate support over the weekend." (A1, staff respondent)

The UK and Denmark models are discharge schemes that incorporate post-hospital rehabilitation services. These schemes are grouped together because all four share the same goals of care:

- Better coordination of hospital discharge
- Continuity of care for older people between hospital and home – meeting needs in the 'grey area' of post-hospital care
- Reduced dependency on hospital sector and expansion of community (non-hospital / extra-mural) services.

The discharge management schemes also shared a number of features. For example, most schemes had instigated multidisciplinary discharge conferences, where staff met to plan care following discharge from hospital. In most schemes, there was at least one coordinating individual, usually a nurse or a care manager, who would negotiate health and social care on behalf of the client. The exception was the Italian WUCC scheme, which was based more around an administration exercise involving nurses and doctors documenting the needs of older people on discharge in an attempt to improve continuity of care after hospital and reduce re-admission. As in the home care schemes mentioned earlier (section 2.1), staff identified that regular meetings (usually weekly), management support, and training (in assessment and rehabilitation) were key features of successful discharge management.

The discharge management teams identified a number of common problems within inter-agency working. Two projects (UK, DK) reported that financing of 'rehabilitation' care caused tension between service providers, because this cost has traditionally been met by acute hospitals. When older people with ongoing rehabilitation needs are discharged early from hospital, the costs for these specialised and expensive services are passed onto the local health or social services budget, or may even be met by the client. One of the main themes to emerge from the UK model was the issue of 'inappropriate' discharge from hospital and to the post-hospital rehabilitation facility. The following quote is a typical example of this:

> "... the hospital need to empty their beds and so they're looking at our service as a way of getting that person out of their bed." (UK1)

This led to a perception that the rehabilitation service was misused, and effectively heightened the tension between the hospital and rehabilitation services. The situation in Denmark was improved by the development of the discharge management team, which in effect managed to circumvent the existing conflict between sectors as the staff got together and developed pragmatic solutions together:

> "Occasionally it happened that some of our citizens with needs for rehabilitation or domestic care were discharged without notice being given to us in the rehabilitation facility or to the domestic carers of the citizens. That was not very satisfactory, either for the citizen, for us or for the hospitals! Now that the coordinating nurse has started to keep an eye on our citizens at the hospital we don't experience that any longer." (DK1)

This example illustrates some of the complexities of dividing long-term medical and social care between sectors. In the UK model, the costs of rehabilitation have been passed on to the primary and social care sector. In Denmark the same divisions exist, and a similar debate affects counties and municipalities, affecting the strategic development of integration services. Another issue was the difficulty of incorporating home carers into discharge management meetings. In the relatively small area of Søllerød in Denmark, it was possible to include community care workers in these discharge meetings, and this had benefits for the client in terms of consolidating their recovery:

> "The great thing about it is that you can arrange with the domestic carer to help the older person with some of the exercises that he needs to do to stay in good condition." (DK1)

The same approach was tried in Vienna, but the wide diversity of providers meant that this could not be achieved. The UK project also had difficulty liaising with the carers who visited clients after discharge, and reported that carers were not allowed sufficient time to help clients do things themselves – instead, they would do things for the client. This could mean that the advances the client made during his/her rehabilitation in terms of 'self-care' were lost once the client returned to living at home with carers visiting.

121

2.4 Case Management/Case Coordination and 'Single Information Point' Models

Several PROCARE teams identified models of coordination or 'case management' within their countries, and the data from these projects is considered here. The models that come under this heading are:

- 'Home care Nürnberg' practice network (D1)
- Kerkrade 'Case management – chain of care' (NL2)
- ACAFPA – Coordination of assessment and advice for older people (F1)
- ILG Phalempin Network – Coordination of assessment and care providers (F2)
- 'Single point of access' – Collaboration to provide health and social care (I2)

This is a fairly diverse group of models, and most of these organisations have dual roles of:

- collecting information about clients by generating assessments, and
- providing opportunities for professionals to exchange information, or pool their knowledge, and plan care accordingly.

These organisations therefore have some overlap with 'home care' provision (section 2.1), but their primary goal is different, because their focus is on the coordination of care through efficient communication amongst separate providers, rather than sharing the care between a multi-professional group working together. In other words, the providers remain separate, but the care they offer is integrated. In the words of one staff respondent:

> "The 'network conference' aims to increase opportunities for colleagues to meet and exchange information, to achieve total client-centred care, by creating a common platform of communication and information". (D1)

The model of 'case management' is of course already fairly widespread across Europe in the social care sector, but these networks are moving one step on and integrating information about health and social care services, either for (on behalf of) the client, or for the service providers. The aims of the case coordination networks are as follows:

- Increase communication between different providers (F, NL, D)
- Assess the needs of clients (F, NL, I, D)
- Share or 'pool' knowledge about clients (F, D, I)

- Negotiate with health and social care services on behalf of clients (D, NL, F, I)
- Reduce unnecessary or 'preventable' hospital admissions (F)

The networks range considerably in size, and bring together a wide range of people, as might be expected. The French ACAPFA model includes council representatives, directors of elderly services, social workers, medical staff and lay/voluntary members, and its assessment work is carried out by a coordinator who works in liaison with referral agents from health and social care agencies. The German association in Nürnberg is much smaller, with two employees responsible for its coordination activities at present.

Staff in the case coordination models valued the opportunity to get to know other professionals, and the development of these relationships facilitated inter-agency solutions to client problems:

> "It is important to move beyond the specific interests of each association, in order to work together in the interests of all old persons (...) we need common aim, and a common gerontological culture." (F2)

One respondent from the German model noted that although individual practitioners had previously tried to meet other people working for their clients, there had not previously been any formal *'individual case conferences'* (D), and this opportunity made it much easier to work collaboratively. In the Dutch Kerkrade project, the care of clients is allocated to particular professionals whose expertise makes them best placed to manage the needs of individuals, and this is an example of how interagency working can lead to an iterative process of *expanding access* to multi-agency care (which in itself reduces fragmentation) and making increasingly *specialised* care available to clients at home.

The coordination networks felt confident that their work was beneficial to the older people in their areas, and identified their role as 'inter-organisational integration' at the management and strategic level in their regions. In this sense they were different from the models that provided direct, hands-on care to clients, but remained essential to drive service development towards collaborative and integrated care.

Issues and Problems within Coordination Networks

The difficulties that these coordination networks encountered were mainly related to organising inter-agency work within the networks themselves.

The German project at Nürnbergwas quite revealing in this respect, and a staff respondent made the following comment:

> "In my opinion, the collaboration was sometimes excellent, but there were also prejudices against other professional groups, competitiveness and insufficient frankness." (D1)

Similarly, one of the French respondents noted that:

> "Coordination is a real investment; but few participants would agree to change their own way of working to establish a true partnership." (F2)

Despite the focus on inter-agency working within the PROCARE project, it was in fact fairly unusual for respondents to explicitly mention inter-professional conflict. The Dutch Kerkrade project also identified that staff were not entirely happy with integrated case management, but in this case they expressed concern at increased workload and reduced opportunities for informal contact. According to some of the care workers, providing integrated care means more 'paper work' and more rigmarole. This way of working together means more administrative work and their workload seems to be increasing. One common complaint was that there is no time left for socialising with their co-workers or for listening to each other's problems (NL2).

It may be that these difficulties are related to local arrangements for care provision, but these extracts suggest that inter-agency case coordination can be problematic for staff. There appear to be differences of inter-agency culture between, for example, home care teams (where opportunities for informal contact were considered to be a strength of the model by staff) and case coordination networks. The German model at Nürnberg identified a number of factors that were necessary for effective case coordination to take place. These were:

- standardisation and harmonisation of care services and communication processes,
- a lot of motivation from the staff involved,
- sufficient time for staff to manage working together,
- support from managers and staff, with acceptance that investing time in inter-agency working now leads to saving time later on, and
- a readiness to accept blurring of traditional professional roles and boundaries.

Although idealised within this account, these factors can be considered as a starting point for identifying some 'pre-conditions' that need to be in place before integrated case coordination can be successful. Some of the difficulties that 'case coordination' models experienced seem to relate to their structure – that is, keeping services separate, but integrating information and collaborating in care provision. This provides an example of 'inter-agency collaboration', a form of joint working that operates across the traditional boundaries between the health and social care sectors. This can be differentiated from the 'home care teams' and 'discharge management teams', both of which have merged professions *within* their organisations, which results in 'intra-agency' joint working. The former approach to joint working is easily established but fraught with communication barriers, whilst the latter approach appears to be more difficult to establish, but easier to maintain. This theme was identified in many of the PROCARE model projects, and will be elaborated upon further in section 3.

A further aspect identified by the German and French case management teams was that their clients could not always afford the complex care arrangements that their assessed difficulties warranted (F) or that their service providers could not meet the needs of clients (D):

> **"With regard to the organisation of individual case conferences, actually providing the care can be difficult because the service providers don't always have sufficient staff or time to provide the level of care the client needs" (D1, staff respondent).**

2.5   *Summary of Findings Related to Integrated Care Arrangements*

Pulling together findings from a diverse group of models is difficult, and the small and localised nature of these models must be borne in mind when the data is considered. However, what became clear during the PROCARE research was that there were distinct 'groups' of services that had developed to provide integrated care. The three main groups identified here were:
- Integrated home care teams
- Discharge management teams
- Care management/coordination networks

The first two groups showed evidence of similar integrated working strategies, which were based around communication, training and management. The types of organisations that developed were based around staff with separate professional identities but similar status. The prescription of care (assessment) was usually conducted by this allied professional group (nursing, care management, occupational therapy, physiotherapy) and sometimes delegated to care support workers. Medical management tended to be an external specialty, and medical workers sometimes contributed to the organisations but were rarely employed outright. The next section identifies what staff felt the results of these arrangements to be.

3 Staff Experience of Working in an Integrated Care Organisation

Considering the different types of joint working identified in the study, we might anticipate that different types of models would have a variety of experiences of integrated working. In fact, although there were some local issues that affected specific projects, it was possible to identify a number of themes across the entire group of projects. We have separated these into tables of 'advantages' and 'disadvantages' identified by mainly front-line staff and key workers at the model projects.

3.1 Perceived Advantages of Integrated Working

The main advantages of joint working, as perceived by staff at the 18 model projects, are illustrated in Table 3. In order to investigate whether the experiences of joint working are contingent on the organisational features – inter-agency vs. intra-agency joint working – the models have been divided into these two sub-groups.

The main advantage reported by staff was that their 'job satisfaction was improved through integrated working, because their service was able to be more responsive to the needs of the client'. This was the main benefit of integrated working at 10 of the model projects. It seemed to represent one of the key differences between integrated models and traditional, 'non-integrated' service provision, from the perspective of staff at least. Furthermore, this 'advantage' appeared to be more prevalent in the models that primarily can be characterised as intra-agency models as compared to the experiences of staff in the models that are organised along the lines of the inter-agency type of joint working.

Table 3: Model Project Staff's Views of the Advantages of Integrated Working

	Inter-agency Joint Working											Intra-Agency Joint Working							Total
	I	I	NL	A	A	F	F	UK	DK	D	D	NL	EL	EL	DK	FIN	FIN	UK	To-tal
	1	2	2	1	2	1	2	1	1	1	2	1	1	2	2	1	2	2	
Job satisfaction – responsive to clients' needs	✓	✓						✓	✓			✓		✓	✓	✓	✓	✓	10
Good team work	✓	✓	✓											✓			✓		5
Good communication (within models)		✓		✓							✓		✓			✓			5
Enhanced co-operation with other agencies	✓			✓	✓						✓							✓	5
Shared culture developed/Reduced status differences between professionals						✓	✓		✓				✓		✓			✓	6
Better relationships with clients					✓								✓	✓					3
Improved autonomy for staff													✓			✓			2

Other advantages that were commonly expressed across the group of projects included 'good team work', 'good communication' (within models) and 'enhanced cooperation with other agencies'. This separation between 'communication amongst us' and 'communication with external groups' marks the difference between 'intra-agency joint working' and 'inter-agency joint working'. Although the difference is only very slight, 'intra-agency' models (single or 'stand alone' organisations) identify communication *within their own* organisations as a benefit, whilst 'inter-agency' models (which might be virtual, or working across multiple boundaries) found that they were able to communicate better with other agencies – and this was likely to have been one of the aims of establishing the model project.

Staff at six projects identified that the development of a 'shared culture' was beneficial to them. This was linked to conceptual themes such as 'believing in the model', 'sharing' and an altruistic motivation towards integrating care for the benefit of clients. Staff might refer to this as a *'blurring of the boundaries'* or *'increasing mutual respect'* between the professions:

> "We have a competency framework for the rehabilitation workers, and all the different professionals contribute to the training...it's learning, and blurring boundaries and roles really." (UK2)

The development of a shared culture between different professionals also had an impact on staff perception of professional hierarchies as an emphasis on inter-professional complementarity – as opposed to inter-professional competition – appeared to establish itself in the models:

> "... for instance the nurses tell us which activities they have planned for the day and that prevents the rest of us from believing that the nurses just sit and chit-chat with older people and so on. I think it is a very nice way of working together multi-professionally. And that gives a better working environment – just like that!" (DK2)

Finally, inter-professional joint working also appears to have an impact on the relationships between staff and clients and the level of autonomy granted to individual carers in integrated organisations.

3.2 Perceived Disadvantages of Integrated Working

Table 4 presents the main disadvantages of integration experienced by staff. Again, in order to investigate whether the experiences of joint working are contingent on the organisational features – inter-agency vs. intra-agency

Table 4: Model Project Staff's Views of the Disadvantages of Integrated Working

Disadvantage	Inter-agency Joint Working											Intra-Agency Joint Working							Total
	I 1	I 2	NL 2	A 1	A 2	F 1	F 2	UK 1	DK 1	D 1	D 2	NL 1	EL 1	EL 2	DK 2	FIN 1	FIN 2	UK 2	To-tal
Problems working with doctors	✓	✓		✓			✓	✓	✓	✓	✓	✓				✓		✓	11
Negotiating the boundaries between model and other services/agencies is troublesome	✓	✓		✓	✓		✓	✓	✓				✓					✓	9
Concern about feasibility of 'model project' aims			✓		✓					✓			✓	✓	✓	✓			7
Not enough time allowed to achieve integration of care			✓									✓		✓	✓	✓			5
Short-term contracts, low salary or poor career progression	✓													✓		✓		✓	4
Shortage of staff				✓				✓						✓					3
Reliant on will of others to collaborate						✓	✓												2

joint working – the models have been divided into these two subgroups in the table.

In spite of the perceived advantage pertaining to the development of a shared professionally integrative culture, there seemed to be consensus across models that 'integrating doctors, hospitals and the medical profession generally into a collaborative approach constitutes a general problem' in the evolution of a genuinely integrated health and social/personal care model. An interesting illustration of this was the German model (Home care Nürnberg), which considered that the support of doctors was a strength of the model, but reported that the integration of medical staff had inhibited the involvement of other, non-medical staff, who considered the project to have been 'taken over' by doctors and no longer integrative.

This issue of the 'care/cure divide' is a historically recognised barrier to interagency working, and appears to continue to trouble 'front line' staff in the real world of care integration. There are a number of factors involved in this divide, including geographical separation (between hospitals or GPs and model project schemes), the communication difficulties that stem from this separation and the continued hierarchical dominance (or 'immense professional power') of the medical profession (Holtom, 2001: 433). Hudson (1999) suggested that this is changing over time, that 'although there is considerable evidence of continued professional tribalism on the part of GPs, there are also indications of a move towards more collectivism and accountability' (from Holtom, 2001: 434).

There were some examples within PROCARE models of 'solutions' to this problem being negotiated[1] but overall, the model projects identified ambivalence towards integrated working in their medical colleagues, and questioned whether or not it is realistic to try and integrate medical and social care at the level of care provision in view of the scarcity of medical practitioners compared with other allied health professionals.

Although five model projects considered 'enhanced cooperation with other agencies' to be an advantage of integrated working, eight projects reported that negotiating 'the boundaries between themselves and other

---

[1]   The UK CART team has developed relationships both with consultant physicians specialising in care of older people and GPs. The team arranges rapid access of clients to outpatient consultant assessment clinics – or may even arrange a consultant home visit for a home-bound client. At the same time, the team and consultant keep the client's GP informed of any changes to the client's medical and social care.

agencies' constituted another stumbling block of care integration – a stumbling block that obviously primarily manifests itself in the models that can be characterised by the organisational feature of 'inter-agency joint working'. The fact that each of the five projects who reported enhanced cooperation also mentioned the problem of negotiating boundaries as being a major disadvantage illustrates the difficulty of maintaining support for collaboration, and the momentum and energy that is required to work at service integration with other agencies. This feature of joint working is difficult to draw out of the research data, but is linked to frequently mentioned issues such as 'not enough time is allowed to achieve integration of care':

> "It is often a time problem, to really commit oneself to these issues, because this takes a lot of time and one would like to find good solutions." (A2)

> "In the beginning, the development of new structures is time-consuming – even, if it enables effective and time-saving working later on." (D1)

Perhaps not surprisingly, some staff expressed concern about the 'feasibility of model project aims', and this could constitute a de-motivating factor that needed to be addressed by the management. This concern was two-fold: staff referred to pressure on themselves and their colleagues, and also thought that the process of collaborative working could lead to unrealistic expectations amongst their service users. During the group discussion (NL2) it was mentioned that, to meet the needs of clients, the care providers regularly have to come up with new products and services. It became apparent, however, that staff grapple with this innovation process. They ask themselves how far they should go in meeting the wishes of the clients by creating new facilities and services when the already existing ones are sometimes under-utilised.

This discussion points to the awareness of finite resources amongst model project staff. Several projects commented that 'integrated working' and tools to facilitate this such as 'single assessment' meant that many client problems might be identified, but that the organisation had to ration its resources and decide which issues to tackle within their cost constraints.

Other problems detected were short-term contract working, and a lack of clear career structure within integrated care. This was usually linked to related areas such as ongoing training and education of staff. In both UK projects, data from 'rehabilitation assistants' (who are not professionally trained, but who undergo specialised rehabilitation courses as part of their work) suggested that their role brought a great deal of job satisfaction, and was better paid than 'traditional' care work. However, professionally quali-fied staff (nurses, occupational therapists, physiotherapists, care managers) tended to find themselves in 'flat' organisational structures with promotion dependent on leaving the 'model project' organisation. In other words, the relatively small size of integrated organisations contributes to improved team-working and multi-professional working, but at the same time limits the careers of those who work in them.

In summary, the main disadvantages perceived by staff of the PRO-CARE 'model projects' were firstly collaboration with hospitals, GPs and the medical profession, and secondly, negotiating the organisational boundaries between care providers that are engaged in inter-agency joint working. Anxi-ety about the feasibility of the project's aims was also evident, although this could be a feature of 'model projects' rather than being related specifically to integrated health and social care. Other problems were related to staff employment and the resources of the organisation in terms of time, money, training and education. Some staff maintain that the satisfaction of working for a responsive organisation outweighs the drawbacks of low pay and poor career progression (the altruistic motivator) – whilst other projects report more serious instability and threats to their immediate future.[2]

3.3 Professional and Organisational Cultures: The Divide between Health and Social Care

The analysis of the main advantages and disadvantages thus points towards two barriers that impede integrated care:
1. Negotiating the differences in organisational cultures between provid-ers of cure and care. In the present context this barrier refers to whether or not providers of health and social/personal care are structurally separated across agency boundaries as this is expected to have a bear-ing on the collaborative patterns of the professionals involved and on the evolution of a joint organisational culture that will potentially supersede the idiosyncratic cultures of the professionals involved in the provision of integrated health and social/personal care.

---

2   The Greek 'Help at Home' model faced short-term funding difficulties and its future was uncertain after 2003.

2. Negotiating the differences in professional cultures between health care staff and social care staff. This barrier that is often referred to as the cure/care divide, denotes the differences in status, power, means of documentation and access to resources that characterise health and social care professionals respectively.

According to Leichsenring (2004) the cleavages between health and social/personal care professions and organisations can be characterised as being cultural, hierarchical and structural in their nature. Although these issues have been the cause of conflict in the model projects of the PROCARE field-work, the problems that were related to cultural, hierarchical and structural differences between health and social care have proved at times surmount-able and solutions have been devised in order to bring the modes of joint working forward in the individual projects.

The Structural Divide between Health and Social Care

In spite of the differences in welfare mixes between the PROCARE countries the rift between the provision of primary health and social/personal care systems and the provision of secondary health care appears to constitute a constant feature across the individual systems. Across the PROCARE countries, the delegation of responsibilities for the provision of health and social care from central to local levels of government reproduces the structural divisions between providers of primary health care, secondary health care and social care. The following quote from the general description of the situation in France illustrates the problem:

> **"The different initiatives taken to coordinate the gerontological interventions collided with the fracture, which separates activities on the medical side from those of the social sector".**

This structural divide furthermore contributes significantly to sustain the differences in professional and organisational cultures and hierarchical differences between providers of health and social/personal care. This is so insofar as the structural divisions between health and social care providers hinders inter-professional and inter-organisational exchanges that can contribute to foster integration in the field.

However, few legislative initiatives to bridge the gap between providers of health and social care have been taken by central governments in the PROCARE countries, as few of the model projects that form the PROCARE fieldwork are subject to specific legal regulation and accordingly mainly are catered for on an experimental basis. As the following section shows, the integration efforts that have been undertaken in the PROCARE model projects have been located in a setting characterized by differences in perspective, status and power of the engaged professionals.

The Cultural and Hierarchical Divide between Health and Social Care

These structural divisions hamper the likelihood that providers of health and social care will engage in formal exchanges that could alleviate the cultural and hierarchical differences between professions and organisations. The *cultural differences* between health and social care mainly relate to differences in professional logic and scope of health and social care professionals respectively, with social care professionals applying a broader scope on the general social situation of the older person than their peers in the health sector who generally restrict themselves to a more narrow somatic scope. The *hierarchical differences* between health and social care professionals primarily relate to differences in professional status that are largely determined by the educational backgrounds of the respective professions. These issues of cultural and hierarchical cleavage are exemplified in the quote below:

> "There are several facets to such professional and cultural barriers. First are differences of ideology and model of care, the most obvious being between the medical and social (psycho-social) models of care – with allied differences in view about involvement of patients and users in the treatment and care. Second are inter-professional disputes about service domains, areas of competence and related issues of status. Most obviously there have been some persistent tensions in joint working between the medical profession (the canonical 'full' profession) and the 'semi-profession' of social work." (Godfrey et al., 2003: 153)

The medical profession is traditionally described as holding a dominant position in the health and social care hierarchy, and the data from PROCARE respondents suggests that this is still largely the case. Firstly, this dominant position stems from the fact that health care professionals subscribe to highly specialised scientific knowledge whereas social care professionals rely on a body of knowledge of a more intuitive and commonsensical nature. Sullivan and Skelcher (2002: 211) thus identify *'differences in training, values and notions of good practice between professional groups'* as problems that limit integration of health and social/personal care staff, that again often are seen as a major barrier to joint working. Secondly, the effects of medical/health care interventions lend themselves to systematic documentation far easier than the mainly preventative effects associated with the typical interventions of social care. These characteristics in combination – scientific specialisation and documentative abilities – place the professions of medical science and health care in a superior position to the profession of social care. This is so insofar as the discourse of medical science constitutes a series of more coherent and legitimate and hence powerful 'truth claims' than the so-called 'semi-profession' of social care, and consequently places medical science (and health care providers) relatively highly in the societal hierarchy of knowledge and in the political process of allocation of scarce societal resources. This is also reflected in the fact that health care professionals – generally across the PROCARE countries – have better regulated educational and job profiles, higher pay and higher status than staff in the long-term social care services.

These differences were also reflected in the reactions of some of the interviewed key workers towards engaging in joint working with other professionals. However, as the following quote indicates the initial scepticism towards the introduction of multi-professional joint working was overcome as the staff also realised the associated benefits:

> "So, in the beginning I was very angry and I actually applied for another job because I had had enough of this. But suddenly, the tide turned and the benefits of the new mode of caring and working with other professionals became evident to me. And this clearly changed my perception of my job as I got another sense of self-esteem as I felt that the work we did with older people rested on a more professional foundation than before." (DK2)

The collated material of the PROCARE fieldwork is rich with examples on conflicts and hierarchical asymmetries that stem from differences in professional and/or organisational backgrounds. These examples cover a variety of conflicts and differences, but generally relate to a) engaging Medical Officers and General Practitioners in patterns of joint working with long-term care services, and b) power asymmetries between staff with their professional background in health and social care respectively. Indicative of this latter issue is a remark from one of our Finnish colleagues:

> "In integrated care, home-helpers (social care staff) usually ask consultation help from home nurses and not vice versa" (FIN2).

4   Conclusions and Perspectives

4.1   In Support of the 'Optimistic Tradition' – Integration of Health and Social Care Is Possible

The very fact that integrated health and social care services are successfully being provided across Europe – as the model projects indicate – suggests that the cultural, hierarchical and structural differences between providers of health and social/personal care can be overcome. Obviously, this has not happened on an entirely voluntary basis, and the emergence of 'New Public Management' appears to have contributed to challenge the traditional dominance of the medical profession (Holtom, 2001) in order to facilitate viable models of integration between providers of health and social care. Indeed, in several of the model projects of the PROCARE fieldwork the managerial level has played a significant role in pushing and mitigating between different professional groups towards a more integrated mode of production:

> "Education has been one of the absolute key-concepts in integrating the differ-
> ent professions by softening up the professional identities that dominated in
> the old care regime [that was characterised by extensive professionally based
> departmentalisation]. However, that doesn't mean that these professional iden-
> tities are gone. They still play a role, but now that role is more productive in
> a necessary division of labour, as you still have some professionals that are
> qualified to provide care that others are not qualified to provide." (DK2)

Thus, the existence of differences in professional and organisational cultures and related differences in status, may not constitute insurmountable barriers towards the provision of integrated care delivered by a multi-professional team. To be sure, inter-professional integration can be a demanding exercise that challenges the professional worldviews and identities of the engaged professionals, but – as is illustrated by the following quote – the element of inter-professional learning processes is highlighted in several model projects as an added bonus to inter-professional joint working:

> "For me, as a physiotherapist, it can sometimes be a bit difficult to agree with
> nurses, occupational therapists and social-and-health assistants on how the state
> of a given citizen is progressing, as we all have our perspectives, opinions and
> experiences. But the great thing about joint working on citizens with compli-
> cated needs for rehabilitation is that it is very inspirational to work with other

professions. It offers insights into the situation of the rehabilitant that you otherwise would not have had. And when it really works, you get the feeling that you have really gone all the way around the citizen. Because I have my perspective, the citizen adds his perspective and the others have their perspectives. And when they all come together you really get a buzz." (DK1)

The empirical evidence collected during the PROCARE fieldwork thus challenges the traditional 'pessimistic' view within the literature of entrenched professional cultures representing an insurmountable obstacle to collaborative working, because of professional groups acting in self-interest in order to maintain professional boundaries and distinctions (Rushner/Pallis, 2002). As discussed above, there were problems of professional integration and joint working, but these were mainly found in relation to external organizations – i.e. in the *inter-agency* mode of joint working. Within collaborative organizations – i.e. in the *intra-agency* mode of joint working – multi-disciplinary teams had developed many strategies for managing inter-professional collaboration. These included the creation of a culture that valued the complementarity of the individual professions, formal strategies of communication (daily or weekly meetings, access to each other's notes and paperwork), informal communication (sharing staff room, meeting throughout the day, mobile phone contact). Furthermore, staff reported improved job satisfaction, because of improved understanding of each other's roles, and being able to see that their holistic approach made a difference to clients. This is illustrated in the following quotes from a nurse and an occupational therapist respectively:

137

"This way of working is completely different ... and what it's taught me is ... I am a nurse by background, but I just don't think like a nurse anymore. I feel I can see the wider picture and how we meet needs together ... in community nursing, we were very task orientated, and we would deal with the task and not look at the wider picture. Now I couldn't possibly look at a patient without looking at every element of their needs." (UK2, nurse)

"What has become better and better (within CART teams) is that we know enough about each other's professions that we can provide each other with the information we need ... without treading on each other's toes." (UK2, occupational therapist)

The integration of health and social/personal care professionals in multi-professional teams with shared staff bases ('co-location') thus locates the individual professionals in an environment of regular interactions with colleagues of other professional backgrounds. The material collected in the

PROCARE fieldwork points towards the evolution of collaborative patterns of the professionals involved and the emergence of joint organisational cultures that appear to complement or even supersede the idiosyncratic cultures that the professionals brought along as they initially engaged in joint provision of integrated health and social/personal care.

It is evident that this conclusion is largely based on the *intra-agency* mode of joint working – a solution that is not feasible or affordable in the provision of all kinds of health and social/personal care for older persons. Nonetheless, the conclusion is significant as it indicates that organisational development towards integrated care provision is a real possibility, as professional identities, cultures and boundaries do not constitute insurmountable barriers towards integration. Rather, these entities can be replaced by overarching organisational identities, cultures and boundaries – much to the satisfaction of both providers and recipients of the care services provided.

The lessons that can be learned from the PROCARE fieldwork are that organisations respond to the demands of integrated health and social care in a number of different ways, but the services that evolve appear to be generally driven by local political demands. Despite this, there are relatively few permutations of integrated working models. Those featured within this research are mainly concerned with assessing, rationing and providing home-based care for older people with complex needs. Integrated care organisations are usually found where intransigent problems exist – at the hospital/community interface, in the 'grey area' between community health and social care and again at a commissioning level, where the organisation tries to pull discrete groups together for the purposes of joint planning and evaluation. It should come as no surprise that 'integrated health and social care' is as complex as the problems it intends to tackle, or as changeable as the prevailing political wind. We have been able to identify some commonalities, and to recognise that integrated organisations form, develop and specialise in response to the needs that are identified in the client groups. As new needs or 'gaps' are recognised, the services proliferate and develop again to meet those needs. The reflexive nature of older people's services across Europe represents a considerable strength of care provision, and seems a poorly recognised source of innovation. The downside for those who would evaluate it is that these rapidly changing services continually evade all our attempts to measure or define them.

4.2 Implications for Practice

- The shared challenge of demographic change and its implications for resource use in health and social care has led different countries across Europe to develop very similar strategic approaches to care integration. These services focus on the development, extension and specialisation of community-based health and social care for older people.
- The high rates of bed occupancy by older people in acute hospitals across Europe have led to specific developments in meeting the needs of clients in the 'grey area' between hospital and community care
- The existing literature reveals that the barriers to integrated working are well established, that there are tensions between policy and practice, and that there is a lack of robust empirical evidence about the costs, efficiency or the effectiveness of integrated care. Measuring success is difficult in methodological terms and consequently the 'case' for integrated care is intuitive rather than evidence-based.
- The 'pessimistic tradition' (Hudson, 2002) can be supported by PRO-CARE data, because the models studied reported that the traditional barriers between agencies persist, and that it is difficult to negotiate and maintain integrated working because of these structural, financial and professional barriers. Working across the 'medical/social divide' remained a universal challenge. This could be due to either differences between medical and social care professionals *or* to the difficulties of communicating across the hospital/community divide.
- There was also some data to support the 'optimistic tradition', and this provided examples of multi-disciplinary working for clients with complex needs, where finance and agency barriers have been successfully negotiated. This tended to be within smaller 'stand alone' integrated working organisations. The long-term costs and benefits are uncertain.

Key Points Related to Establishing Successful Integrated Working between Health and Social Care

- Integrated working is facilitated where there is an effective legal and policy framework in place – this is a key barrier if absent.
- Integrated working requires continuing financial and other resource investment.

- Integrated working is facilitated where there is an effective structural framework in place. Small, single organisations are one example of a supportive structure, but these may be unaffordable, or unsustainable in the longer term. Paradoxically, the existence of stand-alone integrated agencies creates a further barrier for other health and social care providers to negotiate.
- However, 'inter-agency integration' initiatives (working across organisational boundaries) appear to be more widespread. Staff report many benefits for themselves and their clients, but also continued organisational and structural barriers. The more barriers that have to be negotiated, the more difficult it becomes for staff to remain motivated to work with other agencies. Common barriers include multiple agency involvement, geographical separation, different financial arrangements, impediments to shared documentation/data, and lack of organisational resources.
- It is not always clear to staff that integrated working will necessarily benefit their clients, or that the effort required to sustain cross-agency relationships will match the rewards to themselves or their client group.

Factors Which Facilitated Effective Joint Working in PROCARE Model Projects

- Integrated working was helped by 'co-location' (where different staff groups share the same premises and clients). This leads to informal communication networks that became integral features of interdisciplinary working. Respondents also reported development of 'shared cultures' and 'blurring of professional boundaries'.
- Daily or weekly meetings, individual case conferences.
- Knowing other professionals personally.
- Active management support for joint working.
- Training, education, 'in-house' workshops..
- An ethos or 'belief' in the model and its goals.
- Allowing staff time to overcome initial scepticism.
- Allow enough time for the 'integration process' to be managed and for meetings, travel, development and management of networks, contacts and jointly-agreed protocols and strategies.

- Job satisfaction, and seeing clients get better and become more independent.

Factors Which Inhibited Effective Joint Working in PROCARE Model Projects

- Integrated care is inhibited when key actors work in separate agencies, particularly if there is a high turnover of staff.
- Integrated care requires specific skills, and some staff felt there was a real lack of education/training.
- Lack of clear career pathway for professional staff – integrated working is not rewarded in financial or career terms despite the multidisciplinary skills that are gained.
- Uncertainty and job insecurity.
- Concern that the needs identified can't be met using the resources available.
- Low self-esteem in relation to other professions involved.
- Lack of money, time and equipment.
- Short-term contracts/short-term planning for organisation (fear of closure).
- Shortage of staff.

141

Key Innovations in Integrated Health and Social Care Models – Instruments and Methods

Giorgia Nesti, Natalia Alba, Steen Bengtsson

Introduction

Organisational solutions and formal tools to support the whole process of integrated care are crucial to develop coherent and user-oriented strategies. By introducing some degree of formalisation within the care process, such instruments provide a support to professionals in order to plan the individual care project, to define clear and meaningful goals and to monitor progress. They are a strategic resource for promoting the dialogue between different key workers. They also allow "the reduction of redundancies, the enhancement of continuity and customising services within the process of care provision as well as the empowerment of the users of the care services" (Leichsenring, 2004: 7).

This chapter aims to identify and analyse key innovations that have been adopted by selected countries to introduce and support integrated care approaches. By comparing their main characteristics, their ways of working through an analysis of methods, structures and instruments, and their strengths and weaknesses, we will also try to point out lessons to be learned across countries. The focus of our comparison is both on the organisational impact and consequences for the users, and our analysis concentrates on two main areas:

1. Integrated care methods and structures that are adopted by selected model ways of working related to *organisational development and quality management*. In this area, the following types of key processes could be identified:

   • A case manager, i.e. a single professional who is responsible for the entire care management;
   • Multi-professional teams in charge of needs assessment and / or the complete care process;
   • Regular meetings among professionals for exchanging information about the user, his / her care plan, his / her improvements or set backs;
   • Written procedures to clearly define roles and / or processes;
   • quality management systems that develop and control mutually agreed objectives, procedures and outcomes;
   • Training, seminars and conferences to allow organisational learning and mutual exchange of experiences among professionals;
   • Information and communication systems formally structured by using a common database, data coding, and network systems;
   • A structured follow-up process, through regular meetings and reporting systems for example, and communication within the network of regional services.

2. Integrated care instruments related to the *care process* focusing on user's needs. We identified the following solutions that are fostering integration in the selected model ways of working:

   • Multi-dimensional tools for needs assessments, i.e. valid and reliable instruments or forms to assess users' needs;
   • An individual written care plan;
   • Indicators and forms for monitoring the care process;
   • Indicators for the final evaluation and discharge;
   • An overall information and communication system with users and caregivers for informing them about needs, the whole care process, final outcomes and follow-up care.

A further fundamental dimension in integrating health and social care services that has been highlighted during the research process of PROCARE is the development of a person-centred approach. Those model ways of working that were chosen for in-depth analysis were supposed to be organised according to an holistic method, putting the user at the centre. However, the organisational and procedural integration of social and health care is realised by professional care workers, by technical, administrative and managerial staff within a professional system that is shaped by the respective cultures of the organisations involved. Furthermore, care delivery is predominantly carried out by specialists with their 'own' professional methods, skills and specific professional knowledge. Thus it has to be underlined that methods, structures and instruments that are used in order to integrate social and health care are often to be added to the 'toolboxes' of professional care workers. They also have to be added to the organisational heritage of the organisations involved, and thus become an important challenge to organisational change in health and social care organisations. This is a strong theme for PROCARE and is captured in Chapters 3 and 7.

As a corollary, the mere process of organisational innovation towards integrating health and social care services might easily become an obstacle for 'user-centred care' as professionals might become too much involved in additional organisational or technical activities, rather than putting the user at the centre. We should therefore be aware of this ambiguity and of the fact that integrating health and social care is not an end in itself but a means to help the user as a social being to communicate and to take part in family life and society.

145

1   Organisational Solutions for Integrating Care

We started our analysis by comparing the 18 model ways of working with respect to methods and structures adopted to foster integrated care. Table 1 provides an overview of key methods and instruments that were identified as being used systematically or at least informally. The most widespread methods documented in 14 out of 18 model ways of working were 'multi-professional teams' and the implementation of an 'information and communication system'. We use this section to elaborate on these systems.

Giorgia Nesti, Natalia Alba, Steen Bengtsson

Table 1: Key Innovations Related to the Organisation of Health and Social Care Services

Methods & instruments / Model way of working*	Case manager	Multi-professional team	Joint meetings and training	Quality management system	Defined procedures	Joint training, seminars and conferences	Information & communication system	Follow-up system with external services
A1	√	√	√		√	√	√	(√)
A2	√	√	√	√	√		√	(√)
D1	√	(√)				√	√	
D2						√	√	
DK1	√						√	√
DK2	√	√		(√)				
EL1	(√)	√	(√)				(√)	
EL2	(√)	(√)						
F1	(√)	√	√			√	√	
F2	√	√	√		√	√	√	
FIN1		√				√	√	
FIN2		√	√	(√)			√	
I1	(√)	√	√		√		(√)	
I2		√	√		√		√	
NL1	√	√	√	(√)			√	(√)
NL2	√	√	√				√	
UK1	√	√	√				√	(√)
UK2	√	√	√				√	

Notes: √ = formal presence of the instrument; (√) = informal presence of the instrument.
* See the complete list of model projects in Annex 2.

146

1.1 Multi-professional Teams

Multi-professional teams usually take the lead in the assessment process, except in Austria, where assessment was made by the discharge manager while the multi-professional team was responsible for the provision of integrated services (A1) or for the discharge process (A2).

Multi-professional teams generally consist of a social worker, a nurse, a therapist, a GP and a geriatrician; sometimes they also involve an occupational therapist (see NL1) and/or a family assistant (EL1). Two main distinctions need to be taken into consideration:

- Services with internal multi-dimensional assessment teams: ad hoc teams created within the service as integral part of the service, e.g. the Finnish models FIN1 and FIN2, the CART team (UK1), the WUCC team (I1) and the KAPI (EL1).
- Services with external multi-dimensional assessment teams: these are central or regional services, assessing needs for all older persons in the region like for instance in Denmark, in Italy with the Territorial Assessment Unit/TAU (I2) and in the Netherlands with Regional Assessment Agencies/RIO.

All users, carers, key workers and researchers agree on stressing the relevance of such a multidisciplinary approach. Single multi-dimensional assessments and regular meetings are crucial in order to define a holistic care plan and to share information between professionals:

> "As a team we are quite lucky because we can get in and get things done. We can achieve a lot more in our position than say perhaps a GP or district nurse working on their own." (UK1, staff member)

On the other side, when different assessments are to be made, coordination and sharing information became difficult:

> "Some problems with multi-sector care planning included keeping all the paperwork together and accessible, avoiding duplication between professions working in parallel (especially when specialists teams are visiting)." (UK1, staff member)

1.2 Information and Communication Systems

Information and communication systems (archives, database, statistics, and users' reports), supported by modern information technology, are an important modernisation strategy that could be retrieved in a number of models (A1 and A2, D1, DK1, EL1, FIN1 and FIN2, I1 and I2, NL1, UK1 and UK2). Particularly innovative seems to be the German 'Internet Compatible Data Base' (see D1) which provides online information to each facility of the network on every user.

As previously mentioned in Chapter 2, a further interesting innovation in this context is represented by the creation of the Unified Information System (I2), characterised as follows:

> "Goals/objectives: every citizen who is being assisted by either the GP, by social-sanitary services, by the hospital, or by the rehabilitation infrastructure, can potentially be followed and traced back through one unique users' archive that is constantly updated. In the future it will be possible to have access to a databank through mobile phones or hand computers. Success criteria: (a) the database is available on the net for all the operators in the territory: in this way collaboration is facilitated and the passage of information between offices are reduced; (b) the administration and bureaucracy is simplified; (c) data about the citizen are collected and entered only once; (d) the territory and hospital services are put on-line." (I2)

A computer assisted database represents a crucial resource in fostering integration for three reasons. Firstly, it makes the whole process more transparent for users and caregivers, as the Austrian example underlines:

> "Documentation of statistics and compiling a yearly report seems to be quite useful to make the work of the discharge management transparent and to allow them to demonstrate what has been done." (A1)

Secondly, it facilitates communication between different professionals: data represent an evidence-based common ground to exchange information about user and case development. Finally, statistics and reports can be presented to management and administrators, providing evidence of integrated service provision which is particularly relevant in case of innovative services that need to show their benefits.

In this context, it is also useful to agree upon commonly used forms such as, for instance, a 'transition sheet' used in both German models (D1 and D2). The form contains general and current information about the patient, such as his/her current state of health in case of transfer to/from the hospital is filled in by staff of the transferring agency and sent directly to the responsible staff of the receiving facility.

1.3   *Needs Assessment and Individual Care Planning*

Needs assessment and defining individualised care are processes that are meant to produce a better and more cohesive care for users (Baldwin/Woods,

1995; Baldwin, 1998). These processes are, however, becoming placed within the wider political arena, as the following quote from the Danish discharge project illustrates:

> "The training-plan contains some 89 questions that we have to assess ... It differs quite a lot from person to person on how long time the assessment takes, but it takes time from the actual time we can spend with our patients ... But what I have been told is that we've now got a tool that is able to produce statistical information that the politicians can understand. Instead of us telling the politicians that this or that person had a nice stay at the facility and that the person was trained to do a lot more than he could before – in prose – they now get some statistics. So in that sense it is mainly beneficial for the politicians."
> (DK1, key worker)

Thus, formalised procedures to assess needs and to define individual care plans may facilitate the communication between the service and the political level, giving more evidence also to successes achieved to justify the allocation of money.

In Finland (FIN2) and in the Netherlands (NL1), each user has a message booklet "where the care giver writes her messages to the other helpers and to the family members" (FIN2, key worker) or a care record at home:

> "It contains data about their health and social conditions (like health problems, disabilities, medication), care needs and telephone number of relevant persons (like the informal carer, GP and medical specialist). The staff members continually record information in it. After every visit to the client, they note what they have done and, if applicable, which things need special attention. The next key worker looks at these notes before beginning his/her task. Moreover, a copy of the care records is transferred to the office, where the care mediator reads it to determine whether any special actions might be required for the client." (NL1, key worker)

1.4   Case Management

Another important method adopted in many projects is the presence of a case manager, playing a key role in coordinating all care interventions, in taking care of the user during the transfer from one service to another, and in managing relationships with users and caregivers. The case manager is present in almost all the services considered, but his/her relevance varies from a formal to an informal recognition of his/her role.

For instance, in the Austrian discharge project, the main innovation is the installation of a discharge manager who is in a key position between the hospital and extramural care at home in order to help organise all discharge issues. This position is based on the idea of case management, which aims to create a holistic, concrete and individual plan for help and care. The idea is to allow one person to be responsible for all discharge issues who can be contacted by hospital staff, patients and family members when needing assistance with discharge issues. The case manager supports these actors in making all the plans and decisions in connection with hospital discharge and further help and care at home. The most important tasks of the discharge manager are (Stricker et al., 2002):

- coordinating and organising the phase of discharge from the hospital,
- assessing the patients' previous situation concerning help and care at home,
- assessing the patients' future care needs,
- counselling the patient and his/her family about further possibilities for help and care, medical aides, food, transport etc. as well as organising these services,
- support in applying for attendance allowance and to nursing homes,
- contacting family members and involving them in preparing the hospital discharge, and
- systematic development of cooperation with external partners.

A similar role is performed in Denmark by the coordinating nurse (DK1) and by a so-called contact person (DK2); in the Netherlands by the care mediator (NL1) and by the case manager in the UK models (UK1 and UK2). Case managers are usually social workers or nurses. A more informal co-ordinating task is played by the social worker in Greece (EL1 and EL2) and in Italy (I1).

1.5   Joint Meetings, Training and Organisational Learning

Regular meetings are often associated with multi-professional need assessments and usually take place monthly (A1, NL1), weekly (A2, FIN2, I2, NL1) or daily (UK2). In the French (F1), Italian (I1) and Greek (EL1) cases, meetings are more informal and their frequency is based on need:

> "Doctors and discharge managers are of the opinion that this is an important tool for making interdisciplinary decisions concerning hospital discharge and were satisfied with it (...) We have a weekly team meeting. Doctors, nurses, psychotherapists as well as physiotherapists are present (...) In this framework, we discuss all patients from different perspectives, with inputs from everybody.

> Together we plan a date for discharge which suits the patient (...) We discuss things that are unclear, and how each team member sees the patient and then make decisions as a team. Because each individual team member might be missing small pieces of information, the whole picture becomes clear, if one can talk about it in the team and accept each others' suggestions. That is an important process. It is usually a long meeting, about two hours." (A2, key worker)

The organisation of conferences and specific training for professionals as forums where they can discuss and exchange their experience is another important tool for realising integration. During such meetings professionals enhance mutual learning and contribute to making results evident both to the public and users / caregivers. Forums for interdisciplinary communication are also present in Denmark (DK2).

A particular way of joint working can be observed at the German Geronto-psychiatric Association Oberspreewald-Lausitz (D2) through the enhancement of organisational learning. This is seen as an innovative way to pursue integration:

> "In the course of the association conferences different subjects are discussed which are relevant for the members of the association (such as ways of improving everyday collaboration, quality standards common to all). Shared training and educational conferences (FB/WB) are offered to all employees from the participating facilities. Individual representatives of GPGV collaborate in subject-related working groups following association conferences, if indicated (elaboration of cooperation agreements, reflections on patient transfers, public work). Further Education: 25 training meetings focusing on geronto-psychiatry were offered, the participants can get certification from the geronto-psychiatric association which gives them a basic qualification." (D2, key worker)

Educational programmes are fundamental which is underlined by key workers from several countries:

> "All key workers of the three organisations can participate in the Red Cross further education programme; likewise, staff of Caritas and Volkshilfe may offer further training programmes also within the Red Cross." (A2, key worker)

> "The role of rehab workers is very specialised because of their training. They have the basics in nursing, occupational therapy and physiotherapy. And they are with the client every day, so they can see the changes and report back (...) if the client is deteriorating, the rehab worker will know whether to call in the nurse or the care manager." (UK1, key worker)

Another interesting experience crosscutting the dimension of organisational learning and the presence of a follow-up system with external services is represented by the Danish 'Multidisciplinary Discharge Conferences' (DK1). Such conferences are intended to be:

151

> "... an organisational development aimed at providing quality assurance when citizens are discharged from the rehabilitation facility. Upon completion of the rehabilitation programme the individual citizens' needs for services are assessed and the objective of the discharge conference is to inform the relevant service providers on the condition of the citizen and the required service provision. The citizen and relatives are also invited for the discharge conference." (DK1, key worker)

External integration is informally promoted in the Austrian example (A1) through cooperation between the Red Cross and other organisations. In the Italian model (I1) the integration between the WUCC and the region is considerable in terms of informal feedback and reporting to the management. There is also a follow-up system with other services, limited to the transfer of user's final evaluation results. In A2, NL1, and UK1, coordination with external services is enhanced by the presence of the case manager.

1.6   Quality Management

Specific quality management systems for integrated care delivery have not yet been developed. However, what could be retrieved are applications of quality management systems to steer the formal care process, or single parts of it, by defining formal procedures such as in the Austrian case (A1) or in the Italian models (I1 and I2):

> "There is a written protocol explaining how to involve the different Hospital Units into the process. The Unit where the older person is admitted send a filled form to the Geriatric Unit, asking for the needs assessment." (I1, key worker)

> "(...) the Local Health Agency (LHA) 11 of Empoli made a protocol of protected discharge from hospital. In this protocol the following definitions are given: objectives, procedures of discharge from hospital, criteria for the activation of the home care service, target group of intervention, used resources, information instruments, criteria of check-up, etc." (I2, key worker)

Some models are making preliminary moves towards quality assurance. Within the Austrian model (A2), for instance, the discharge management has developed the Standard Procedural Plan that regularly evaluates processes and related impacts in internal "Quality Conversations". In the Danish model (DK2):

"... the 'Common Language' assessment tool ... and its guidelines for the assessment process can be viewed as a handy tool in terms of quality assurance as it systematises both assessments for services at the health centre 'Bauneparken' and the contacts that have to be made and the information that has to be shared with the other providers of the required care." (DK2, key worker)

In the Dutch model (NL1) and in the Finnish model (FIN2), quality control is guaranteed by monitoring clients' satisfaction, gathered through surveys and formal complaints.

2 Key Innovations Related to the User

Long-term care cannot be 'applied' to the user like a medical intervention or operation to a patient can. The user is an indispensable co-producer of the service, assisted by professional workers. As specific instruments used in integrated care are mainly developed by professionals, it is of utmost importance to consider whether and how they are involving the users. Table 2 provides an overview of those instruments and their application in the selected model ways of working.

153

The main aim of these instruments is to involve the users and their families in the care process, in choices that have to be made – at best based on complete information – and in planning procedures. Only if users and their families know what is expected from them as co-producers it is possible to monitor and achieve the aims defined in the individual care plan. Still, as we can gather from Table 2, monitoring and evaluation of these processes have been developed only at a few sites, while multi-dimensional needs assessment and individual care planning seems to be a general standard within integrated care approaches. Following the table we go on to outline issues relating to needs assessment, individual care planning and user-centred care.

Table 2:   Instruments Related to the User

Model way of working*	Multi-dimensional needs assessment	Written care plan	Indicators/forms for monitoring	Indicators/forms for evaluation and discharge	Information and communication system with users and caregivers
A1	√	√		√	√
A2	√	√		√	
D1	√	√			
D2					
DK1	√	√			√
DK2	√	√			√
EL1	√	√			√
EL2	√	√		√	
F1					
F2					
FIN1	√	√			
FIN2	√	√			√
I1	√	√	√	√	
I2	√	√		√	
NL1	√	√			√
NL2	√	√	√		√
UK1	√	√			√
UK2	√	√		√	√

Note: *   See the complete list of model projects in Annex 2.

2.1   Needs Assessment

The identification of need is central to the organisation of care. The concept of need builds a bridge between what a person wants, and what society (the Welfare State) is able and willing to provide. Therefore, tools for needs assessment and identification are an important feature when it comes to steering the quality and quantity of care provided to the individual user.

Interviews and conversations with users are particularly useful for grasping clients' needs and defining the care plan. From this point of view, models undertaking home visits seem to be more effective than the others in understanding care needs.

Moreover, assessment forms enable workers to collect and exchange systematic and detailed information. As an Italian key worker points out:

> "The WUCC realises integration using instruments and strategies to achieve goals. Instruments usable by everyone. (...) Such instruments (...) are filled by single professionals and then discussed to define a common goal." (I1, staff member)

Nevertheless, if assessment tools are too time-consuming, as in the Danish (DK1) and the English case (UK1), they become an unexpected threat, as the Danish report clearly enlightens:

> "The training-plan contains some 89 questions that we have to assess. (...) It differs quite a lot from person to person on how long time the assessment takes, but it takes time from the actual time we can spend with our patients (...)." (DK1, key worker)

Discovering the user experience of needs assessment was difficult in this project because, for many, the assessment process took place a long time prior to the research interview and users often could not remember what happened during the initial stage. For instance, in the British models only a few respondents remembered an assessment, or assumed that an assessment must have happened, as this example suggests:

> I: "When you got here, were you aware of any assessment being done, by the nurses or the physician?" – User: "No. But you see, what they do ... when you are getting washed and dressed etc ... they keep an eye on you. You're not aware of it at the time – they are crafty! But they don't know that we are keeping an eye on them as well!" (UK1)

In this same example the nurses have a different view of what happens. This nurse was talking about assessment and care planning in general:

> "The patients understand what the care plan is about to a certain degree and often they need to be reminded that they are actually taking part in a rehabilitation programme. And helping families understand what it's all about. So that definitely goes on when it's working well. And they take ownership of the transfer across to the Limes as well and there's a lot of work done to help them understand what's all about." (UK1)

In many cases the clients knew nothing about the assessment process because their sons or daughters had arranged it for them. If users/clients had managed it themselves, they only remembered that "a lady" had come to their home and had asked them questions (FIN1). They could not remember any details, and showed no interest in the subject. The only important thing for clients was whether or not they could get what they wanted. In this respect, the Netherlands' Regional Assessment Agencies (RIO) worked well: all clients asserted that the type and amount of care requested was given.

In the Greek project with Open Care Centres for the Elderly (KAPI), needs assessment was separated into different health and social dimensions with each professional taking responsibility for their area: the social worker for the social needs and for their social history, the nurses and the health visitors for the medical needs of the users, the family assistants for the service to the clubroom, the physiotherapists for functional improvement. The professionals involved are also the collective providers working in a team; the team leader is the social worker and the whole team works on the basis of a shared collective responsibility. According to the users, everything operates informally. This example shows how difficult it still is to really work in a team for integrated care and to overcome professional approaches, that is to delegate single activities to, for instance, a small 'assessment-team', rather than having each single professional assess specific needs. Similar problems arose in a French example:

> "Everybody tries and pretends to collaborate but not everybody is able to do it. We all do our work individually, but not as a team. The doctors don't get involved." (F2, key worker 2)

> "... it is difficult to listen to each other, we are not talking the same language." (F2, key worker 4)

Attempts to overcome this problem have been made, such as introducing more formal instruments. The Danish home care project of Skævinge is using the so-called 'Common Language' assessment tool that was developed by the Danish Ministry of Social Affairs in cooperation with the National Association of Local Authorities. The Common Language assessment tool focuses on the following overall dimensions of the functional abilities of the service user in performing instrumental and physical activities of daily living (IADL and PADL): personal care, cooking, mobility, housekeeping, capacity for planning the tasks of everyday living, social relations, participation in social life and interests, mental functions, and ability to monitor own health situation.

Furthermore, the 'Common Language' assessment tool is associated with home assessment that covers the following dimensions: access, stairs and thresholds within the residence, the suitability of the arrangement of the rooms, and the location of the residence in relation to shopping and transport. 'Common Language' operates by assigning time to each single function, such as cleaning hall, cleaning kitchen, bathing the person, etc. – therefore it has been criticised by Danish professionals for being too mechanical and producing an inhuman service. In the Skævinge project (DK2), however, this effect is overcome by combining the instrument with a person-centred approach.

In some cases needs assessment is clearly separate from service delivery, if the services are contracted out for example, or if a third party is purchasing services. A typical example for a clear-cut separation between needs assessment and care delivery is the care system in the Netherlands, where Regional Assessment Agencies (RIO) work independently from the service providers and thus act as gatekeepers for care provision. RIOs thus could also be considered as an instrument for integration of care as they assess the entire situation of the older person and his/her care needs. The RIO is trying to achieve an integral assessment. An assessment advisor visits the applicant on request and asks about his/her situation and care needs. In the case of a simple application the assessment advisor makes the decision. In more complicated cases a multi-professional team is called in. Following ongoing reform, however, the relationship between RIOs and the providers will be further diminished as the assessment result will no longer describe the services that should be delivered, but the 'functions' that have to be supported.

The English CART team (UK1) has developed its own assessment tool that could be characterised as multidimensional. Similar instruments are used in Finland (FIN1) or in Italy (I1 and I2):

> "The assessment is made during the WUCC meeting. It consists of: an analysis of information collected by the Geriatrician and the Social Worker and the elaboration of the SVAMA form, a multi-dimensional evaluation test, including: personal data, health assessment, social assessment, cognitive and functional evaluation (Barthel Index, Short Portable Mental Status Questionnaire). Each part of the SVAMA is filled by single professionals and then discussed during the WUCC meeting in order to define a common goal." (I1, key worker)

It was of interest that clients participating in the interviews from vertically integrated projects seemed to be much more conscious about the needs assessment processes. For instance, the main instrument used by the discharge manager in Vienna (A2) was extensive interviews and conversations with the users, often including their families, in order to assess their needs with respect to services at home, applying for attendance allowance and so on.

The role of the discharge manager is to assess the patient's and the family's needs regarding care and support after hospital discharge and to organise the service provision. This is clearly understood by the users themselves:

> "... and then I realised I have to talk to the discharge manager. And I filled out a questionnaire, what we have at home and what we don't and that was it ... she also helped me fill out the application for attendance allowance." (A2, user)

2.2 Individual Care Planning

A central feature of an integrated care process is that the result of the needs assessment is translated into an individual care plan, which combines the different types of intervention that are needed. The advantage of this way of working is that the person's situation is viewed as a whole. The plan gives the user and the relatives a tool to see what the care provider is offering, and what can be expected from the care. In an ideal world it secures the social rights of the user, and makes the user and the relatives feel safe. Furthermore the care plan would connect the individual professionals' efforts, and it would ensure that the needs of the user are central to the plan, rather than one single professional's perspective. When the users are given the opportunity to compare, they appreciate the benefits of having a care plan:

> "At first we had a private care service. It was horrible. Then we contacted the home nurses of the Red Cross and they provided us with the care plan. We have really good cooperation with the home nurses." (A2, user).

Often users had a less than clear picture of what happened during the care planning stage. In the Finnish home care project, one older lady remembered an initial home visit and a lot of things that had been written down on paper. Some remembered the first assessment visit, but did not remember any plan being written, while another user did not remember the written plan, but felt that the content of care had not changed since the first meeting.

In the Greek Open Care Centre, the social worker is responsible for the whole care process. She keeps a personal dossier (their 'social history') which is later updated with data about the user's marital and financial status, relationships with his/her family, health conditions, personal data, needs and social status and any other associated problems. The social worker consults this dossier very frequently and carries it with her even on visits, in order to have all the necessary information relating to the users' needs and health problems at hand. She can contact the family when the situation is considered urgent.

In the Danish home care project, the coordinating nurse plays a similar role, whereas in the Dutch 'nursing home without walls' they allocate every client a staff member, who acts as a contact person for that client. This staff member is supposed to be the first contact for questions and complaints about the care.

Another common tool reported in the Finnish discharge project is a team file, which contains information that can be of use to the home carer or the team. The team file is a kind of action plan and a guide for all phases of home care. Similarly, in Germany (D1) they use transition sheets containing general and current information about the user. They represent a good instrument for exchanging information between professionals.

Tools for needs assessment and individual care planning are most important from the user's point of view and the fact that both these methods are present in virtually all the model projects could be interpreted as an indicator for their good practice. However, work still needs to be done to further older people's understanding of the process and to promote meaningful involvement on their level.

2.3   *Creating An Integrated Care Process Putting the User at the Centre*

The central feature of the user perspective is stressed in all integrated care models. Thus, the manager of the department for social services in the local government of the Hartberg district (Austria) said about their project:

> "For us the user perspective is the most important point of our work. It is important to offer help for older people in need of care directly at the local level. This and the permanent personnel contact with our clients are the focus of our work." (A1, manager)

The strong ethos towards user involvement and user-centred care which can be retrieved throughout the data is not enough, however, to guarantee that the user is in fact an active part of the care process. A care process can easily become a professionally dominated process, where the clients take passive roles. In order to ensure that the user is more of a partner, a number of instruments with this specific purpose are needed. In this section we shall give an overview of the instruments that have been used in the projects for orientating the care process more towards this end.

The home care projects are examples of horizontal integration. In these projects a number of carers with different professional background come into the clients' homes to promote client-centred care. A lack of coherence between the single interventions will immediately reduce client-centred-ness. For example, if the care process is discussed and planned only among professionals, the needs and requests of the client can easily be pushed into the background.

The Greek home help project (EL2) is typical of other home care projects in the way it addresses these potential difficulties. In this project, staff have identified the following aspects which contribute towards active involvement and a client-centred approach:

- The policies are started from a user perspective.
- The needs of the users are fully respected, i.e. person-centred care is a basic component of the "Help at Home" programme.

- The team operates as a coordinated and cooperating team that is fully aware of the user's conditions.
- There is flexibility in adapting to changes in physical or mental conditions of the client.
- All documentation is shared between the relevant players involved.
- Mutual trust is actively developed and user satisfaction is constantly being monitored.
- A friendly atmosphere is created by open communication channels between the clients and staff.
- Further education for all staff is guaranteed.

In some of the projects the concept of self-care plays a prominent role. The Finnish home care project (FIN2) reports that several clients stress the importance of being active in their care and being able to discuss needs and wishes. In the Danish home care project (DK2) the values of self-care have also played a central role in the reorganisation of the elderly care services. A staff member explains:

> "Having a starting point within the self-care principle forced us to focus a lot more on the needs and capacities of the individual than we had previously done. When we started working from the self-care principle the needs of the individual were at the centre and formed the basis of the explicit starting point of the way we assessed and planned care with individuals. And when you force yourself to be more aware of individual needs and solutions you get a much better understanding of the person you are dealing with. And it increases your appreciation of yourself as a professional." (DK2, key worker)

If self-care and user involvement are made central aims, there is greater potential for the user to become more prominent in the process of care, and professionals become more aware of the needs of the user. The Dutch example of Zijloever (NL1), a 'virtual nursing home without walls', illustrates how a virtual concept can be an instrument for horizontal integration with the user at the centre. This 'nursing home' consists of a day centre plus the users' own homes where they get domestic aid. Although all these users have a nursing home place, they manage with this virtual home because they have an advisor and they can get the help they need. In some cases this help is rather modest, but clients are reported to be satisfied because they can remain in the areas they know. The interview results show that this is mainly due to the fact that communication channels are open, and the clients feel free to use them:

> "If I want something or if I do not like something, I simply call N.N. [name of the person who is in charge]." (NL2, user)

3   Learning from Failure: The Need for Organisational Development

As mentioned in the beginning, instruments and methods can only be applied successfully if they fit to the organisational and managerial guiding principles of the organisations involved. In models that are focusing on horizontal integration, for instance in Finland (FIN2), staff made explicit reference to the fact that shared values and guiding principles had been agreed upon. These are:

> "- based on the needs of the client ..." (FIN2, key worker 15)

> "- the aim that the customers can live as long as possible at home ..." (FIN2, key worker 8)

> "- makes the care complete for the client ... not fragmented care." (FIN2, key worker 14)

We have witnessed that, the more that vertical integration is realised the more difficult it becomes to construct coordinated or integrated approaches:

> "Improvement amongst CART team members is better than communication within the multi-disciplinary team in the acute hospital. There are fewer personality clashes, we have better information, a better level of staffing and fewer

staff turnover problems, where hospitals tend to use agency staff a lot." (UK2, key worker).

In this context organisational features become predominant – and often lead to failure or to reduced cooperation. A typical example is the UK Limes Livingstone Integrated Care Project (UK1), a community hospital and a residential home with an emphasis on recuperative care. This model's intention was to form a strong partnership and to create a seamless service between the acute and the recuperative part of care. The aim was to pool funds, to install a single management structure, to share resources and skills to the benefit of patients. Furthermore, the idea was to develop a new type of 'generic worker', i.e. a non-qualified rehabilitation assistant who would learn basic skills in nursing, occupational therapy and physiotherapy and then work flexibly between the two units. It seems, however, that most basic organisational structures and processes towards cooperation have not been realised to date:

- Funds have not really been pooled, though some jointly funded posts have been created.
- No single management structure has been created, though senior managers meet and liaise (but operational management of the two units occurs separately).
- There are generic workers, but these are mainly in the social service unit. There have been problems with the proposal to share staff, because the units use different contracts, and staff in each unit have different salaries and terms of service.
- Mainly the Livingstone hospital staff felt excluded from cooperation: they did not know the staff at Limes (social care), and felt they only saw visiting professionals occasionally – there was no weekly meeting or daily handover:

    "You're not allowed to go to any of the meetings for the planning." (UK1, health worker 11)

- Organisational and professional boundaries thus remained constant:

    "... the whole ethos of this project has not been planned, it's not been organised and it's failing." (UK1, health worker 9)

    "I mean we went through a very bad patch where actually we weren't carrying out our perception of rehabilitation. We were caring for folk who were waiting to be placed in long term care facilities and a lot of our beds had that kind of a patient so we weren't able to actually offer the rehabilitation facilities or expertise we have." (UK1, health worker 10).

"There's no give and take over there." (UK1, health worker 9).

From this example it can be learned that organisational cooperation – and sometimes integration – is a process that has to be actively and constantly planned, structured and confronted. Communication and mutual developmental work with respect to shared objectives, procedures and cultural approaches are indispensable to overcome the traditional cultural divide between the health and social care sectors:

> **"The cultural element is crucial but this is a process requiring time. You start from filling a form and then you solve a problem. It seems a simple and banal thing to do but it isn't: it requires the doctor to sit down in front of the table and think about the patient, even if the surgeon usually thinks only about the operating theatre and the rest does not matter." (I1, key worker)**

In this context it is most important to balance the organisational and structural preconditions for cooperation and integration with the concern for the provision of a user-centred service. While we have shown a number of examples where organisational 'tools' were successfully implemented, it is much more difficult to show evidence for developments towards user-centredness as these are much more value-laden, 'soft' and less concrete but they are dealing with 'awareness', 'respect', 'atmosphere' and similar concepts. Further research is needed to identify the way in which these values are or could be translated into the daily work of integrated long-term care services and facilities.

163

4   Conclusion

From the evidence given by the analysed model ways of working it can be said that progress has been made with respect to 'technical' solutions for some of the most pertinent problems in integrating health and social care services:

- Multidimensional assessment instruments are used in all countries, collecting data with a valid and reliable assessment form, generally including personal data, health assessment, social assessment, cognitive and functional evaluation.
- The multidimensional assessment represents the point of departure for defining an individual care plan, including the coordination between different providers.

- Multi-professional teams and/or a single case manager (see also Chapter 3 and 7) have been defined and installed as a focal point for coordination and integration processes.
- In some cases data are already collected, processed and stored using information technology, in particular the internet to foster information exchange at all times from different places. A step forward will be finding a way to use IT-solutions (see Chapter 2) that can also be controlled by the users and/or their caregivers.

Still, the methodological 'hardware' alone cannot solve what has been described as the 'soft' aspects of integrating health and social care services. Only in rather general terms can we suggest that all activities that improve communication and use an organisational development approach are useful, even though they have to 'fit' with the respective national and regional approaches.

CHAPTER 5

The Role of the Family in Integrated Care

Cécile Chartreau, Marie-Jo Guisset, Andrea Kuhlmann,
Monika Reichert, Aphrodite Teperoglou,
Eftichia Teperoglou, Alain Villez

Introduction

The focus of this chapter is on the role of the family, which was a clear emergent issue within the PROCARE analysis. The main objectives of this chapter are:

- to give an overview of family care in Europe, concentrating on the PROCARE countries,
- to examine the relationship between family care and integrated care.

This chapter provides an account of the analysis in three main sections:

The *first section* provides a description of general tendencies with regard to family care and the role of the family in general, an overview of national policies related to older people's care by families and some socio-demographic data. The culture and ethics of family care are discussed in a transnational perspective.

The *second section* examines support given to family carers in a transnational perspective; it gives a description of services provided to families in different countries, especially integrated care services.

The *third section* deals with the main tasks of family care with respect to experiences, influences and expectations; it contains a description of what is done by family members (informal help) in a transnational perspective and reflects the level of interdependency of formal and informal care. This section deals with the following questions: Do families accept different kinds of support? Will their expectations be fulfilled and are families satisfied with services?

The chapter ends with concluding remarks and provides recommendations relating to best practice in dealing with the informal caring relationship in integrated care models.

On the basis of these findings we try to point out the link between integrated care and family care with regard to differences between the countries. Finally, the future of integrated care services with regard to socio-demographic trends is debated.

1   The General Role of the Family in Long-term Care

In most industrialised countries we have experienced significant changes in patterns of family formation and family structure. Families have become less stable and more diverse, changing roles and relationships are apparent with respect to paid employment (Ponzetti, 2003: 768-778), cohabitation is increasingly common. As well as the percentage of non-married women, we can witness a growth in the number of lone parents and an increase in the number of people living alone. Further challenges concern the continuing decline of the traditional family model of a male breadwinner and a dependent wife, and the rise of the two-earner family. Added to this are women's increased economic independence, not to speak of the impact of feminism, the changing sexual norms and general attitudes towards families and children.

Moreover, the age distribution of the population has changed substantially during the past decades with a growth in the proportion of people aged 65 and over. All the visible outcomes of the changing patterns and the demographic trends have led to a renewed interest in the family in both the sociological and policy literature as well as in the political and popular discourse. A source of much concern is the care and welfare of older people by the family while, empirically, the importance of family care has increased immensely during the last 20 years: the increasing long-term care needs have mainly been shouldered by family carers (Philp, 2001).[1]

---

1   Though mainly dealing with family carers, by carers we generally mean people who look after a relative or friend who needs support because of age, physical or learning disability or illness, including mental illness (http://www.carersinformation.org.uk/).

Historically, care of older people has been considered a private matter. Concerns about the implications of demographic trends, together with the influence of feminist analyses of family-based care have ensured that the issue is now a subject for public debate across Europe (Ditch et al., 1994: 73-74). Still, in most of the European societies, informal care provided by the family is the main source of care. The family is predominantly responsible for meeting the needs of older people or disabled relatives. Families are the largest 'care service' and partners are the most important carers, followed by the caring generation of children. The integration of informal care is a critical area for integrated care delivery due to the fact that many family carers often do not see themselves as carers, also professionals do not see the caring family as partners, and finally because of the rising number of non-family informal carers, who are often immigrants (Leichsenring, 2004: 31). The relationship between state policies and measures on the one side, and family behaviour and family ethics on the other hand is being debated. New needs arise and new institutions oriented towards older people are necessary. The next two sections of this chapter address both the new needs which are related to the changing sociodemographic trends as well as the main national policies in relation to family care in the PROCARE countries.

1.1   General Data on Family Care

Ageing of the European population has become increasingly important on the EU agenda. In the 50 years between 1960-2010, the population aged 65 and over in the 15 EU Member States will have more than doubled, from 34 to 69 million, while the population as a whole will have increased form 315 to 385 million (Whitten/Kailis, 1999; see for a general overview OECD Health Data, 2004).

It is the increasing number of very old people that propel the need for action in long-term care. In France, according to the study HID/INSEE (1999), 5% of the inhabitants over 60 years old have to stay in a bed or armchair or need help for washing and dressing. Out of these 628,000 people, 223,000 live in institutions and 400,000 in their own house. In Germany nearly three out of four people needing care are cared for in the domestic environment; in 1999 this was equivalent to approximately 1.44 million older people needing care. The percentage of people reporting a disability (all levels) increases with age. Finland shows the most rapid progression and reaches the highest level of disability prevalence from the age of 40 onwards, with more than 52% of 60-64 year-olds reporting a disability. Belgium, Greece, Ireland and Italy have the smallest percentage in each age group (about 20% for people between 60 and 64 years of age) (Eurostat, 2001). More than half of the Netherlands' population of 65 years or over report a physical disability; 15% of those people have a severe, 22% a moderate, and 24% a minor disability (de Klerk, 2000).

Overview 1: Features of the Main Carer[2]

1. **Women are more likely to be carers than men:**
- In the Netherlands 60% of the carers are women and 40% are men.
- In Germany approx. 80 % of the caring family members are women (partner or daughter- (in-law).
- In Austria, daughters and daughters-in-law carry the main burden of care.
- In the UK 58% are women and 42% are men.
- In Greece caring is a family affair and the daughters, daughters-in-law and grandchildren are the main carers.

2. **The age of informal carers is relatively high, compared to the adult population as a whole:**
- In the Netherlands the age distribution among informal carers is: 18-34 years 17%, 35-44 years 23%, 45-54 years 31%, 55-64 years 17%, 65-74 years 9% 75+ years 4%.
- In the UK a fifth of all adults aged 45-64 provide informal care: under 30 years 12%, 30-44 years 20%, 45-64 years 41% and over 65 years 27%.
- In Germany approximately half of the carers are already between 40 and 64 years old, a third older than 65.
- In Austria about 59% of all family carers are between 40 and 60, one third above 60 and about 15% are younger than 40. Altogether about 1.5% of all employed people are carers of older kin.

In the UK there are nearly 5.7 million carers[3], in Austria according to the evaluation of the long-term care allowance scheme currently about 90% of the recipients are mainly cared for by a family member (Badelt et al., 1997). In Italy between 1983 and 1998, the number of people involved in taking care of a relative, is estimated to have grown by 21%. In the Netherlands a large-scale survey confirmed that informal care is still very common.[4] On the basis of the results the number of people who provide informal care is estimated at 3.7 million (total Dutch population: 16 million). In France, 3,700,000 people are family carers: this amounts to 60% of all the carers (HID/INSEE, 1998-1999; Dutheil, 2001).

1.2 National Policies Related to Care of Older People by Families

Policy responses vary widely and are informed by different attitudes to the role of the family. Specific legislation on integrated care and national policies related to elder care provided by the families is scarce. In recent years we can observe initiatives which support an increasing number of policies and respective legislation with respect to supporting (or not) informal care networks. The analysis of this section was based on national policy initiatives concerning the support of family carers that were reported from the 18 PROCARE model ways of working.

The number of countries with long-term care schemes has grown remarkably during the last decade. These schemes tend to provide cash payments to the person in need of care – not only older people – and/or their family carers as a way of acknowledging the role of family care and the fact that complete professionalisation of long-term care will not be feasible. Furthermore, such schemes offer people the possibility of deciding independently which kinds of services to use. When services are integrated choices may become less clear. Some of these schemes, in particular the German Long-term Care Insurance and the French 'APA' (Allocation Personnalisée d'Autonomie), are – at least partly – based on voucher systems (Leichsenring, 2004: 34-35). [5]

---

2   see also http://www.carersinformation.org.uk/; Timmermans, 2003; Badelt et al., 1997; Nemeth/Pochobradsky, 2002.

3   More information on http://www.carersinformation.org.uk/

4   See the survey among informal carers (N=1,211) by the Social and Cultural Planning Office (Timmermans, 2003): the majority (65%) of the respondents cared for an elderly person (65 years of over). The informal carers were not only family members of the recipient (partner, child, parent, sister, brother or other relative). Some of them were friends or aqaintances (12%) or neighbours (6%).

5   For further information see also www.plan-retraite.fr/apa.htm (France) and www.bmgs. bund.de/eng/gra/long/4293.php (Germany).

The establishment and development of networks of national policies related to family care, could be polarized into two 'camps': in the Mediterranean countries and their prevailing 'family ethics', which will be looked at in the next section, only minor efforts to integrate family carers in providing systems are being observed (Leichsenring, 2004: 30). On the other hand we can identify a group of countries (UK, Austria, Germany, Denmark but also regions of Italy) with mechanisms and initiatives which are crucial for family and informal carers to organise care for older people at home.

Analysing the different approaches towards the national policies which support or impede the provision of family care, it is interesting firstly to draw upon some examples of legislation which support the central role of the family in the provision of care. We can find specific legislation both on a national and a regional level. In Italy, informal care networks, in particular the family, are the core resource for older people, also underpinned by Law n. 328/2000, the Social Plan 2001-2003 and the local legislation. In France the concept of solidarity is a key to understanding informal social support. According to the French legislation, the notion of 'solidarity' emerges as an obligation or duty between members of a family, parents toward sons and daughters (even adults), and sons and daughters toward their older parents. In Greece the family is responsible for the care of its dependent members of all ages under civil law. Where the family cannot provide such care, then Social Security policy comes into play. This legal responsibility of the family is specified in the Constitution of 1975, amended in 1986 and 2001.[6] In Austria, the direct legal responsibility of the family has been reduced during the past few years. Apart from the introduction of the long-term care allowance scheme in 1993, this lessening of family responsibilities can be shown by the fact that, in many provinces, siblings are not asked any longer to contribute to nursing home fees. Even if the pension and the long-term care allowance of the older person do not cover all costs, social assistance schemes will step in. Support services for family care have been increasingly

---

6   Although the constitution itself does not mention the concept of 'social security', the family is under the protection of the State. The State will care for the health of citizens and will adopt special measures for the protection of young people, the elderly and invalids, as well as the needy. People with special needs are entitled to take advantage of measures, which "guarantee their personal autonomy, employment inclusion and participation in the social, economical and political framework of the country". Despite responsibility being delegated to both the family and to the State there is great difficulty in enforcing these provisions since it requires action by the public legal service (legislator).

developed, for which both Austrian models analysed ('Social and Health Care Districts in Hartberg' and Discharge Management at the Hartmann Hospital, Vienna) are examples of how family carers can be supported to help older people stay at home.

Also in the UK, it is expected that spouses and other family members will care for their partners or older relatives. Still, there is growing awareness about the need to complement this type of support by means of formal services, since it is known that there are about 5.7 million carers in Britain that save up to £57 billion per year.[7] In the UK the government established a national strategy for carers and a substantial policy package as well as a new legislation to allow authorities to address carers' needs. In the communities, the networks of giving, of caring, and of supporting relatives, friends and neighbours are part of the glue that helps join society together. Also in the selected models of the empirical research in the UK that are helping older people return to independent living, staff are increasingly aware of the important role of family members.

In Germany, after a long discussion the Long-term Care Insurance came into force in 1995: the purpose of the respective law is to help those in need of care to lead as independent and self-determined lives as possible. The intention of the law is also to facilitate freedom of choice between residential care, community care services and cash benefits. In reality, a large majority of entitled people choose the cash benefit as services often are not available or not available at the right time and to the extent needed. The German Model of Home Care Nurenburg looks for solutions in the relationship between users, carers and services, in particular during the transition to home after a stay in hospital. As the development of mutual trust is key to a complementary relation between services and family carers, staff and management in this model way of working put special emphasis on this issue.

In the Netherlands the national policies in relation to 'informal' welfare are not evident. Certainly, the supply of formal home care relieves family carers, and thus may be considered as a kind of support but there are only a few services focusing on the needs of family carers. Current political debates, however, are tackling the extent to which the existing and/or potential resources of family or informal care should be taken into account when shaping future policies. This debate will have important practical consequences for both older people who are in need of care and their (potential) carers.

---

7   see http://www.carers.gov.uk and http://www.carersinformation.org.uk.

In the Mediterranean countries care for older people continues to be a 'family affair'. Care is provided by the family and there is no direct support from the state. One of the best examples of this situation is Greece, where informal care provided by the family is the main source of care. The cost of care is undertaken by older people either from his/her savings or from the pension, or by the family. Older people play a reciprocal role, by providing capital or property, or by assisting with child care, so the relationship is not perceived as one of dependence. In societies like the Greek one, where historically a Welfare State did not develop compared to the most of European countries, there is a great necessity to develop services to support informal care (Teperoglou, 1990; 1993; 1996; 2003; Sissouras et al., 2004: 342). To this end, certain positive steps have been taken by the provision of pilot schemes (Model 2: Help at Home, pilot programmes supporting carers). One of the Greek Models analysed (KAPI) emphasises the neighbourhood and its social capital in re-building social solidarity.

171

Also in Italy, informal care networks, in particular the family, are the core resource in caring for older people. However, family care is increasingly supported by special schemes. The regional legislation in Veneto, the region where one of the Italian model ways of working is situated (I1: Working Unit of Continuous Care, from Hospital to Care Facility/Home), provides economic support for families and for people with physical and/or psychological problems if they need particular health and social care at home. In order to maintain older people at home, the Region Veneto assigns a daily fee for community care services. This provision includes home help, admission to a day centre and support to family carers. These services are provided by the municipal social service or the Local Health Units that have to assess the older person's means and needs. Although at an experimental stage, the regional administration (Deliberation of Regional Assembly n. 1513/2001) has instituted a monthly fee for people with Alzheimer disease and behavioural disorders, financed by the Local Health Unit. This provision is means-tested and dependent on a medical assessment. Finally there are experimental economic provisions supporting family carers (Deliberation of Regional Assembly n. 3960/2001) covering expenses for medicines, short-term care in a nursing home, and home care for terminal patients.

Also in Finland the legislative framework moves towards a differentiated way of supporting family care. According to Finnish legislation, sons or daughters are not responsible for their parents' care. However, also the largest group of helpers caring for older people are friends or relatives

(Salonen/Haverinen, 2004: 194). Thus they are also considered to be important partners of the Finnish model ways of working. On a more general level, political debates increasingly stress that the responsibility of family members as caregivers will increase in the future (Mäkinen et al, 1998: 52; Ministry of Social Affairs and Health, 2002: 115). On the municipal level, however, Finland still provides advanced support to family carers of working age by 'employing' and paying them a fee (more or less equivalent to a minimum wage), and by providing additional services. The municipality and the caregiver draw up an agreement, including a plan of care and services. The caregiver has the right to at least one day off per month, and the municipality is responsible for providing the care during this period. In recent years cooperation has intensified between family members, volunteer workers, the public sector and provider organisations (Ministry of Social Affairs and Health, 1999a).

Another interesting approach is the basic tenet in Danish social policy in general and elderly policy in particular: emphasis on ensuring individual independence. In order to avoid putting older people in need of care into a relationship of dependence, the family is assigned a residual role in the provision of care services for older people. However, in cases where older person are living with spouses who are capable of performing activities of daily living, they will be expected to perform these. Only when help is needed for personal activities can the older person needing care decide who should deliver the care, either spouse or a professional. This is to ensure a dignified solution to care. In our data, among people interviewed in the Danish model 1 (municipality of Søllerød), we found that those who were living with their spouses and needed personal care preferred assistance from a professional carer. In Søllerød, day-care facilities (one also specialised in people with dementia) are also available to provide respite for spouses who care for their frail partner.

To sum up, care policies in all countries rely heavily on the availability of a spouse or other family members. However, while the direct responsibility by legal regulations has diminished in some countries over the past 20 years – in combination with the development of respective formal services and benefits – other countries have only just started to support the ever present willingness of family carers to take their role in the caring process. To a large extent, this has to do with the culture and family ethics in the different countries which we will analyse in the next section.

1.3   The Culture, Ethics and Responsibilities of Family Care

With respect to the cultural and ethical or moral perspective of informal care, some interesting issues appear to be evident from the PROCARE data. The concept of 'caring' seems to be emerging as a specific activity, which is concerned with establishing, increasing and/or developing services both for the provision of care and the support of carers, yet remains to varying degrees not fully formed. Within this shifting and translucent context, what is clear is that families are trying to maintain the care as long as possible.

The importance of family ethics as a driver to this situation is apparent and in our data appeared to be a prominent factor why informal family care remains the most preferred and accepted way of long-term care for frail older people. In all the participating countries of PROCARE and from all informants, it became clear how important the role of the family is and that organising care as well as providing care (at home or not) is almost impossible without some informal help from family or friends. More specifically, in Austria the status of informal carers remains precarious and specific, and systematic measures to acknowledge and support family care are still lacking because of the strong family ethics, moral values and their perceived caring responsibilities (Bahr/Leichsenring, 1996; Rosenmayr/Majce, 1998). On the one hand, the family carers interviewed seemed to take their responsibility for granted; on the other, for some there was a price to pay and it was evident they could not do everything and were relieved to have help through home help and care. The following quotes illustrate these views:

> "I have given up my job because it was not possible anymore to do caring and a job. I looked after both my mother and father in law at first. Then my father in law died. I have two sons and one little daughter. All in all it is an enormous burden. And the relatives don't help me. They only say: 'You can do that. You are at home.' It was clearly up me to help." (A, carer 4)

> "I take care of my mother and the care the home nurses give helps me a lot. If my mother needs more help I will have to give up my own little coffee shop. I am in my coffee shop from 6 pm until midnight. As I have to get up every two hours in the night to see to my mother, it's such a burden and sometimes I think I can't do it for much longer." (A, carer 7)

> "Mrs D. has lived in my neighbourhood since my childhood. I have given her my promise to take care of her if she needs it so now I take care of her – that's all." (note: Mrs D needs heavy care round the clock) (A1, carer 5)

Also in France, the family has a dominant caring position: services only intervene if the family support is weakened. Another example of strong family responsibilities is in Germany: family is the largest 'care service' (BMFSFJ, 2002: 193). The family's readiness to care is on the one hand due to feelings of solidarity and family attachment and on the other hand to feelings of obligation. Even when the older person is admitted to an in-patient facility, family members continue to feel responsible. Tensions often exist in these situations, mainly due to the nursing home staff not including the family in care decisions or recognising their expertise as carers. In addition, general communication between nursing personnel and family members is often very difficult. One carer (C6, D1) criticised that her requests, though agreed upon with the head of the home care service, were only taken into consideration by the home nurses after she had vigorously insisted on them.

Recently, with the introduction of care insurance, the caring work of the family has become more valued and accepted by society. It should be mentioned that the third sector is playing an important role in identifying and complying with social needs in Germany. For example the Federation of Advice Centres for Older People and Family Carers (BAGA) has published a manual for professionals on how to support carers, in particular those caring for older people suffering from dementia (Meyer, 2004: 27).

Though family members are taking on caring responsibilities with a great deal of physical, emotional and financial consequences, it has also been recognised that, in many PROCARE countries, economic migration has led to a situation where families are separated by long distances, so that the provision of hands-on care is impossible. The same is true in certain cases where the type of care needed by the older person cannot be provided by untrained family members. Still, moral judgements by neighbours, friends or even care professionals with respect to family members who are reluctant to care for any reason are the main cause for family members to feel guilty if asking for a place in a nursing home or sometimes even when applying for home care services. The following quotes provide examples of some of the issues discussed here.

Discussing her mother's admittance to residential care, one carer appeared suspicious of the care given which was connected to some separation anxieties:

> "It looked a bit fishy to me to bring my mother there ... For me it was terrible at that moment, you simply get rid of somebody." (D, carer)

A member of staff seemed to be empathetic towards families and their feelings of guilt:

> "Sometimes you build up a rapport with the families as well ... I really believe that we are here to help the client, but we're here to give their families a bit of moral support too, because I think they do need it. Sometimes there's a guilt trip with the families ... they ask why haven't we done this, why haven't we done that for their parents – but we look after them as well as we possibly can here ... I think a lot of it is guilt, especially if a parent goes into residential care, because they think they're letting their parent down." (UK, S26, generic carer)

Evidence of the tensions was clear in this quote:

> "... families are more concerned about what we're doing with clients here than the clients themselves because we let the clients takes risks and the families are very worried about them." (UK, S5, care manager)

Sometimes carers do not even accept the slightest help due to their feelings of guilt. A caring husband called for the home care service only when he found out that his wife cooperates better with external agencies: "I am of the opinion that for my wife it is sometimes easier to be treated by a specialized nurse or by any of her friends than by me, the permanent partner." Once the services were accepted, the husband could also comply with the fact that he needed some free time, too:

> "We have also discussed this with our two daughters and they have supported me by saying: 'Dad, you must have some free time for yourself.' (...) Despite all the love you cannot always hold her hand." (D2, carer 5)

In the Netherlands morals around informal care were evident in the criteria for the allocation of professional care. In particular partners, sons and daughters provided a substantial part of the care for the frail elderly living at home. Traditionally, professional care was considered additional to the care that is or can be provided by the primary network (family, relatives, friends). Criteria for assessment were formulated accordingly. Since the 1990s the norm has been questioned and some modifications have been implemented, for example informal carers should only adopt those tasks that can reasonably be asked of them, but this is rather vague. It offers no clear guidelines that could be used in an assessment. As a consequence, the regional assessment agencies follow different rules.

Moving to the Nordic countries (Finland and Denmark), it is not common for sons and daughters to be the primary carers of older relatives, instead care is based on a municipally agreed delivery level. The concept of high level family networks is under discussion. In Finland there has even been speculation that the service contribution, which by social legislation is at the moment the responsibility of society, has to be moved back to family members (Salonen/Haverinen, 2004: 194).

In spite of the unfavourable legislation towards family care, there is a general trend of informal intra-generation care: spouses are generally expected to help each other and are in reality the most important source of help and care. In Denmark there are some variations on the level of family care depending on the marital situation of the individual in need of care. For older people who live alone there are no legal obligations for sons and daughters or other relatives to provide social or personal care. Nevertheless, in both countries, the moral obligation is evident.

In contrast to these situations are the two Mediterranean countries of PROCARE: Italy and Greece. According to the Italian ethical position, the family networks guarantee a real and continuous process of care provision and the family dimension of care is based on the right to choose the preferred care arrangement. Due to its flexible structure, it is easy to involve individuals in the process of care provision, and it is at the core of society, where individual interests are protected. Very recent research confirms the importance of the family network as an important web both financially speaking and in terms of concrete help in daily life. In particular, this research points out how home care of both younger and older generations is taken care of by the generation of women who at the end of the 1990s were in their sixties: 'the grandmother generation'. In Greece the long-standing traditional cultural beliefs prevail and the family takes care of their older people, preferring for them not to be living in a hospital or a residential care institution. Traditionally the proportion of older people living in residential care institutions is very small – less than 1% of the total number of older people (Ministry of Health and Welfare, 1999). During the interviews with users living with their family we identified the importance of family ethics in Greece. The concept of caring as a specific activity with the relevant support of the State is both new and alien in Greece. The sons and daughters are taking care of their parents and now start to encourage them to participate in the KAPI centres, for instance when a husband died and there was the potential for social isolation (EL1, user 6, 69 years old; EL1, user 8, 81 years old). In another Greek case, however, the carer's mother suffered two strokes, was heavily dependent, but the daughter's responsibilities were clear:

> "My life is totally concentrated on my mother and I have less time to care for my child and husband ... I do everything for her." (EL2, carer 1/U3)

177

In summary, despite changes in the modern family such as decreased family size, increased geographical dispersion and extensive employment of women, families remain the most important source of help to older people in all PROCARE countries, a result which can be found in other European studies on family care like EUROFAMCARE (Lamura, 2004) and OASIS (Motel-Klingebiel et al., in print). However, the caregiving tasks provided by family members vary enormously from country to country and also within countries. While some families provide nearly all kinds of support and help which are necessary for an older person – *"I am the caregiver for everything"* (D2, carer 5) – others concentrate only on specific tasks like emotional support. Strong moral and ethical views around the perceived roles and responsibilities of the family towards care-giving were influencing the care. Whatever role families provided, it was always evident that caring means a heavy burden for the whole family who needed support and respite.

2   Supporting Carers: The Range of Help and Support

As was briefly presented above (see 1.2), the range of help and support for people with long-term care needs varies between the selected countries. This is even more so in relation to services that are to support family carers. Apart from formal home care, services that are specifically focusing on carers' needs are still quite exceptional. If available, they should cover information and advice, respite and financial support, and these aspects were found within the selected PROCARE model ways of working.

2.1   Information, Advice, Counselling

In Vienna (Austria), the Municipal Health and Social Centres offer advice, counselling and support for family carers. Normally, there are fixed times when family carers can come to the Centre. However, if there is something very urgent, the social worker tries to deal with it immediately and find quick solutions though facing serious time constraints. The Home Nursing Services of the Municipal Health and Social Centre offer advice for patients and their families on issues such as diabetes and dietary counselling. The principle is that the Home nurses also give advice to family members in the home when they need it. They also try to actively include family members in nursing care, but also help with the organisation of additional provisions and give them information they need. In the case of a discharge, the patients and their families receive a 'made-to-measure' maintenance schedule for care at home from the discharge manager. The discharge manager works in cooperation with patients, families, hospitals and social care services. The personal confidence between discharge manager, patients and their families helps to reduce the fear and the insecurity caused by the new personal situation of the older person and their families at home.

In France, information is given through local information centres (Centres Locaux d'Information et de Coordination Gérontologique/CLIC) like the ones in Châlus (F1) and Phalempin (F2). The main mission of CLICs is to welcome, inform, listen, advise and support the older person and his family. Following the introduction of the APA (Allocation Personnalisée d'Autonomie) advice is now increasingly given during the assessment procedure in the home of the applicant and his/her family, but also by Alzheimer family associations, GPs or social services. Also in France, discussion support groups are available in several places for family carers (Guisset et al., 2003; Guisset, 2004). The primary function of these self-help groups is to tackle participants' emotional problems and feelings of guilt. Many carers are, however, reluctant to attend a support group, feeling that their stories are intimate and not to be shared with strangers.

In the Netherlands where support to people who care for an older person is limited, some counselling is still possible. The counsellors visit the carers to discuss their concerns and give them advice.

In Denmark, if the tasks of taking care of a spouse or a family member are straining the family carer, they – and again this will typically be the spouse of the person in need of care – can receive psychological support from the care staff at the health centre or staff delivering personal care services. Relatives of people with dementia can also get advice and support from the local dementia coordinator who is employed by the municipality in association with some of the neighbouring municipalities like in Skævinge (DK1).

2.2   Respite Care

Temporary care provides some relief to family carers for a brief period (day-centre or day-hospital for medical care) or for a longer time (temporary residential care). For instance, in Denmark, the municipality of Skævinge offers day-care facilities for 'normal' older people. If they are living in their own homes, they can be admitted in cases of sudden illness when the older person would need to be under continuous observation. In Finland, the permanent family caregiver is able to have a small vacation every year, at which time the municipal home care service will take care of the older person.

Over the past three years France has developed the day-centres, mostly through the Alzheimer national programme though not all day-centres are for people with dementia. Furthermore, some French associations organise stays in a holiday village for older people and their families. Respite care has existed for many years. Originally, temporary residential care was available in winter for older people who had limited resources at home. The availability of this resource was however restricted as it was complicated to organise and manage financially. Nevertheless it was seen as a good support for carers and an opportunity for the older person to develop social contacts. This was demonstrated in a German report, which stated that day care or short-time care is useful to advance and maintain social contacts (BMFSFJ, 2002).

In the United Kingdom, if a carer is under strain, then 'respite care' may be provided. This means that the older person is admitted to a residential or nursing home for a short period, typically a week or two. This may occur if a carer is unwell, or wants to go on holiday. Where the carer is an older person, or has ongoing health problems, then the respite care may be put in on a regular basis – perhaps one week in six or similar. The downside to this is that the fees for residential or nursing care for the older person are means-tested. In other words, if the older person has savings (about 17,000 EUR or above) then they will pay for some of the residential home care (about 300 EUR per week) or nursing home care (about 500 EUR per week). If the carer is a spouse, then in effect they will be paying for the respite care and this can put some people off.

If a carer is looking after an older person with dementia then the situation is slightly better. There is a charity called 'Crossroads', which can provide sitters for the older person for an hour or two, on a regular (weekly) basis. This means the carer can go out without worrying about the older relative. However, provision is very limited (1-3 hours per week) and was being cut further by local councils for funding reasons.

For those with dementia or physical problems, most areas offer some day-centre provision. This can be arranged either to prevent social isolation, or to reduce carer strain – usually a bit of both. This service is often provided by charitable organisations (notably Age Concern in the UK) or sometimes by Social Services centres. People usually attend for 1-3 days per week. There may be a waiting list, and they may have to contribute to patient transport minibuses, or to meals.

2.3   Financial Help: Care Allowances

In some countries, there is financial help in the form of allowances or tax reductions. In Finland, regular monthly financial support for the permanent family caregiver is available, but it is limited and dependent upon the monthly household income. In France, the allowance APA (Allocation Personnalisée d'Autonomie), which provides money for care is very important even if insufficient to buy all the services and provisions needed. In Germany, the long-term care insurance is fulfilling the same function, that is to partly cover care-related costs.

181

In Italy, individual costs for long-term care are provided through an 'allowance for accompanying needs'. Also, in some regions special funds for families caring for Alzheimer patients have been created.

In the United Kingdom some financial support for carers is available if they care for a person receiving disability allowance.

In some countries, there are incentives to acquire tax refunds to cover part of the expenses for domestic collaboration (F, UK) or the possibility of reducing the amount taxed through having a dependent (F). Regarding other countries (DK, EL, NL), the family carer is less able to get financial help. For instance, in Denmark, apart from the fact that care services are provided for free by the municipality, there is no general source of financial support for family carers. However, if a family member is diagnosed with a terminal illness, a care allowance is available for family members who wish to care for a dying relative. In such instances primary health and social/personal care services are still available from the municipal elderly care services.

2.4   Admission to an Institution

It should be mentioned that, as a last resort, admission to a nursing home has to be considered as a support for the family. One carer in Austria illustrates the point at which this sort of help becomes necessary:

> "I could not have stood it anymore. You know, this getting up and having to go, like when I was working, this never ending 'MUST DO'. At some point, one says, actually I do not want this anymore. For me, this is a big relief. Why? I know that she is cared for. I know she gets her breakfast. I know that the nurses are there, that she has a neighbour, (...) and that it is warm."

This, of course, does not mean that the older person would be completely abandoned. Just the opposite, there are still a lot of opportunities to integrate family carers in activities and daily routines in residential care settings.

3   The Caring Environment: Experiences, Influences and Expectations

3.1   The Experiences of Caregiving

The extensive literature on the burden of caregiving experienced by family members is well documented. What is clear is that the extent and nature of the burden depends on many variables (Halsig, 1998; Pearlin et al., 2001). Alongside the level of care needed by the older person, caregivers in all PROCARE countries found caregiving especially stressful. A summary of salient issues is given below, showing that caregivers felt particularly stressed when they had to:

- sacrifice privacy and free time to care so that they do not have any time for leisure activities, relaxation and / or social contacts,
- care for an older person who suffers from dementia,
- combine care for older people and care for other family members (e.g. when child care responsibilities are present at the same time),
- combine employment and elder care,
- provide caregiving without support from other family members and / or professional care services,
- practice long-distance caregiving and / or
- care for older family members who refuse external help and support.

In other studies, the effects of burdensome caregiving on the physical and mental health status were often problematic, with caregivers reporting heart trouble, sleeplessness, depression, headaches and feelings of exhaustion particularly as the care recipient became more impaired (for an overview see Diözesan-Caritasverband für das Erzbistum Köln e.V., 2003). In addition, there are feelings of guilt towards the frail older person and towards other family members, as seen in previous quotes. It is small wonder that according to a German representative study, 41% of the caregivers felt very strongly burdened and 42% strongly burdened (Schneekloth/Leven, 2003).

On the other hand, the PROCARE study showed that older people in need of care also felt stressed about the situation. This is explained not only by their disability and illness but also by their loss of autonomy and independence. In addition, previous surveys from Denmark (Colmorten et al., 2003) and many interviews with care receivers, for example in Finland, showed clearly that care receivers usually *do not* want to become a burden to their family, they want the families to lead their own lives. Their resistance against family care is especially strong when it comes to physical care.

Despite all the burden caregiving can be accompanied with, it has to be acknowledged that family caregiving can in contrast be a positive time in the lives of the caring family member (Buijssen, 1996; Schulz, 2001). For example, some caregivers experienced caregiving as rewarding because they

- are able to repay for help and support they once got from the care receiver (reciprocity of help),
- are able to do something useful and help to improve or stabilize the health status of the older person,
- are rewarded by a positive feedback from the care receiver and the social environment,
- feel emotionally near to the care receiver,
- have financial advantages.

183

3.2 Influences on Using or Not Using Professional Care Services

Results from most PROCARE countries illustrated that the missing mediation between informal care and professional help and the insufficient transparency of the services as a whole (such as of the offer of services) and within the services (such as flow of information between the employees) are a continuing major problem. Further, many caregivers and care receivers in all PROCARE countries complained about *insufficient* integration in the caregiving process. Feelings like not being taken seriously or being powerless can result in a difficult relationship with professional carers, as previously mentioned.

Especially against the background of increasing impairment the data collected in our study showed, however, that an *interdependency* of formal and informal care can be noted. In these cases home and professional nursing care are *complementary*, that is family caregivers and professional carers share the caregiving tasks although the proportion of work for each 'party' can differ. As a rule professional carers are mainly responsible for physical and medical care – the family caregivers does 'the rest'. One example from the Netherlands illustrates this. The user is a 78-year old woman with severe health problems. She lives alone. Every day staff members of Zijloever dress and undress her, prepare her breakfast and supper, and check her medication. One of her daughters does the shopping, laundry and cooking for her mother. Also, she accompanies her if she has to visit the doctor or hospital (NL1). The following quotes give other examples of the division of care:

> "I get four visits a day from the health centre. We decided to accept the offer for personal care because I didn't want my wife to have to help me going to the bathroom and things like that. Because I don't want to be a burden to her ..." (DK, user)

> "A municipal home-care assistant comes in the morning and in the evening. My daughter comes each weekday at midday to cook and help with eating. She lives at a great distance, and the question is how long she will manage ..." (FIN, user)

> "I go shopping and do all the organizational, administrative and financial matters for my mother. That is what I do, or when a letter has to be written, I do it at home on the computer." (A, carer)

While these divisions may seem practical, they may also be fragile and easily disrupted, as seen in the second of these quotes. Also, as explained earlier, there are limits to this 'teamwork' when cultural orientations in terms of professional care prevent an appropriate use of available services. In many cases, the use of professional services fails due to reservations felt by people in need of nursing care or their families with regard to the provision of help and care by strangers. This fact is mentioned here once more because it is one of the prominent results of the PROCARE study:

> "I know that it is not good for him." (D, caregiving daughter about not using respite care for her father suffering from dementia)

> "I think that would be the end of him. He'd go downhill. He would think we have all given up on him." (UK, caregiving wife about not using full time residential care)

In Greece, the moral position of the family and their strong cultural responsibilities as outlined in the previous section are indeed a powerful driver that influences the notion of formal and informal interdependency. What is perhaps more influential in this setting, however, is the extent to which services themselves have evolved, and the amount they have to offer, which may make the choices more limited. In Greece there is no direct support from the State or the local authorities to the family carers. The cost of care is undertaken by the older person him/herself, either from savings or from the pension, or by the family. Only in recent years, some pilot programmes supporting the carers have been implemented. In the framework of the Programme *Ageing Well Europe*, the Gerontological and Geriatric Institute implemented a programme developing preventive health services and psychosocial support for older people and their families in 1996. Similar programmes are implemented in some regions on a pilot basis (Emke-Poulopoulou, 1999; Sissouras et al., 2004). Although there is no universal policy on services for older people, attempts have been made to fill this gap and give families some relief from their responsibilities. Some initiatives have been made from the Greek government (Ministries of Social Affairs, Interior) to introduce some corrective measures. In 1998, the implementation of a 5-year pilot programme began, 'Home care for older people', which brings together the Ministry of Health and Welfare, the Ministry of the Interior and the Municipalities in a 'tripartite model' responsible for organizing and providing the services (EL2).

A further important issue connected to factors influencing the care environment concerns decision-making and choices. The question was raised as to who made the care decisions. Some themes from the data emerged about the extent to which person-centred care was in operation, in the context of family and carer decision-making.

In some countries, it appeared that the family was primarily responsible for making care decisions. Despite the fact that 'client-centred care' and client choice appeared to be central to their service provision, users spoken to about admission to these models did not feel they had a choice, having a view that their families tended to make the choice on their behalf. The following quotes from users from the UK provide an illustration of this. For example, a 89-year old man felt:

> "My son talked me into going. He said 'you won't be able to manage on your own'." (UK2, user)

> "My daughter arranges everything...she organised everything ... she arranged
> for me to come here." (UK1, user)

Paradoxically, the view of staff was quite different – they felt the clients made choices, and that they managed care on behalf of the clients with these choices in mind. A quote from a member of staff in the Netherlands sum up the general view of other PROCARE countries:

> "The needs and when possible specific wishes of the clients are the starting
> point in the planning and providing the required services. Flexibility and speed
> in adapting to the physical and psychological changes of the client are seen as
> an essential pre-condition to achieve this goal." (NL2, key worker)

It must be recognised that older people are often passive recipients of care and are content to let the family take care of the decisions (Ham/Alberti, 2002), which may fly in the face of the 'client-centred' movement and appear disempowering (Bytheway, 1995), but may in fact be acceptable to older people. On the whole, the challenges surrounding respecting and acting on the older persons' choices and decisions, and what ultimately are the decisions made in the best interests of the older person remains a difficult issue. For instance, in the United Kingdom, a user's family and doctors strongly recommended admission to a residential rehabilitation centre. She initially didn't want to go, but after staying at the centre, she felt they were right to insist that she had some rehabilitation care, and with hindsight agreed that she would not have coped at home. In addition, a simple reason that influences use or non-use of the services is information, an issue that features as a general deficit in the models of integrated care researched in this study (see next section). A key worker from the UK illustrates this:

> "... people say, 'oh I've been like this a long time, I wish you'd come to me
> earlier' – because of that, I think we could assume that there are a number of
> older people out there that are deteriorating and don't necessarily have services
> involved." (UK, key worker)

So, whilst the PROCARE data provide the variations of care arrangements and factors influencing them, the wider literature provides another perspective. It appears that despite the effects of the burden of care, a significant number of caregivers providing care for older people are not or hardly supported by professional care services, such as daily in-home services, day-care centres or institutions for short-term care. However, aside from the moral position of the family and national policies on family care – certainly one of the most important factors – the following factors can also influence the use of professional assistance (see also Lamura, 2004):

- level of information on services available,
- quantity and quality of services available in the community,
- level of impairment of care receiver,
- general availability of family social support,
- employment of caregiver,
- gender of caregiver,
- family relationship between caregiver and care receiver,
- financial reasons.

Further, it should not be overlooked that factors such as higher incomes, higher educational level and individual preferences geared toward fulfilling oneself and achieving emancipation, tend to strengthen the inclination not to become a carer of an older relative. The willingness to use professional services is therefore much greater in the 'bourgeois milieus' than in the 'lower-class-milieus' (Blinkert/Klie, 2000) – a fact that should be valid for nearly all PROCARE countries. However, where there is an economic incentive, the choice between informal and professional nursing care can be influential. For example in Germany in some cases, the long-term care allowance plays an important role as an income component in lower social classes, which is a major reason for them to choose the familial nursing care option.

3.3 Family Members' Expectations of Services and Integrated Care

In general, family caregivers in all PROCARE countries had some views about what they should expect from the service. From their point of view, professional carers should ease the emotional and physical burden of care faced by family members by providing care of high quality. Help was expected with regard to the physical and medical care but also with regard to care-related information and advice. Further to this, feelings of gratitude were also expressed alongside expectations, with caregivers seeming to be thankful for every small bit of support and help they could get, and for friendly and respectful treatment of themselves and the users by the professionals.

When it came to integrated care, family caregivers or users included in the PROCARE study *hardly ever* formulated expectations of the service in specific terms. Sometimes, what they expected from a service was articulated as a feature not being evident, or a complaint. For example, common complaints in our interviews (for example, in Greece or in Germany) referred to a lack of clarity and information as well as to an insufficient coordination between services. Issues relating to dissatisfaction are described in more detail later in this section. However, the Italian interviews gave a different picture. The caregivers here stressed that the professionals were coordinated. In addition, the advantage of integrated care was seen as different professionals having specific competencies and different perspectives.

One of the *main reasons* for this 'speechlessness' is that the term and the concept of 'integrated care' is not or hardly known by family caregivers; the integration of services is relatively new in most PROCARE countries. This is mentioned in Chapter 1. Even if family caregivers or older people use integrated services they are simply *not aware* of it. In addition, an information deficit can also be observed with regard to the different provisions of integrated care (such as discharge management).

If specific expectations towards integrated care exist they do not seem to be very high. According to the findings from Austria – which were more or less concurrent for the other PROCARE countries – many family caregivers see themselves as the main person responsible for care. Furthermore, most of the time caregivers *do not* want to give up caregiving completely and there is relatively little empirical support for the notion that professional services cause family members to provide less support for their relatives (Denton, 1997; Penning, 2002).

What was, however, apparent from the data were issues arising when expectations were not realised. The PROCARE data revealed instances of dissatisfaction with services that was variable. According to the results of the interviews in Germany for instance, the following aspects were highlighted by caring family members:

- insufficient safeguarding of intimacy; insufficient empathy of the nursing personnel,
- no time for personal communication and heart-to-heart talks with family members especially with nursing personnel,
- insufficient consideration of the needs of the caring family members,
- regarding out-patient care: lack of punctuality, organizational problems,
- insufficient time given for families to react, such as getting medication for discharge,
- insufficient integration of caring family members , caring family members are not taken seriously, missing possibilities of influencing care resulting in feeling disempowered,

- care is not always aligned to the need / the requirements of the user,
- insufficient transparency of the services as a whole and within the services, such as flow of information between the employees,
- long-term and difficult discussions regarding financial matters.

In Greece, it appeared that the most important factors that generated feelings of dissatisfaction were the lack of information and the bureaucracy the older person has to go through to get access to services. It was seen as a strongly discouraging element. Presenting certificates and going to bureaucratic appointments was onerous and took many hours of family holiday time or leave. In addition, there seemed to be a degree of bureaucratic inefficiency, with people having to cope with large queues and waiting lists.

In the Netherlands, support to family carers is limited. In 2001 a large-scale survey among informal carers (N=1,211) was conducted. The results were published by the Social and Cultural Planning Bureau (Timmermans, 2003). The investigation focused not only on informal care for older people, but also for younger people with a disability or health problem. However, the majority (65%) of the respondents cared for an older person (65 years of over). Secondly, the informal carers were not only family members of the recipient (partner, child, parent, sister, brother or other relative). Some of them were friends or acquaintances (12%) or neighbours (6%). About a quarter (26%) of the respondents felt (over)burdened by the care tasks. Many of them experienced time problems, with limited time for recreation or for running their own household.

Most respondents received support. About 40% made use of facilities which provide information, advice or emotional support, 17% used care attendance services, and in 10% of the cases the care recipient visits a day-care centre. Among the respondents who did not use support services about 70% stated that they had no need for it. The most common need for (more) support concerned information provision.

4   Conclusion

Despite significant changes in patterns of family formation and family structure families still are the largest 'care service' and predominantly responsible for meeting the needs of older people or disabled relatives. The importance of family ethics is crucial and it could be argued that this could be a main factor why informal family care remains the most expected and accepted

189

way of long-term care for older people in Europe, even in countries with a traditionally developed system of social and health services.

Beyond the moral economy of care, it is certainly the extent to which support services are available which influences their use and the knowledge about their usefulness. With respect to the issues connected with integrated care, it is most important to notice that, at least in the selected model ways of working, long-term care is not seen any more as totally a 'family affair' but as an interplay of formal and informal care. Of course, family carers are not yet calling for integrated care. They want information and the right service at the right moment in time, with access mechanisms that are transparent and user-friendly.

Even if most of the PROCARE model ways of working focus on meeting the needs of their older clients (e.g. tailor-made services, client-centred care) we still have to emphasise that too often professionals abstain from integrating family carers in 'their' care processes for a number of reasons (prejudices, complications, misunderstandings, etc.). This needs further research and development. While not all models explicitly involve relatives, some have started to deliberately focus on the integration of family carers in their practice, in particular those working with clients suffering from dementia. Given the demographic and epidemiological expectations services will need to rely more and more on relatives in the future, as one key worker from Austria highlighted:

> "One can deal less with the patient ... we are more and more dependent on cooperating with the family to know how the situation was before." (A, key worker)

Against the background of these findings we indicate characteristics within the models which facilitate cooperation between informal and formal caregivers as 'best practice'. From the families' and the older persons' point of view, integrated care should help provide care at home for as long as possible. Therefore, in general, the following conditions should be considered by the different stakeholders involved.

National policy should ...
*   integrate family care into family policy,
*   acknowledge the tasks and efforts of family carers (such as by financial help),
*   support the development of high-quality services (such as by consumer protection, financial incentives),

- support the integration of services on different levels (especially on the regional level),
- inform carers about the advantages of integrated care and promote their use (through the help of family doctors).

Services should ...
- include family carers in the caregiving process (such as in assessment of needs, care planning),
- respect the rights and choices of care receivers and carers,
- provide better information about policy and address carers directly,
- improve coordination and communication,
- provide support services for carers and encourage carers to use them (such as counselling and respite care).

Non-governmental organisations (NGOs) which represent family care should support family carers regarding their rights, offer practical help and assist with helping family carers to lobby. Furthermore, there should be more robust measures in place between all European countries to exchange information and best practice about family care

The Outcomes and Benefits of Integrated Care – In Search of the Service Users' and Carers' Point of View

Riitta Haverinen, Nasrin Tabibian

1   Introduction

The views on the quality, benefits and outcomes of care services vary from one stakeholder to another. The discourses on human service policies and reforms have addressed the issue of *quality* (Donabedian, 1980; Ovretveit, 1998; Qureshi et al., 1998; El Fakiri, 2000; Nocon, 1997) and the *outcomes* of services (Evers et al., 1997; Ovretveit, 1998). Different approaches to outcome measurement have been presented to the public and private sectors especially in the context of growing efficiency and financial constraints. Today, the discourse on outcome measurement is entering the service arena and gradually reshaping the clinical and administrative practices in the social and health care sectors. While some researchers have addressed more managerial aspects of outcomes and benefits, others have concentrated their work on accountability issues. It is only recently that measuring and assessing the outcomes of services have turned up on the care policies agenda for older people as a result of demographic changes, growing costs in the care sector and the gap between supply and demand. The human and financial aspects remain closely intertwined in this discourse.

The main interest of PROCARE was in analysing the procedures in the allocation and delivery of services and how different stakeholders perceive the benefits of integrated care. Though outcome measurement, as such, was not the main focus of the empirical research, benefits for the user were at the heart of our interest. In this chapter we try to focus on the views of the users and their family carers from an outcome and benefits perspective. The underlying idea is that the users and their informal carers are indispensable for improving the quality of care and service delivery, in particular since the position of the care user has gone through a transition in the last few years – the user has evolved from a 'patient' to a 'service user', a 'consumer' and even sometimes to a 'commissioner'. This indicates the rising importance of care users' and their carers' opinions in the quality discourse, in particular with respect to models that have been developed and are claiming to deliver integrated, person-centred care.

2   Research Questions and Empirical Data

The main questions in this chapter are:
* How do frail older people perceive integrated care?
* What seem to be the most important characteristics of quality of care for the users?
* What is the place of empowerment and social integration in our models of care?

The data gathering for PROCARE was not originally carried out from the perspective of the outcomes and benefits of home-based integrated care, but this perspective became relevant during the project. As home-based services are the policy aim in the care of older people in a European context (see Leichsenring/Alaszewski, 2004), we were also interested in knowing whether interaction with family, friends and neighbours was actively encouraged by the model projects.

For reasons explained in the methods chapter, there were insufficient data with direct quotes from users to provide a robust analysis purely from the user perspective. We overcame this by combining empirical and theoretical approaches. Firstly, the national researchers, who know the national and local contexts of the model projects, provided us with valuable analytical data about the user experience gleaned from local professional and organisational sources. An additional dimension was to analyse all data sources within a social constructivist theoretical framework, to add depth to the emerging explanations.

By choosing a social constructivist approach for analysing our data (Berger/Luckmann, 1996) we were interested in discovering the significances and meanings given by the carers and users despite the limitations of the empirical evidence. The significance of everyday language and perceptions made by the service users and their experiences of care bring the life world perspective into the focus of our analysis. The answers and quotes provided by the respondents are used as illustrations of the socially constructed reality for our conceptual framework. Integrated services are, in the first place, socially constructed realities in the 'systems world' (Habermas, 1981) which is represented by organisational structures, legal and financial frameworks, quality management and service delivery procedures designed by the professionals in an organisational perspective. When evaluating the outcomes of projects, researchers often concentrate on these aspects, so that policy improvements remain based on issues from the systems world. What we attempted was to reconstruct a life world perspective as a counterpart of the systems world; hence we combined the 'real' world with the 'systems' world, through the blending of user and organisational viewpoints.

195

3   User Perceptions of Integrated Care

Classical literature on quality issues (Donabedian, 1980; Ovretveit, 1998) distinguishes between structural, process and outcome quality and thus contributed mainly to the organisational and professional discourses on quality development. In these discourses, outcomes are conceived as the end results of a defined process that, if it comes to care services for older people, should be – as Donabedian puts it – affordable and effective interventions beneficial to the defined target group (Alaszewski et al., 2003). Also Ovretveit (1998) defines *service quality* as meeting the needs of those who are most in need and at the lowest cost, within regulations.

Still, a number of different perspectives on outcome quality in the area of care services can be identified. Nocon et al. (1997: 5) observe that the users' and carers' organisations stress the importance of choosing and monitoring outcomes because they advocate a shift in "the focus of attention to users' and carers' needs and away from organisational issues". Qureshi et al. (1998) point out, however, that it is easier to identify outcomes in cases that fit into a conventional treatment or intervention model. In the first report on recommendations of the Commonwealth Fund's International Working Group on Quality Indicators (2004), the authors present an overview of the quality criteria for the performance of the health care system. These criteria, however, mostly relate to the structure and organisation of the care and pay only partial attention to the view of the users themselves.

Many researchers are applying the concept of user satisfaction as an indicator for a successful project. El Fakiri et al. (2000) address the migrant specific quality criteria. Rossi (1997) points out that service user satisfaction measures are useful but usually not worth being regarded as evidence of success or failure. Also Ware (1997: 46) points out how difficult and unreliable it is to measure user satisfaction since the desired results of satisfaction surveys can be easily achieved by manipulating the measures used. Ovretveit (1998) has a more positive view on user satisfaction and considers the measuring of these aspects as essential and significant for the success of the care process. This can occur if measuring satisfaction includes the following features:

- looking at the types of services which people want, expect and need,
- features of services that are important to users,
- users' actual experiences of what happens to them,
- users' knowledge or ignorance of the services provided to them,
- how to access the service,
- the benefits users gain from the service,
- users' good and bad experiences of the service,
- problems caused by the way the service was delivered.

We adopted Ovretveit's approach to examine the opinions of people who used the services provided by the different model ways of working. Our point of departure is, however, that the users are not concerned about quality concepts as suggested by professionals but they show their (dis)satisfaction with the care they have received on several levels that we have classified under the headings *integration, empowerment* and *social inclusion* which we will elaborate on.

3.1 Integration

Early on during the PROCARE project it became apparent that the concept of integrated care had different meanings in different settings. Integration is widely accepted as a policy aim for the care of older people in Europe. The hypothesis behind the ideology of integrated care is that integrated service delivery models produce maximum benefits to the service user. Van Raak et al. (2003: 11) see integrated care as referring to a coherent and coordinated set of services that are planned, managed and delivered to individual service users across a range of organisations and by a range of cooperating professionals and informal carers. Thus, integrated care delivery is mainly needed by older people with complex care needs, using a wide range of services – varying from nursing, therapy, medical care and treatment, to domiciliary care and social services – over a longer period of time, usually also from different providers. In this context, three elements are common in the objectives of all the analysed model ways of working and were key issues identified through workers' definitions in Chapter 1:

- older people have the right to live independently at home as long as possible;
- care should be user-centred; and
- social and medical care should be integrated with aspects of well-being.

Despite this, our question is whether these elements are also important from a user's perspective. First of all, it seems that older people find it difficult to evaluate the process of integrated care (FIN 1, 2) because the concept is too abstract for them and not being used in the context of everyday life. Examples from the data, however, point out the value of the model projects to the older people:

> "I am 94 and have a lot of health problems, I do not have anyone to look after me and I am in your hands, in the hands of the programme. I felt I was saved. My participation in the programme has changed my life because I was obliged to my neighbours since I was not capable of performing any daily living activities alone because of my health problems. I fear the programme being stopped and I will be lost," (EL2, user)

Furthermore, it can be seen from the data that the notion of integrated care relies heavily on the user's own resources which can vary from time to time. According to the carers, attention to the integration of social aspects of care – in the form of guidance and support – plays an important role in making their task less burdensome and offering an opportunity to improve their social life. According to the users and carers, integration also means the transition from one type of care to another so that the older person continually profits from one or the other form of care:

> "A nice lady came to help. I do not know from which organisation she was".
> (FIN1, user)

> "If there is something I would like to have done differently, I just tell them.
> And they say: We'll figure out something – and they do." (DK 2, user)

The great majority of services users in the selected model ways of working seemed to be satisfied with the care they received. However the impression was that they were grateful to have received any care and did not want to complain. In addition to this, our data seemed to infer that users did not seem concerned about the organisation providing care and often did not know to which organisation the professional carers belonged, as the quotes illustrate. One of our main assumptions was that the service users have a different way of looking at the results of care and cure services than professionals. We did not find evidence for this. It might be that users were very satisfied while – according to professionals – the care they received was not the ideal form for them. This is partly due to the fact that most older people play the role of passive recipient of care and seldom know about alternatives and sometimes even are afraid of services being reduced if they complain. This does not, however, mean that they do not have an opinion on the benefits, products and sometimes even on the process of integrated care. It was crucial to the service users, for example, how everyday care was given and who provided care and information on the type of services and products. The continuity of care by the same professionals and teams was of utmost importance to the care receivers:

> "It is very important to me that it is someone from the same group of carers that shows up." (DK2, user)

> "My domestic carers are the same as I had before I was taken to hospital. [...] It is very important to me that it's the same person who comes. Because the things they help me with are quite personal, so I don't like it when a substitute comes around. Fortunately, that doesn't happen very often." (I1, user)

The change of helpers was stressful for the service user:

> "New helpers continued to show up and that was quite stressful because I had to go with them all the time and tell them what to do and how to do it. In the end I decided to call off the domestic care and hired a lady to clean the house instead." (DK1, user)

Further elements came to light in the data. For the users, evidence of integration was reflected in the way the individual care plan was set up in collaboration with the professionals, the service user and/or the carer. The fact that the service user received the right amount of care, at the right time, seemed to indicate that person-centred care was at the heart of care organisation. The users and carers also appreciated being involved in the decision-making process. The role of information was also essential in the way the users perceived the outcomes of care: older people needed to be informed about the nature and decisions made by care organisations and workers. Person-centred care therefore also meant that service users felt their views were taken into the consideration:

> "Every time I have a problem I discuss it with the professionals and they listen to me carefully and encourage me and they advice me how to deal with it dynamically and not to be upset ... I can sort out personal problems and find psychological support." (EL1, user)

> "Comforting! Yes it is, and I think that is a good thing." (DK1, user)

From these quotes it can be inferred that in some cases the coordination of care services with rehabilitation units and the hospital worked satisfactory. Not all the care receivers were, however, so satisfied. There was evidence of a lack of seamless care when services did not seem to function according to plan, and some disorganisation was also apparent:

> "I have neither home help nor meals on wheels." (A2, user)

> "It was little annoying to be dragged from one system to another and have to get used to a new place ... And I was ill! (D1, user)

In addition to this, Chapter 4 has highlighted the difficulties in involving users in the needs assessment process in a meaningful way. However, active use of communication channels helped:

> "If I want something, I simply call." (Nl1, user)

From an organizational perspective, meeting and respecting the needs and wishes of the user and carer contributes to improving the sense of well-being. In some projects (NL) organisational care policies promoted autonomy as an important principle when caring for older people, encouraging users also to be viewed as commissioners. This was manifest as the user/carer themselves are at the forefront of choosing products and services.

When looking more closely at outcomes, there will inevitably be a difference between the user, carer and organisational perspective. Despite a person-centred approach, the data demonstrated that service outcomes reflect a number of activities of everyday life and functioning ability. Outcomes for maintenance or prevention consisted of issues like meeting the basic physical needs, securing personal safety, being able to live in a clean and tidy environment, staying alert and active, having access to social contact and company, and being in control of one's life (see Chapter 1 for how outcomes were defined by workers). There was a consensus that services are responsible for ensuring that people who are not able to carry out their own self-care are personally clean and comfortable, and have enough to eat. Although this reflects a life-world perspective, with elements of quality being practical and rooted in daily life, it is difficult to tease out what the outcomes could be from a user perspective, and whether autonomy and self-sufficiency are imposed rather than desired.

Table 1:   **Elements of Integrated Care from Two Perspectives**

Elements of integrated care from the life world	Elements of integrated care from the systems world
- Have a say in the needs assessment and views taken into consideration - Have a say in how services are delivered - Smooth running of everyday care services - Personal attention and home visits - Social needs addressed - Alternative services offered - Continuity of workers - Financial aspects taken seriously	- Access procedures - Information and transparency of service access - Qualified staff and key contact person - User choice on care alternatives - Explicit and seamless procedure and process of care - Attention to staff permanence - Feedback procedures on place - Attention to social and financial aspects of care - Quality systems at place and assessed
Risks of integration	**Risk reducing**
- The needs of the user not heard and lack of flexibility to act accordingly - Regulated standard service for individual needs - Changing staff and hasty visiting times because of the personnel deficit - Social needs uncovered - Dependence (on services, on financial situation) - Isolation and loneliness at home	- Needs assessment procedures and continuous assessment - Individual care plan and coordinating key person - A named own worker, team responsibility and service coordination - Alternative service options available - Feedback and complaint procedures - The reasonable contribution of informal carers

The elements of integrated care based on our data are summarised in Table 1. For clients receiving integrated home-based services, the core elements of the life world are associated with process factors and the way the services are provided, and also with economic considerations. Drawing on the empirical data, the table sums up the core elements of the clients' life world as points of departure for the provision of services. The table also shows the systems world or organisational counterparts of these elements, which should be taken into account when implementing the client-centred service integration in the life world. In addition, based on the data, the table lists risks involved in the implementation of integration and corresponding ways of reducing these risks.

In order to arrange services so that the demands from a life-world perspective are met, the system world needs to incorporate these demands in policies and procedures. Unfavourable conditions seem to have a lot to do with limited collaboration between health professionals and poor continuity of care. For instance, as has been previously highlighted, service users complained about the continuous change of staff members. In order to guarantee continuity, the concentration of all facilities at the same place (one point of access) might prove beneficial.

The empirical findings of this study relate to previous research findings (Harding/Beresford, 1996; Patmore, 2001; Evers et al., 1997; Qureshi et al., 1998). The outcomes of integrated care must be about meeting the needs of an older person in a continuous way, the admission to residential care is to be avoided, service personnel should seek to meet the individual quality expectations taking into account different values, circumstances and aspirations of older people.   .

From the life-world perspective, user satisfaction relates strongly to the way in which services are delivered. These process outcomes are important because of their impact on the feelings and satisfaction of people receiving services. Being able to live in a clean and tidy environment is of considerable importance to service users since they live 24 hours a day in their home. This often runs counter to the objectives of the systems world which is not able to meet all expectations. It thus becomes the task of professionals involved in integrated care organisations to communicate potentials and possibilities and to negotiate them with users who may then decide on priorities.

ZonMw (2002) points out that, in order to make the right choices in care, the users and their family carers need sufficient and accessible information. The care world and available information on existing organisations, products and services are, however, mostly directed towards the 'white' and better-educated care user and his/her needs. Thus information and communication become a vital aspect in improving outcomes of integrated care models by involving users in making the right choices, if possible by also involving the surrounding neighbourhood or voluntary services into the care system of the single user as takes place in the Greek KAPI model.

3.2   Empowerment and the User Perspective in Integrated Care

Nies and Berman (2004) have developed the concept of integrated care by adding the aspect of *empowerment* to it. They see integrated care as a well-planned and well-organised set of services and care processes, targeted at the multidimensional needs or problems of an individual service user, or a category of people with similar needs or problems. People expect services to provide the right care, at the right time in the right place. *Empowerment* has become a relevant concept (Nies et al., 2004; Beresford, 2000; Beresford et al., 1997) in referring to the changed status and position of the service users. The concept is also used in referring to the integrity and self-respect of service users and a holistic and solution-oriented working model (Adams, 1996).

Current debates about empowering service users tend to focus on developing instruments that seem better suited for service users who have more social, intellectual and physical resources to fit the role of the critical consumer. This development ignores the fact that most of the service users are frail, very old people who are not always aware of existing opportunities. However, the concept of empowerment consists of a multitude of elements both as a process and an outcome. For the service user, this includes

- sustaining autonomy (example: being able to live independently and safely in one's home as long as possible);
- sustaining functionality (example: being able to care for oneself with some help from outside);
- maintaining or regaining self-respect (example: service user being pleased/proud to be able to live independently or care for oneself); and
- receiving sufficient and accessible information on the care process and products and involvement in the decision-making process;
- having the economical options to regulate the service use.

While these are worthy values, we remain unsure whether empowerment is a concept understood, accepted and internalised by older users, or one that is socially constructed by professionals and policy-makers. It is also a very difficult concept to operationalise especially when organisational barriers are in the way. For example, Chapter 2 made clear that users did not know how to access services which flies in the face of an empowering, autonomous ethos. However, when using the life-world perspective, elements of the data have been used in an attempt to illustrate how empowerment can be viewed from the user perspective, and this section sheds some light on this.

From our data, it seemed that, in the words of the users themselves, empowerment meant being informed and getting involved in decisions about the care process. On the other hand receiving help is a paradoxical issue in the life of older people:

> "On the one hand my mother was relieved that the home help came. On the other hand she protested. She said the home-helpers are always in a hurry. I wanted to see what the home helpers do ... She had 15 years of experience and I like her. The main thing is that my mother is doing well. I cannot wash her, like the home helpers can." (A2, carer)

From a professional perspective, client empowerment is clearer and could be illustrated through the following quote:

> "One saw that the patient started to cheer up the closer we got to her apartment (...) The first thing she wanted to do was look into her mail box. She was very active, opened her mail box and we let her unlock the door by herself. It took a while, but she could do everything. That was the proof for us that it would work at home. She was very active and had a positive attitude." (A2, discharge manager)

The interplay between dependency and independency is an important factor in relation to empowerment. On the one hand independency should be promoted, on the other hand frail older people are very dependent on the services and care workers for the tasks they cannot perform themselves. In addition as we have seen in Chapter 5, dependency on family members can create its own unwanted sense of disempowerment and reduction in independence and autonomy.

The experience of empowerment was further understood as becoming, as far as possible, physically and socially functional again after treatment. Empowerment in integrated care was also connected with boosting the moral and giving the service users a sense of confidence. Self-confidence and self-sufficiency were two aspects of empowerment boosted by additional services brought to the home of older people, like meals on wheels. Giving moral support and establishing personal contacts with the care users was another way to improve the position of the user:

> "The nursing service would inform me about further decisions, but I have the final say in coordination with the family". (D2, user)

> "When you're ill and away from your own home it's easy to loose your spirit. But when that happened someone from the staff were always able to crack a joke or talk to me and pull me up again." (EL1, user)

203

The impact on a user of when dependency on a service ends was seen in this next quote. The importance of continuing home support is clear in this instance:

> "As I was leaving there, it suddenly dawned on me that I would be on my own. It gradually dawned on me, and on the day they brought me back and left me here on my own, I just went to pieces." (user 3)

> " ... there was an older relative with a desperate family having a case of Alzheimer with a thighbone fracture. The relatives wanted to have the older person admitted to a rehabilitation centre because they didn't feel able to help him. The physiotherapist showed them the right steps to make him move and now the older person is walking. The home intervention avoided the hospital admission." (I1, a staff member)

The financial aspects played a role in social care. What were seen from an organizational perspective as empowering practices of vouchers or care allowance seemed to have a negative side, as it was not seen as enough to cover costs:

> "The home help does not come as often anymore. I have decreased that. Because they made me pay 7,47 Euro an hour and that is 70 Euro a week, I only get 268 Euro attendance allowance." (A2, user)

This is a joint experience shared by the staff members as well:

> "For us it is difficult to have a good conversation or a chat with our service users and/or carers because we have the 'five minutes service charge' regulation. Sometimes it is necessary to talk a little bit longer with the service users but then they ask: Do I have to pay for that extra?" (A2, focus group participant)

From the life-world perspective, the principle of empowerment places the emphasis on clients' self-confidence and self-esteem, and their own will and autonomy. Particularly the role of social functioning becomes pronounced. In the systems world, it is not enough to have empowerment as an underlying principle, but the principle should be applied in practical contexts in such a way that the service user's subjectivity can be maintained. In the care process, everyday activities should be consistent with respect for autonomy and human dignity. Equally important is to show respect for the client's own choices and to promote activities that help maintain social functioning as a precondition of independent action. Capabilities are closely linked with resources. The list of risks in Table 2 makes it clear that it is not enough to have empowerment as a policy aim, but the systems world needs to look for ways in which communication, interaction and feedback mechanisms can be used to support client empowerment. To maintain empowerment among clients is also a matter of staff skills and training. A core element of empowerment is flexibility and sensitivity to people's everyday needs and also possible changes in them. What all these elements in our data suggest is that greater inclusion of the more sensitive experiences of users should be integrated in the systems world in order to really serve the different needs of service users. In the following table we have collected the elements of empowerment based on our empirical data.

Table 2: The Elements of Empowerment from Two Perspectives

The elements of empowerment from the life-world perspective	The elements of empowerment from the systems-world perspective
- Keeping self-respect and self-confidence - Sustaining autonomy despite the dependency and frailty - Sustaining social functionality - Attention to mood and morale	- Empowering as a principle and core practice - Subjectivity of the user - Autonomy and social functionality integrated in the care practice procedures - Autonomy and respect as prevailing care practice perspectives - Self-care as a guiding principle, but sensitivity to individual aspects
Potential risks of empowerment	**Support systems of empowering practices**
- Empowerment rhetoric not practice - Lack of an empowering culture and practice - Insensitivity to the users' changing situation, needs and wishes - The dependency of the frail service user makes them objects not subjects	- Communication, information and feedback procedures - Training on empowering practices - Flexible service structure - Sensitivity to needs and wishes of older people in the daily practice

The support systems for empowering practice mean open communication channels with the relevant care providing organisations, provision of ample information on the different kinds of care products and services and lastly but not least supporting the care users and carers in their choices. One-window information centres (a single access entry) and procedures for information and simple complaint systems are some of the tools for achieving empowerment. The aim of enabling older people to live independently cannot be achieved without attention to empowering and well-being of the users.

The attitude of the care staff towards autonomy and respect for service users is an important factor in the way towards empowering practice. Evidence for such an approach could be found in the Danish and Dutch models. In these projects the service and care deliverer are instructed to treat the service users in such a way that they can keep the lead in their own lives. This is sometimes promoted by viewing the service users as commissioners.

Maintaining and regaining self-respect means the service user being pleased and proud to be able to live independently or care for oneself and that the service user and the informal carer received adequate information on the care process and products. Involvement in decision-making means that the client had a say in the sort of services he/she received, when and how much. The status of a commissioner can be promoted if it is in the core care practice of the organisation. Staff members should not decide for them, but always ask them what and how they want things done. In the interviews the key workers showed this attitude. Several clients stated that they are involved in the decisions (NL1). The security guaranteed by the staff means personal confidence between discharge manager, service users and their families and can help to reduce the fear and insecurity caused by the new personal situation of older people in need of care and their families at home (A2).

From the methodological and conceptual point of view empowerment proved to be an important complementary perspective of home-based integrated care. Sometimes it might look too self-evident to be analysed separately but it was worthwhile to address this aspect both in the care, research organisation and assessment of daily practices of integrated care.

3.3   Social Inclusion as a Perspective in Integrated Care

Social inclusion is a commonly used concept in the context of European social policy. The concept concentrates on involvement in society as a policy aim (Dwyer, 2000; Deacon, 2002; Taylor-Gooby, 2001; Pierson, 2001). The policy aim of social inclusion addresses active participation throughout the whole life span. The elements of social inclusion cover issues like maintaining connection to the family, keeping the social ties active and satisfactory, being able to feel like a citizen and participating in everyday life and continuing to do home tasks as much as possible. Social inclusion means socialisation and staying in the familiar environment and consequently, the prevention of marginalisation. This can be achieved, for example, by attending day care centres, receiving help to go shopping and to spend time on hobbies.

Social inclusion is about maintaining the connection to the community. There were examples of how this can be achieved. In Greece, the establishment of day care centres helped to reduce social isolation, as evidenced in these quotes:

> "The participation in the programme has contributed to the improvement of the quality of life, has given free time and helped me in dealing with my loneliness ... I think the best bit was the feeling of being cared for – people cared about you." (EL1, user)

> "When I came to the programme, my life was a chaos, I was desperately sad because of my spouse's death. However my mood changed later, I felt a human being. My hours were filled, I have changed, and I found happiness." (EL2, user)

The package of services in Italy aims at reconstructing social bonds; 80% of older people living at home share their homes with a personal assistant (a family assistant, mostly an immigrant) and the physiotherapist interacts more with this personal assistant than with the older person's relatives. The physiotherapists teach personal assistants, for example, simple therapy to assist the older people in their mobility. The model project can be a link between the family, the community, the older person and the social services. It encourages socialisation among older people and temporarily relieves families and informal carers from the burden of care. The model project could also help in keeping the morale high after inevitable losses in life.

Model projects (NL1, DK) can offer a kind of care that promotes social inclusion. Instead of being transferred to a new and strange residential setting, the users can stay in their own homes, enabling them to continue their social contacts and activities in the neighbourhood they are familiar with. The growing awareness that older people have the right to live independently as long as possible was the principle idea in the establishment of the project (NL1).

The empirical evidence testifies that some service users are enabled to maintain the close connection to their community via day care activities or visits from volunteers. Home visits by volunteers are seen as having a positive effect not only on the social life of older people but also on that of the informal carer. According to the model project staff, social contacts are supremely important to older people as physical disability prevents them from socialising in the community and leads to loneliness, which became apparent in one Danish project (DK2).

As has been highlighted in Chapter 5, it would seem that only a few model projects (A1 and A2; DK1 and 2) make also provisions for supporting carers and reducing the burden of family carers. The local pensioners' associations and voluntary organisations provided ample opportunities for social inclusion by arranging excursions, talks, bingo and dining arrangements (DK2). Furthermore, voluntary associations also promote social inclusion among lonely older people by, among other things, mediating visiting friends. These facilities are, however, not available everywhere. Social inclusion can be measured, for example, by participation in the different activities and their accessibility. Pensioners' associations gathered older people in the same locality where the services were given. Health centres could run a day care facility for older people where talks, productive activities and coffee drinking were organised.

Well-organised discharge planning pays attention to potential social isolation. In some cases the referrals were made to organisations (mainstream and voluntary) that offered day care which was particularly promoted by the Finnish and the UK models. Some models had a volunteer visiting team for older people in need of care in the district (A 1), in other models visiting by family and friends was encouraged and trips and other activities organised. Needs assessment played an important role in getting the services (DK).

In relieving loneliness the actual helping process was important. In some models the staffing has been planned in a way to guarantee that there was time to have a cup of coffee and a chat with the older people (DK). The municipality also had day-care facilities for older people where talks, productive activities and coffee drinking among other things were organised. The way the staff met the older people, joking, and laughing together made a great difference.

Day care facilities were not available for all older people, however, as needs assessment was conducted prior to admittance (DK). The main criterion for admission was loneliness associated with physical disability that prevented the citizen from socialising in his/her community. Two of the citizens interviewed attended a day care facility. One of them said:

> "I visit the day care centre two times a week. I really like coming there because I got to know quite a few people among the residents and staff there while I was admitted for rehabilitation. And it would be a shame if I lost touch with them." (DK2, user)

However, the surveys conducted among older people in Denmark indicated that solitude associated with ageing was a fairly widespread problem in that country. But this is not restricted to Denmark and was widespread throughout the PROCARE countries.

Having provided a general overview, elements of social inclusion as a perspective in integrated care are synthesised into a table, comparing the life world and systems perspectives.

Table 3: The Elements of Social Inclusion from Two Perspectives

The elements of social inclusion from the life world	The elements of social inclusion from the systems world
- Feeling like a citizen; being able to lead as normal a life as possible - Staying in a familiar setting and maintaining a connection to the family, neighbourhood and community - Participation in everyday tasks (self-help) or getting help without participation - Getting understanding for changing moods - Easy access to socialization opportunities - Getting help in personal socialising needs (shopping, walking tours, café visits …)	- Social inclusion as a policy aim and core practice - Functional and enabling housing conditions - Activation and socially including practices - Support services and options available, helping tools in socialisation - Relevant support systems to family carers - Access to socialising (day care facilities, pensioners' associations, voluntary services)
Potential risks	**Risk reducing**
- Lack of staff and socially including practices - Loneliness and isolation of older people when activation level drops due to problems in physical and mental functionality	- Staffing measures and continuous staffing assessment - Financial incentives to carers, volunteers and voluntary organisations - Social inclusion measures and regular assessment

Social inclusion is not a traditional concept in the care for older people, although from the life-world perspective it contains simple things of everyday life: retaining the citizen status, having an opportunity to live one's own life and stay in the familiar environment, and participating in everyday activities. It also means that thresholds for participating are low enough and that participation is supported. In the systems world, it is necessary to closely analyse the concept of social inclusion so as to identify the ways in which the systems world can support needs in the life world. This support means functioning accommodation, support services and support to informal carers, as well as low thresholds to day care and participation in association activities.

To be able to reduce risks, the systems world needs quality systems that provide feedback on staffing levels and economic incentives, and mechanisms for monitoring the realisation of social inclusion.

It seems relevant that model ways of working actively strive to promote social inclusion. The elements of social inclusion are environmental: instead of being transferred to a new and strange setting, the service users are kept in their familiar setting, enabling them to continue their social contacts and activities in the familiar neighbourhood which seem to be the prerequisites.

Social inclusion is a self-evident aim of integrated care at home, but too little attention has been paid to actual procedures and working methods and how this may become realised in the life of service users. It is not enough to have social inclusion as a policy aim. It means having an integrated philosophy and practice procedures, assessment and measures, and real action to secure materialisation in daily practice.

From the methodological and conceptual point of view, social integration/inclusion provides us with a complementary conceptual framework and essential additional aspects in integrated care. It emphasises the social aspects of ageing and the need to stay in a familiar surrounding as crucial aspects of maintaining social functionality while getting along despite being frail. The concept also reminds the systems world to look at the everyday integrated care practice from a specific perspective.

4   Discussion and Conclusions

This chapter looked at the benefits of home-based integrated care as perceived by older people. Using the wider concepts of empowerment and social integration provided a focus for analysis of the perspectives. It seems that the life world perspective has to comply with the rules of the systems world perspective in service provision: the systems world dictates the terms of integration. However, there are slight indications of a greater sensitivity to the views of older people in the data. In Denmark, for instance, the concept of self-care and a range of services that create and maintain interpersonal relationships were an integral part of the model projects. Older people need services, though they very seldom complain. They are not interested in the organisational aspects of things; what is important to them is the quality of the work, the encounter itself, and that their most important needs are met.

There were indications of elements of good practices. From the life-world perspective, it is important that services are provided using a one-window model, that older people have their own designated worker, that care is received from the same worker at pre-appointed times and that there is sensitivity to personal situations. It is important to create contacts and maintain them, and it is also important to organise activities that promote contacts. Useful tools in achieving this include various meetings and clubs, as indicated by the Danish model projects.

There should be a distinction between the characteristics of good care according to researchers and policy-makers and the way frail older people (and their carers) judge the quality of care. Our analysis has shown how, in the actual provision of care, the systems world does not sufficiently take account of the life world of the service user. Economic constraints and the regulation and standardisation of integrated care can hamper both the working methods used for empowerment and genuine integration in practice.

Quality systems that ensure the systems-world perspective are prevailing. Frail older people generally lack insight into the process and organisational structure involved in the provision of care. They base their judgement, therefore, on the results of the process, that is on the quality of the care they have received. Frail older people and their informal carers are more concerned with whether they have received 'the care they needed, at the right time and in the right way'; they have valuable opinions on the elements of the care process with which they are in direct contact (e.g. home-care workers); and they do not generally concern themselves with the way the care is organised (structure). These points concur with findings in other chapters.

Furthermore, the data suggest that care recipients' situations vary widely, as well as their own resources. There are vulnerable silent clients on the one hand, and empowered, demanding consumers on the other. Versatile research into the roles of the recipients of different kinds of services for older people is needed in order to be able to provide tailored, needs-based services and not standard services in addressing individual needs.

Our results are consistent with the latest evidence-based literature on home care (Godfrey et al., 2000: iv-viii). The authors note that across the studies that considered the user perspectives of integrated care, a range of attributes were identified. These could be classified into those that related to the nature of the service (continuity, reliability and responsiveness); the nature and demeanour of the staff (disposition, competence); and the nature of the process (quality of relationship, awareness of needs, flexibility). For those most dependent, the highest value was placed on staff continuity.

Based on our research, the different aspects of integration, empowerment and social inclusion should be taken into account when creating good practices in the European perspective.

5   Future Research Needs

Identifying and testing elements of good practices is an important future step in European research. In many cases, good practice does not consist of the operational model of a project as such, but of important individual viewpoints, local capacities, collaborative procedures or just certain aspects of the model. Accordingly, research and evaluation are needed before a specific element or model can be identified as good practice. At the moment, the concept of good practice is used in a very broad sense. This will erode the core content of the concept so that much of its meaning is lost. This research project, too, was concerned with identifying good practice. The concept of good practice is multidimensional and problematic. If a thing is described as good, it is also necessary to ask good for whom and under what conditions, what mechanisms and settings are required, and what levels of competence and social capital are needed for it to be labelled as good.

One challenge for research is to analyse the concept of good practice itself. Another research challenge is to give more visibility to older people's viewpoints and gain insights into their life world. What is needed is sensitive empirical research to analyse the interconnection between older people's everyday life and their care needs, and to see which aspects of the process of delivering and receiving care are the most important for service users. A systematic literature review of earlier research alone could provide important cumulative knowledge. The provision of care and integrated services takes place under conditions determined by operational settings and staff competence. The data suggest that the financial aspects of care, such as user fees and various service vouchers, may affect client choices.

The process of everyday care also needs to be analysed from the perspective of service recipients, not only from that of organisations. Different groups have a legitimate interest in studies on the outcomes of care. An important outcome according to the managers might be in conflict with the view of the users as to what is useful to them.

The evidence with respect to the effectiveness of home care is neither extensive nor very robust. This is partly a reflection of the complexity of interventions that come under the rubric of home care. Evaluative studies are needed not only on outcomes but also in relation to service-user conceptions of maintaining valued life choices. Performance and effectiveness on care approaches (Vaarama, 1995; Knapp, 1988) concentrate on effectiveness and outcomes of care. There is a need to explore the impacts and outcomes of integrated care on different users, and different kinds of informal care relationships and socio-economic circumstances.

The process of developing user-led integrated care needs a lot more investigation. A fundamental feature of integrated care is the complexity of the intervention. The inputs are multidimensional, offered by different kinds of staff, in the context of co-production, using different eligibility criteria and allocation practices. It is of utmost importance to refine and combine research methodologies in order to gain an understanding into the processes producing particular outcomes for specific groups of users. The purchasing systems of services are in need of a sustained research endeavour to examine the impact of service delivery and outcomes for service users.

National and EU policies for older people need practical and knowledge-based working methods that cross the different sectors of society. There is a need to embrace a systems approach where the life world and the personal significances of older people really are the focal issue. Vulnerable older people and their carers require their own research agenda. More investigation is required on staffing policies, qualifications, and the adequacy of care professionals and indeed the socio-political aspects of care, and especially in the context of a social policy driven by economics.

CHAPTER 7

Working towards Integrated Care – Working Conditions

Charlotte Strümpel, Sirpa Andersson, Eftichia Teperoglou

1   Background and Methods

In the course of the project work, it became clear that the success of integrated care is closely connected to the workers involved. This entails that the working conditions have an important role to play in providing integrated care and in overcoming barriers to integration. In order to ensure and improve quality and efficiency in integrated care it is important to examine the professional development of staff and its working conditions. This requires a combination of different elements and strategies which we will focus on in this chapter.

While the general framework conditions (e.g. role of authorities, legislation and societal developments) in a country are relevant to the working conditions and have been elaborated on elsewhere (see Leichsenring/Alaszewski, 2004), in this chapter we will focus on the working conditions within the organisations providing integrated care.

Working conditions have been identified as a key factor in any type of care provision, and have been studied quite intensely. Still, less is known about the effects of working conditions specifically in integrated care. Some of our findings are in line with general knowledge on working conditions in the care sector, others show issues particular to integrated care.

This chapter will start with a general overview, containing a description of types of staff involved in the projects, types of tasks performed, as well as an overview of specific 'hard facts' such as pay, and contracts. After that, the specific working conditions of care and case managers will be elaborated on, followed by general issues of positive and negative working conditions in integrated care. The conclusions will consider general ideas and put forward policy recommendations.

2   Overview of Staff and General Working Conditions

This section aims to give a short general overview of working conditions. First, we will describe the different types of staff that work in the models in the different countries. After that we will show which types of tasks are carried out in integrated care. Finally there will be a short overview of staff's satisfaction with working conditions.

2.1   Types of Staff Working in Integrated Care

The starting point of our analysis was to investigate which type of professionals are involved in the PROCARE models. One of the main characteristics among all models was the range of different types of services – from discharge management and one-stop care assessment to integrated care in the community. From this it followed that there were many different types of staff and professionals involved.

However, there were some professional groups that were common to almost all projects, in particular care and case management functions, general managerial and / or administrative functions or specific professional functions (nursing care, medical provision, social work). It became clear that staff – regardless of their profession – could be in case / care and management positions and in positions where they provided the services according to their profession (nursing, medicine, social work etc.). In some models, professionals had some case / care or general management functions combined with hands-on provision.

The most common professional group found in the PROCARE models was *nurses*. They were mentioned in 15 of the 18 models. In more than five models nurses had case management or management functions (see below, section 3). Nurses were involved in assessment and planning as well as home nursing and hospital nursing provision. In some projects nurses played a pivotal role such as, for instance, in Italy 1 where different types of nurses had several distinct functions. Another example could be found in Austria (A1) where a nurse had the discharge management function. In the second Austrian model the so-called 'district' nurses (*Stützpunktschwestern*) had a management as well as a case management function and provided home nursing. These seemed to be quite a number of roles for one person, especially as they were expected to provide a defined percentage of hands-on nursing care yet limit their time with administrative and organisational tasks.

Another common professional group found in our integrated care models were *social workers* who were explicitly mentioned in 10 models. It could be observed that they were engaged in a wide variety of different functions with different tasks. In France (F1) the social worker was a case manager in the community, in Italy (I1), employed by the hospital, and in Greece (EL2) social workers were mainly involved in assessment. In the Dutch models (NL1, NL2) a social worker worked as a motivational therapist; while in Germany (D2) and Austria (A2) social workers carried out 'mainstream' social work tasks such as assisting people in applying for benefits. In some countries social workers were very common in hospitals and/or health care settings while in other countries, such as Italy, it was something very new and innovative to have social workers in hospitals.

A very interesting and less straightforward area was the issue of *key workers providing home help and care*. In at least 10 models staff were mentioned that provided different levels of help with household and personal care activities. Some key workers were integrated in the models, others were associated with the models as outpatient or similar services. This seemed to be the area where countries differed the most. From country to country the care tasks were divided in different ways between various types of key workers, with quite different terms and prerequisites, such as training and education. The following gives some examples:

- In Greece (EL2) we found family assistants that provided help and care for the family at home. Their tasks were – depending on the user – assistance with activities of daily living, such as dressing, bathing and feeding, and in household tasks such as cleaning and shopping (for users who lived at home). The family assistant's education usually consisted of a High School Degree and/or Nurses Training. In the Greek model 1 the family assistants mainly worked in the KAPI clubroom.

- In Finland there were home helps who took on both domestic work such as cleaning, shopping and personal care (dressing or bathing). They undertook a three-year diploma education.

- In Austria there were home helps that provided help with household tasks and had a short three-month training, and home carers who had a two-year training that provided personal help with activities of daily living (washing, dressing). The Austrian law is very strict in prohibiting home helps from providing any medical type of activities such as applying ointment or changing bandages – these activities are restricted to nurses with a diploma, and nursing assistants.

- In the Netherlands there were carers with three levels of respective education: Level 1 were those with training in domiciliary care involving a lower vocational education. Level 2 carers had training in personal care and performed mostly personal help with activities of daily living. Level 3 carers had training in personal care, nursing and social support, which was a special training after intermediate vocational education. In some cases, it was possible for key workers to upgrade their position through training (for example, in the UK or Finland; see training).

Also, we found country-specific specialised jobs with specialised education such as the 'Social and health worker' in Italy who offered direct assistance to older people such as hygiene and mobility, but also gave information and provided training for users. Another example was the 'health visitor' in Greece (EL1) who acquired his/her specialisation during a four-year training and thus was also skilled to take blood samples, to measure blood pressure and to administer vaccinations.

A professional group that was regularly present was *occupational therapists*. They were also involved in different roles. In the UK and France we found occupational therapists in assessment, planning as well as case management and discharge management.

Another dominant professional group involved in integrated care models were of course *doctors*. They were mentioned explicitly in eight models, but due to the nature of integrated care, liaison with medical doctors (for example GPs) was mentioned in almost all groups. Medical doctors were found mostly in their primary function as doctors providing medical services in PROCARE models. In Germany (D1) however the case manager was a medical doctor. In Italy the hierarchical role of the medical doctor seemed to be important – in one model (I1), he was the manager of the project, while in the other (I 2) he was the head of a working group that coordinated all the other professionals.

2.2 *The Range of Tasks in Integrated Care*

From the wide variety of professional groups and different types of models, it followed that staff in these models had a wide variety of tasks: from straightforward administrative ones like phoning, faxing and e-mailing, to complex coordination and management tasks and, of course, hands-on health and social care provision. It became evident, though, that different professional groups could carry out the same task. Furthermore, it became apparent that there was a considerable overlapping of tasks in the integrated care settings, either in case management or in other professional areas. One single professional group hardly ever provided specific tasks; more commonly different people and/or professions undertook them:

> "In this setting there is a blurring of our roles. If a crisis or problem does arise I can't ignore it, because it is not an occupational therapy problem. I've got to address those issues, but I will seek the advice of a nurse or a physiotherapist if the issues involve their area." (UK1, occupational therapist)

Also, the same professional groups had a variety of different duties for which they were responsible. For example in one model (I1) there were three types of nurses: the older people's nurse who carried out the first interview with the user to evaluate his/her social and family situation; the administrative nurse, who drew up and disseminated a multidimensional evaluation of the user; and the nurse who identified 'users at risk of losing their autonomy' in other units and admitted them to a specialised older people's unit.

  With respect to individual duties, with *hospital discharge* it seemed that nurses saw themselves as having a more holistic role:

> "The patient's discharge involves nurses more than doctors, because doctors only see the patient as an illness and don't consider patients as people." (I1, key worker)

As was seen in previous chapters, *assessment* was undertaken by many professional groups, depending on the focus of assessment, with nurses at the forefront:

> "An important task of ours is to visit the patients at home and assess their care and support needs, and to inform relatives and patients about how the care can be provided. In many cases patients and relatives lack the knowledge about the services they are eligible for." (A2, nurse)

219

There were a wide variety of *administrative tasks* involved in integrated care. In some cases there were secretaries and administrative helpers who took on these roles and in other cases, case and care managers and other professionals had to do them. This was sometimes considered burdensome:

> "Our day is filled up with telephone calls, faxes, filling in forms or writing reports, this is such a large part of my work that I sometimes feel like my own secretary." (A2, discharge manager)

2.3 "Hard Facts": Salary, Contract, Working Time and Infrastructure

Looking at the 'hard facts' of working conditions in health and social care, some interesting differences between the various European regions could be seen, highlighting areas of inequality and discrimination in some cases. In the Northern countries (DK, FIN), working contracts were permanent and workers had full-time jobs. Though salaries were perceived as low, workers appreciated that job security was high. Moving towards Southern Europe, salaries were still seen as low – in fact, most care work was done by women, and female work is generally, and in all PROCARE countries, paid less. In addition however many health and social care workers did not even have a permanent contract, with therefore less job security. In some countries part-time employment was quite common; some workers viewed this in a positive light as it was more convenient for those with family commitments.

Salary

It was frequently stated by all interviewees that wages in the care sector were relatively low. In Greece (EL1), staff received pay according to the 'Public Sector Wage Scale', which was reported as being very low. Indeed in one model (EL2), there was no guarantee that workers would be regularly paid as the municipal agency in charge was responsible for serious delays in salary payment.

It must be noted that wage levels are open to subjective evaluation between different workers. Although there is a tendency for people to feel they are not paid enough, we found both key workers who felt their salaries were adequate, and those who felt underpaid. In the Danish models, pay was in line with central bargaining agreements of the respective professional groups and staff interviewed were generally satisfied with their salaries. In the Netherlands however salaries in the care sector were generally viewed as being low. Some key workers (NL2) assessed their salary as low with respect to the high demands and pressures of their job.

Workers tended to use different personal strategies to overcome any disparities in pay, as the following quote illustrates:

> "Because the salary for the evening shift is better, I have planned to start working only in evenings." (FIN1, the only interviewed male key worker)

Striking inequalities both within the medical sector and between the health and social care area have been identified as a major obstacle to integrating different organisations and professionals providing care services. This was also reflected in important differences concerning individual incomes, as was emphasised by Italian key workers who all earned roughly the same while doctors were paid considerably higher incomes. Another aspect was mentioned by professionals in the UK who pointed to the fact that in some cases even workers doing the same job were paid different amounts for weekends and overtime due to disparities in their contracts. Due to the dominance of the health care sector, health care staff were paid better wages than their social care counterparts. This had partly to do with better training in medical care than in social care, but it was also observed that unqualified health care staff have better terms and conditions than social care staff.

Contracts

A wide variety of contracts were found in the 18 model ways of working. While in many cases staff had permanent contracts, for instance in both models in Finland and Denmark, some model ways of working were developed as finite projects with limited and insecure funding. This affected job security of all staff. For example, funding for one of the Greek programmes (EL2) terminated at the end of 2003, which resulted in substantial job insecurity for some employees. All key workers interviewed were quite concerned and felt personally insecure and vulnerable, a situation not very conducive to developing a common future. Also in one of the German models (D2), staff had limited working contracts due to the temporary nature of the model.

One specific feature of contracts and working conditions in integrated care that we have encountered in several models was that staff working closely together or even doing the same job can have different employers. This results in different contracts and working conditions such as amount of leave and salaries.

In Italy (I2) the nurses, doctors, social assistants and physiotherapists were civil servants and they had a contract with the National Health Service. Other staff (e.g. 'socio-medical workers') were private employees contracted by social cooperatives who were contracted-in by the National Health Service.

In Greece not all salaries were paid from the same budget and this resulted in salary differences for employees doing the same job. Those paid from European resources were better paid than those employed by local authorities.

In the model UK1, the respective staff had different employers (Social Services or Primary [Health] Care Trust). This resulted in different salaries as the hospital was more generous for night and weekend duties:

"We were asked, but they wanted us to take a (social services) contract, which meant less money, and the same amount of money whenever you worked – nights, days, weekends, and I feel we are worth more than that ... and that's why I wouldn't change my contract." (UK1, key worker)

"And of course the problem is that we will come in at weekends for the flat money and agency staff get a fantastic amount from their agency, or from us via their agency for weekends and night duties." (UK1, key worker)

In UK2 model, all staff were employed by the Acute Hospital Trust, except the care manager who was jointly funded with social services. Staff here had permanent contracts as the project had become a mainstream service. The key workers had the feeling that they were 'neither one thing or another' as they were hosted and funded by the acute trust, but their work was in the community which actually resembled the work of those in the Community Trust.

In Austria (A1) home helps, home carers and home nurses worked together in a team, though with different organisations as employers. In general this was not seen as a problem:

"We all work together and we are all integrated in our work; the clients do not know if we are from the Red Cross, the Caritas or the Volkshilfe [the three non-profit organisations providing the services]. That is really not important for the clients." (A1, key worker)

"If we have no problem the system is no problem. But if there is a personnel problem we have to inform our institutions and they inform the head of the model way of working, the Red Cross. The system is more complicated for personnel problems and decisions, but for our work with the clients it is perfect." (A1, sub-district nurse)

In the other Austrian model (A2), the discharge manager worked in the hospital and was employed by the Red Cross, while her colleagues in the hospital were employed by the hospital. A positive aspect of this was that the discharge manager had regular contact with other discharge managers working in other hospitals for the Red Cross.

Working Hours

Across all models, there seemed to be a wide variety of hours worked. Staff in Greece (EL1), France (F1 and F2), Finland (FIN1 and FIN2) reported full-time jobs. Greece (EL1) reported that overtime was not paid, but could be taken back as time in lieu. Germany (D2) reported a higher number of hours and overtime.

In Austria most nurses, home carers and helpers interviewed individually and in focus groups reported part-time job arrangements which were considered family-friendly by the professionals themselves. Finland (FIN1 and FIN2) reported shift work, also night shifts which were less family-friendly but better paid, while in France the work was also seen as being less family-friendly.

3   Care and Case Management and Working Conditions

Among the central factors for the development and operationalisation of integrated care networks we found what has been described as care and case management. As this was emphasised during our empirical research we would like to highlight the issue In this section with respect to the specific working conditions of this still developing new professional profile. In particular, we will first look at definitions of care and case management and then highlight the role and tasks as well as the education of the care or case managers, and look at implications for training opportunities.

3.1 *Definitions*

Concerning the conceptual discussion about the definition of the Anglo-Saxon term of *"Care und Case management"* (see also Chapter 4), there is a variety of statements concerning the nature of care management but they are often not explicit, lacking clarity and the definition of the term is much debated. The main aim of an integrated care strategy – as has been extensively discussed in other chapters of this book – is matching supply and demand for older people in complex situations. The methods used are client- and therefore demand-oriented. This approach has also been taken up in other domains such as, in particular, the health sector where it is more known under the heading of *care management* or 'managed care'. This is mainly concerned with introducing steering mechanisms and economic thinking in medical care (Leichsenring, 2004: 22-23).

The basic idea is that all cooperative and organisational tasks are taken over by a single person, in many cases a qualified nurse or a social worker. In this function s/he should be the contact person for the patient, relatives and the internal as well as the external service providers. The term *'case management'* denotes the coordination or integration of help in favour of the individual case (as a case, i.e. not necessarily as a person) and of the immediate personal environment. Conversely, the term *'care management'* denotes the coordination of help and networks of service providers at the level of the general public in a care region. The whole concept has elicited widespread discussion without producing any final definition of the terms (Roth/Reichert, 2004: 290-291). However, as a basic definition we may conclude that care management includes the following features: planning, arrangement and monitoring of care needs across time, place and discipline:

> "It is a coordinator function, which is the responsibility of a specialised unit at each site (referring to model, project) and allocates the long-term care benefit to applicants who meet the eligibility criteria." (Kodner et al., 2000: 5)

3.2   Roles, Tasks and Qualifications of Case Managers

The main starting point of the care-case manager's role description in the PROCARE countries was its multidimensional nature. On the one hand we could identify a group of countries (UK, Finland, Denmark, the Netherlands) where case managers were established within a mainstream service and on the other hand countries like Germany and France where case management was mainly in model projects. Also in Austria, case management was evident, but very often reduced to a discharge management role, acting as an advocate between different care providers (Grundböck et al., 1997: 14; 1998: 101). In Finland, the case manager was mostly the chief home-care officer, not a nurse. She carried out the so-called 'first visit' to assess the client's needs and to set up an individual service plan together with other professionals.

In Greece and Italy there was no evidence of care- or case management and the professionals were not familiar with this role within an integrated care context. Though not called case managers, in the Greek models there was a person in place (social worker), responsible for planning, assessing and arranging services together with the user. In the Italian models there was also a coordinator, leader and promoter of the project (WUCC), as well as a social worker who was responsible for users' social needs assessment, for contacts with social workers from the region, and for a family assessment. However, they were not officially called ‚case manager' and their tasks were less extensive than one would expect of a case manager.

We found a broad range of strategies being applied to foster integrated care, but the respective tasks were not always accomplished by a single person called 'case manager'. For instance, on the operational level, case management initially included responsibility for assessing patients' care needs which took place in all models and usually consisted of an assessment of personal, social and physical situation at home (A, FIN, I) as well as financial assessments (UK, FIN). Once the older person was accepted by the case manager, the 'classical' case manager would undertake a more detailed individual support and care plan together with the user and his/her family. Furthermore, the organisation and coordination of team meetings, discharge planning and liaison with social services on behalf of clients were essential features of a case manager's job description. Further tasks could include the organisation, coordination and participation in quality circles.

In the UK, case managers also acted as 'gate keepers': they organised social care on behalf of clients while the GP performed this function with respect to health care. The case manager was the central person for contacts and arrangements with other agencies and for the coordination of all the social providers. In one of the models of case management (German Home Care Nürnberg [HCN]), the care manager was responsible for setting up a screening service by phone which included taking a detailed record of the case. Also his task was to feed in data and to evaluate the database. Another issue related to case-care management was the idea of 'One-Stop-Windows' involving custom-made care and individual care plans as was evident in the role of the Dutch *omtinker* of the Trynwalden project (Ex et al., 2004: 438).

The vocational background of the case managers was an important issue. In theory, the case-care manager is a single person that takes over all coordination and organisational tasks and is either a qualified nurse, a social worker or from another profession. In the PROCARE models, the following table demonstrates that both nurses and social workers and – to a lesser degree – other health professionals carried out case or care management tasks. Nevertheless, more case managers seemed to have a specialist nurse education than as a social worker. From the interviews and focus groups with key workers and management it was not evident that a social worker background or a nursing education appeared to block or facilitate collaboration, coordination and communication between the different professional groups of the selected models. Only in the focus group of the Austrian model (*Discharge Management in the 'Hartmann' Hospital*) were participants of the opinion that "it is important that the discharge manager (in the case of this model) is a trained nurse with experience in extramural care and not a social worker" (A2, focus group).

226

Table 1: Professional Background of Case and Care Managers

Country	Models	Title and education
Austria	Discharge Management in the "Hartmann" Hospital	Case managers – nursing education
	Social Care and Health Districts in Hartberg	Case managers: nursing education – further education in project management
Denmark	24-hour Integrated Health and Social/Personal Care in the Municipality of Skævinge	Assistant manager at the health centre 'Bauneparken' – Nurse (4-year education) with administrative diploma training
	Rehabilitation of Older Persons in the Municipality of Søllerød	Area manager for the elderly services in the municipality of Søllerød – Nurse with administrative diploma training
Finland	Discharge from Hospital to Home Care – Helsinki	Chief home care officer – 3-year high school (diploma) Doctor
	Elderly Care – City of Espo	Not available but existence of multiprofessionality

Country	Models	Title and education
France	C.L.I.C. Châlus	Case manager, Social worker
	C.L.I.C. Phalempin	Case manager, Ergo therapist
Germany	Home Care Nürnberg (HCN)	Case Manager, Doctor with HCN Case manager, Specialised nurse with HCN
	Geronto-psychiatric-geriatric association Oberspreewald-Lausitz (GPGV OSL)	1 coordinator of the association – social pedagogue 3 spokesmen of the association: inpatient section, outpatient section and clinical
The Netherlands	Care facility "Zijloever"	Care mediator: Higher education in social services
	Chain of care for the elderly in Kerkrade	Care coordinator (BCAR), Education varies; sometimes trained nurses
United Kingdom	Limes Livingstone Integrated Care Project (LLICP)	Social work professional (may be diploma or university degree)
	Community assessment and rehabilitation team (CART)	Social services – diploma or degree (also qualified nurse)
Greece	Open Care Centres for the Elderly (KAPI) Help at Home	Not available
Italy	Working Unit of Continuous Care (WUCC) Single Point of Access	Not available

All professionals interviewed mentioned the following aspects of the case and care management system as useful In facilitating the quality of service delivery:

- a concentration on the coordination of tasks,
- effective joint working, and
- the feeling of being supported by the management.

In the Danish Skævinge model, the organisational emphasis on multi-disciplinarity and inter-professional collaboration, coordination and communication was highlighted in most of the interviews with staff. In the Dutch models, most of the key workers felt they were valued and supported by the management. In the UK, although the problem of lack of training was evident, almost all staff felt positive about management involving staff in problem-solving: case managers had developed the culture of an open door policy and open minded ideas. The fact that the key workers could pass on users' problems, wishes and needs to the management, who could then take all the necessary steps to fill in any service delivery gaps, was evident also in the Netherlands and in Germany:

> "The door is always open and you never feel intimidated asking for help from managers." (UK1, key worker)

> "The head nurse A. contributed a lot to developing discharge management. She wanted the project and communicated from the beginning that it's a good thing, so that the whole team had a positive attitude towards it from the beginning" (A1, discharge manager)

As case managers in Austria and Germany mainly worked in projects at the interface between hospital and community care, it was interesting to see how collaboration within individual cases had improved through better coordination. The following quote from the doctor of the HCN (D1) testifies to the importance of the case manager's role, a central feature of which was the collaboration and coordination of care:

> "(...) currently, one nurse is working for HCN, who has a lot of experience in this field. She can use the database and identify who has to be contacted in individual cases; also a target plan is set up in collaboration with the client and the doctor, which is checked for goodness of fit. *What is important is that the 'case' is terminated by solving the problem.* (...) A relationship based on knowing each other and personal confidence has been established between the employee of HCN and others involved in such a way that the care arrangements can be carried out "without official channels." (D1, medical doctor)

Another quote highlights the positive effects of mediation pathways from the HCN to the patients:

> "... and the patient feels that the services or help offered is excellent – as far as he can understand them. That's the key issue, the patient doesn't feel alone." (D1, ombudsman PNN/HCN)

Here the HCN had taken charge of the case management function; however, she could not offer case management to all, but currently only to people whose General Practitioner was a member of the PNN (Practice Network Nürnberg, doctors association). In these cases questions could be raised as to whether those people who needed case management the most were actually targeted. If not, there was the danger that case managers worked with people who did not actually need their services.

Leading on from this, staff in both UK models reported inappropriate referrals as a major problem in their work. Sometimes patients' who were not necessarily in need of case management were referred to them and to other professionals at the same time:

> "We get quite a few inappropriate referrals, and sometimes it seems that people decide to refer to everyone and see who gets in there first – sometimes, an occupational therapist goes in there and someone from social services occupational therapy has already been in and it's very confusing for the client ..."
> (UK2, occupational therapist)

Other skills acquired by case and care managers consisted of organising daily meetings and developing a common and flexible working culture between staff. From the interviews with key workers and focus groups, we identified common features in all models. In the UK, staff emphasised their satisfaction with regular, open meetings where they discussed clients' cases. Daily meetings were also held in countries where case management was not explicitly evident, such as in Greece. Lack of time was seen as a major problem in some countries. In Germany, communication and collaboration were an essential part of the two case managers' work. There was enough time to carry out working groups/network conferences; but conferences for individual cases could not be organised. This implied that pressure of time prevented staff from communicating in a systematic way about individual cases, so communication was carried out in an informal manner which may not have been as effective.

In the Austrian and UK models, regardless of which professional groups they belong to, the work in an interdisciplinary team functioned well:

> "The work in an interdisciplinary team functions very well. It's a very good working atmosphere, regardless of which professional group we are talking about. You can talk to each other anytime if you need something. That's why it works. That's a very important point." (A1, medical doctor)

In Denmark the most important role of the management (at the health centre) had been to implement common values throughout the entire organisation. Valuing staff input was evident again in the Netherlands where the case manager had a general overview of all the cases and problems, and reacted promptly to staffs' suggestions and concerns. In the French models it was clear that gerontological coordination added value to the role of professionals working for the social and medico-social sector, in relation to information sharing and listening.

Not everywhere were relationships fostered in a positive manner. In the German HCN model, different providers seemed to be in competition with each other. Here was the situation that for the first time doctors had been attached to the project to maintain contact with the nursing personnel. Some key workers found collaboration with the doctors and other workers difficult due to hierarchical problems and culture clashes (see chapter 3 for elaboration on this aspect). Also in the UK1 model there were conflicts because health and social care were organisationally separate.

3.3   Opportunities for Training and Further Education

Opportunities for training and for further education of staff seemed to be dependent on many factors, for example on financial situations, the culture within the model or regional education opportunities. We also found evidence that care and case managers played a role in supporting the training and further education of other professionals. Judging from the interviews, it was obvious however that in most models there were considerable opportunities for training. As staff came from very different training backgrounds, opportunities for training and further education varied greatly from model to model, but also within models.

Staff confirmed that their organisations not only offered them ample opportunity for further education and training, but they also developed innovative training programmes to further integrated ways of working (Netherlands, Austria, Finland and Germany). In Finland, a new form of education was introduced to jointly train health and social care. The home helpers had the opportunity to gain qualifications as nurses alongside their routine work. Also, key workers in Finland reported that they were able to regularly access further training specific to home care. In the Austrian model 1, all key workers that were employed by different organisations participated in the Austrian Red Cross further education programme. However, here it was reported that opportunities for further education were decreasing due to lack of financial resources and time.

The Danish case was particularly interesting with respect to case and care management and the interconnection with further education. In order to support and sustain the drive for a multi-disciplinary approach to the provision of care and in order to increase the professional identity of the organisation and the individual staff, the management of the health centre of Skævinge formulated and deployed a continuous education strategy to keep the qualifications of staff up-to-date.

In some cases (e.g. UK2) it was possible to participate in training and development but there was little opportunity for career advancement, due to the limited number of staff and positions. The lack of career advancement is typical in the field of older people's care (Harris-Kojetin et al., 2004; Frerichs et al., 2004). Also, staff in the UK models highlighted the lack of training for some aspects of their role, and this was connected to the availability of funds:

> "Well we did get a lot of training at one time, but it seems to have petered off
> a bit now." (UK2, staff member)

Staff members in the UK and French models mentioned the importance of recruiting specialised personnel. In the France, the case manager was running training courses for professionals but the opportunity to obtaining a further qualification was limited. In Italy where there was no evidence of explicit case management, there was a process of professional education through conferences and courses.

In Greece (EL1) there were different opinions on the opportunities for further education and training, depending on the municipality in which key workers were working. Some municipal agencies offered good support, in others social workers and health visitors were not happy. Information about courses was scanty and fees were not always covered. In other cases (e.g. EL2) staff had the opportunity to attend courses and conferences, and the municipal council encouraged such initiatives.

To sum up, it is crucial for a successful case and care management, but also for positive working conditions as a whole, to adapt to the salient educational and professional challenges and to develop new initiatives and solutions.

4   Positive and Negative Aspects of Working Conditions

A variety of positive and negative working conditions were found in the consultations with staff of the models of integrated care studied in the PROCARE project. Some of these have already been mentioned in connection with the 'hard facts' of working conditions such as satisfaction with pay and contracts, and in connection with the tasks of case managers such as communication and team work or further education and training. In the following we will highlight those working conditions that were identified as positive and/or negative by staff. The order of the working conditions listed below roughly corresponds with the extent to which they were mentioned.

4.1 Positive Aspects of Working Conditions

Working with Clients and Seeing Outcomes

Staff were very motivated and reported liking their work. This was very closely connected with working with older people and their families and with seeing the outcomes of their work:

> "I can not think of one member of staff that does not pull her weight or work well and has a nice attitude to the residents, which is very, very important in my book, that you do care about them. They are aware that you care about them and they feel loved and it's just a nice working environment really" (UK1, key worker)

> "We would not leave our work to anybody else." (F1, key worker)

In both models in the Netherlands several key workers pointed out that helping other people gives them positive feelings and a lot of job satisfaction. Most key workers felt that they were valued by both clients and the organisation. In Finland for example, key workers felt substantially motivated in their work by positive daily feedback from the older clients and from the fact that the clients were so pleased to have and receive help. In many models in different countries it was mentioned that a good relationship with the older people gave the key workers job satisfaction and motivation. In UK1 most of the generic carers felt rewarded by extra responsibilities, even if they were not paid. These findings are in line with other findings that helping other people and the satisfaction gained from the actual work with the clients are integral to work satisfaction in care for older people (Frerichs et al., 2004).

Specifically, it was important to staff that the goals of work were clear to them and that this entailed working alongside the user and his/her family (IT1):

> "I can give the clients a sense of security, like in 'you need not be worried'. I find it very important that elderly people can enjoy their old age. An that I can give them some sociability." (NL1, key worker)

> "I really have the impression that I mean something to the people here" (NL1, key worker)

Conversely, users' and carers' satisfaction was related to single key workers as reported by users, such as in an Italian model. It becomes clear that the personal relationships between the key workers, users and families played a pivotal role in satisfaction on both sides.

Another important positive aspect of working with older people and their families concerned the outcomes of the rehabilitation process which appeared to hold an intrinsic value that contributed to a pleasant working climate (DK1). The outcomes that key workers reported could be on very different levels. A key worker in Greece was devoted to detecting health risks and preventing negative outcomes, while staff members in other models were pleased by smaller-scale outcomes:

> "Yes, I enjoy my work very much. I can give them care and be nice to them. Elderly people especially need that. It also gives me a pleasant feeling. For instance, if I have washed a client, so that she can go to the day centre clean and fresh. That is my motivation. Also, to acquire insight in human characteristics. It is very challenging and interesting work." (NL1, key worker).

Having enough time to spend with clients and to be able to elicit their needs without pressure was generally seen as being positive in the two models in the Netherlands and in UK1:

> "We have got time to sit and discuss things with patients that you don't get on the ward and that makes a difference" (UK1)

The aspect of taking time for the users was a very important aspect which became even clearer when looking at negative aspects of the work in integrated care, since the lack of time and time pressure was something that many of the studied key workers over most countries experienced (see below).

All in all, we saw how important it was for workers to have a good relationship with clients. The high intrinsic motivation of staff could mainly be explained by these relationships, which played a meaningful role in the integrated models. It was important for staff to see that the model way of working was useful for themselves and for the older people in need of care as extrinsic motivation, and to counter more negative features such as low salaries.

Autonomy, Independent and Varied Work

Many key workers across all models expressed satisfaction with the high level of autonomy in their work. Within the limits of their job description, many were able to make autonomous decisions about care in consultation with the client. For instance, in the models studied in the Netherlands, the key workers unanimously said that they had a lot of independence and responsibility. They highly valued this aspect of their work. The opportunity to plan and arrange one's own work was found in models in different countries such as Denmark, Greece and Austria:

> "I feel totally independent and I can arrange my work according to my own decisions, although sometimes I have to follow the doctor's program" (EL1, key worker)

> "The nurses make their own work plans and coordinate this with other social services. Twice a week all nurses are in the Health Centre and carry out administrative tasks as well as having team meetings." (A1, manager)

Some key workers that had already experienced work in an institutional setting valued the possibility of being totally responsible for their work:

> "Before I worked in the institutional care system. The rigid structure and not being responsible for the work weren't satisfying." (A2, key worker)

> "It's pleasant to go into the district. I feel free. If you have that sense of responsibility, you can work independently" (NL1, key worker)

Similar comparisons with research undertaken in the US can be made. Certified nursing assistants working in the clients' homes appreciated the flexibility of their work schedules as well as having more time to spend with clients, compared to working in a nursing home (Kopiec, 2000).

Another important inherent facet of work in integrated care was that the job was not considered monotonous (I2) or boring, but varied. Key workers in D1 reported a good working atmosphere in surroundings where new innovative concepts and forms of collaboration could be tried out. Their colleagues from D2 saw their work as diverse, varied and independent and that they were able to make decisions and integrate their own ideas. A key worker from Greece viewed it In the following way:

> "(I like) the fact that despite many years of service I keep learning a lot of new things." (EL1, key worker)

Another specific issue connected with integrated care was the satisfaction gained in relation to providing home care. This was especially the case when an outcome resulted in an older person staying at home rather than having to be admitted to an institution. At the same time however it could result in feeling isolated or unsupported. Staff in the Netherlands, Germany, Greece and Italy described these phenomena and also the risk of working alone in a person's home, which also engendered feelings of dissatisfaction:

> "In our job there is professional loneliness, since we all make decisions on our own" (EL1, key worker)

At the same time integration, communication and joint working could improve professional loneliness. For instance, in France gerontological coordination helped to combat professional loneliness and staff knew "that they are not alone helping the frail elderly" (F1, key worker).

Communication and Teamwork

Communication and teamwork – as mentioned repeatedly within this book – are the core issues in integrated care and one of the key determinants of working conditions and staff satisfaction. It was therefore no surprise that staff interviewed repeatedly mentioned teamwork and networking as important parts of integrated work. Although some aspects in connection with the roles and tasks of a case manager were mentioned above, we will elaborate on this issue in more detail.

Many staff members reported their working atmosphere to be warm and friendly. Austrian and German key workers in both models reported good teamwork with colleagues and managers. This seemed to be especially pertinent regarding communication within the model. External communication with other services is elaborated on in more detail below.

In UK1 staff communicated every day in meetings and informally, while different professionals valued each other's input. They reported good relations between all staff, an 'open door policy', and equality among staff. Connected once more to outcomes, staff felt rewarded in their work and positive in their working environment as this key worker explained:

> "We always discuss things and work together for clients and we can see the results. It means so much when a client comes in unable to walk and leaves walking unaided" (UK1, key worker)

Following on from this quote, one aspect that was seen as important in teamwork was seeing the achievements reached as a team that would not have been possible to attain as an individual:

"As a team we are quite lucky because we can get in and get things done. We can achieve a lot more in our positions than say perhaps a GP or district nurse working on their own. We've got multi-skilled people and we can provide more than just our basic skills, and we have good support networks and resources at our resource." (UK2, key worker)

As mentioned above working together in a multi-disciplinary and multi-professional team was viewed as a very favourable aspect of working in integrated care:

"For me as a physiotherapist it can sometimes be a bit difficult to agree with nurses, occupational therapists or social and health assistants on how the state of a given citizen is progressing, as we all have our own perspectives, opinions and experiences. But the great thing about joint working with citizens with complicated needs for rehabilitation is that it is very inspirational to work with other professions. It offers insights into the situation of the rehabilitant that you otherwise would not have. And when it really works, you get the feeling that you have really gone all the way around the citizen. Because I have my perspective, the citizen adds his perspective and the others have their perspectives, and when they all come together you really get a buzz." (DK2, physiotherapist)

236

Prerequisites for working together successfully across disciplines were a clear and shared language by different professionals and respect, cooperation and equal footing:

"I think everybody is equal. This is the only team I've ever worked for where I've got immense respect for everybody. Although I might be a professional, the rehab workers do just as good a job as I do, and I don't see those boundaries so much." (UK1)

It was also very important to focus on the needs of the users and not on competition between professionals. In A1 the discharge manager stated:

"From the beginning onwards there were absolutely no problems. Not one single ward nurse said that I am taking their work away or that something of their competence is being stolen. My work was taken up very positively by the doctors as well as by the nurses. I liked that. I could develop my work the way I wanted to and it went very well." (A1)

The features of interdisciplinary work that were beneficial to communication within projects were also those which were important in contacts with external collaborators. While there were quite a few positive aspects mentioned in connection with this, external collaboration was also an issue which elicited many negative remarks (see below).

Some key workers had experienced positive contacts with external partners, such as the friendly relationship with the municipal councillor, who helped solve problems, and communicated and cooperated well (EL1), or general good quality collaboration with other services (D2):

> **An important aspect of collaboration with external partners is knowing the partners personally: "(...) but the most important factor is – as I have experienced it – to be able to enter a meeting room and to know the people there."**
> **(D2, key worker)**

Other research has shown that the principles of teamwork include entrusting work performance, coordination and implementation to the workers and providing a commitment to them. Commitment to the work is improved by a common definition of goals, planning, and participation in decision-making. In the team, the duties must be clearly defined: this encompasses collective responsibilities on the one hand and individual responsibility on the other. A good team provides opportunities for workers to develop their different skills and areas of competence (Shonkin, 1994).

4.2 Negative Aspects of Working Conditions

While close contact with users and their families, alongside the large amount of autonomy and variety connected with the work in integrated care were mostly seen positively, the issues of teamwork, communication and joint working have both positive and negative aspects. Negative aspects of working conditions that integrated care workers in the PROCARE models were confronted with were: lack of resources and pressure on time, the 'dark side' of joint working, too many administrative tasks and a lack of infrastructure, especially the kind needed for communication (cell phones, email and so on).

Lack of Resources and Time Contraints

A *lack of resources* was the most often mentioned aspect which impeded the work in our integrated models. This could be a lack of finances, personnel or infrastructure. This lack of resources in the care of older people has been repeatedly stated all over Europe (e.g. Zellhuber, 2003). Lack of financing leads to lack of personnel, which in turn leads to time pressure at work and was a problem specifically mentioned in Greece, Italy and Germany. Also, pressure on time were mentioned many times in our interview material. Only in models in Denmark and the United Kingdom did staff say that they had enough time to spend with their clients (see above). The lack of personnel was seen as being especially grave because care needs were increasing at the same time. A constant lack of resources could also have a frustrating effect on workers:

> "Whenever I came up with a suggestion to improve my work or submitted a report, the management due to lack of resources rejected it." (EL1, key worker)

Generally, it was hard to recruit and retain 'hands-on' key workers in many models. This was for example mentioned in F2 and A1 where it was hard to recruit new people because of low pay and working conditions:

> "It is not only us (Red Cross) that do not have enough personnel in home care: other associations also have this problem. At the moment, we are in the situation where people have to stay in the hospital, because they cannot be cared for at home. That is the current situation on the Viennese market." (A1, manager)

That aside, some models lacked specialised staff due to lack of funds. This was for instance evident in EL1 where additional specialised personnel were needed to provide a service in the afternoons and at weekends. All requests and needs could not be addressed due to lack of time and personnel. In UK2, a lack of specialist staff resulted in a waiting list for some services. The lack of one therapist meant that the service could only take on half the clients it normally would:

> "There are lots of [types of rehabilitation] we could do for specific problems, but there is just no money available." (UK2)

Time constraints and, hence, not having enough time for clients was a particularly disturbing aspect of staffs' work:

> "For us it is difficult to have a good conversation or a chat with our clients and their carers because we have the "five minutes pay system" for our work. But sometimes it's necessary to talk a little bit longer with the clients, but they then ask: Do I have to pay for that?" (A2, key worker)

> "Because of time constraints, you can't be as patient as you would like to be. When several telephones ring and several clients stand in front of the door, you tend to lose your patience." (A1, social worker)

Staff in the two Dutch models did not usually experience time constraints, except when colleagues were ill or on holiday. This meant that the remaining staff had to take over their work, so only essential care could be carried out with no time to chat to clients. Staff regretted the heavy workloads and stress in these periods as well as the fact that they had too little personal contact with colleagues.

Lack of time and constraints on time are not phenomena to be found specifically in integrated care, they are also present in other types of care for older people and caring environments (Zimber et al., 2000).

Lack of Role Clarity and Communication Difficulties

One aspect of negative working conditions was a certain confusion that some key workers felt about their work in integrated care. They felt they lacked clarity about what was operationally meant by integrated care, for example how they were actually supposed to go about "joint working". It is interesting that workers were able to define what they understood by integrated care in chapter 1, but the actual detail of how to carry it out was less tangible here:

> "No formal joint working, workers operate by themselves."
> (EL1, key worker)

Staff members in Austria, Denmark, Greece and Italy mentioned that much of their work depended on informal communication and in some cases they missed systematic opportunities for cooperating with each other (see also above):

> "The problem is that the area of rehabilitation has grown enormously over the past decade so a lot of informal procedures have evolved, and this means that a lot of knowledge is tied to certain people and not written into more formal procedures. This can make it difficult for new employees to find their way around the general organisation of older people's care or in the relationship with the hospitals." (DK1, key worker)

While internal communication was mostly seen as positive, as mentioned above, external communication with other services could be problematic:

> "Communication and collaboration with other services is difficult, meetings do not take place regularly." (D2)

There was also a lack of coordination between KAPI and other institutions (EL) as well as a lack of transfer of medical information between the hospital and rehabilitation centre (UK1). In D1 distrust and old-fashioned structures impaired collaboration with other services and thus made life difficult for staff members.

The *position of medical doctors* was discussed in many models (see also chapter 3), and in our analysis it seemed to be connected to status and difficulties with collaboration. In one Italian model, doctors' attitudes were seen

239

as a problem (I1), while in Finland (FIN1) a lack of doctors was noted. Key workers in the UK found it hard to rely on GPs who did not refer patients to them and found a lack of communication with external agencies, such as GPs or community care managers.

Key workers in A2 had made an effort over the years to improve co-operation with GPs. It was a long process of talking to them and explaining their roles, but they felt they had made improvements:

> "The cooperation with the general practitioners is much better then 3 or 6 years ago. Some are really interested in our work. We always try to contact our clients' GPs." (A2, key workers)

The Burden of Administrative Duties and Extra Roles

Staff in several models mentioned that they found they had too many clerical and administrative tasks, combined with a lack of support and lack of infrastructure. Staff felt that this took time away from clients:

> "You have too little time for the patients, and too much administration." (A1, discharge manager)

> "The five minute reports are traditional but now the stress is more intensive. We have more administrative work, but not more time for it." (A2, key workers)

In one of the models in Denmark (DK1) training plans were introduced which involved a great deal of documentation, and this raised fears:

> "This project – the training plan – has taken a lot of time. The time it takes to fill in the forms takes time from our time with the users. (...) In my view, the training-plans are not for the immediate benefit of the rehabilitants and it is not for the benefit of the practicing therapist." (DK1, key worker)

In Greece and the UK some staff members had to carry out tasks that they were not trained for. These were for example prescribing drugs when the doctor was absent or doing certain types of paper work:

> "We're not actually doing our job as we should be doing it, because its taking longer to put everything into place before we can actually do what we are employed to do." (UK1)

Lack of Infrastructure

Too many administrative tasks could also be connected with a lack of technical equipment, which would help communication. In NL2 and A2, staff did not have cell phones at their disposal and had to use their private phones. The discharge manager in A2 did not have access to email:

> **"Often it is quite difficult, you try to call someone but the line is busy. Then you call the next person. One has 4-5 people that are discharged at the same time. It is always hard not to forget somebody. If I could email it, it would be finished immediately." (A1, discharge manager)**

In several models there was a lack of access to electronic data (D1). In A1, access to the municipalitie's client database could have eased staff's work considerably. In I2, the integrated system, especially in this experimental phase, was very slow. Furthermore there was little time to input data into the computer, when staff were busy carrying out the interventions. Now the situation is slowly improving because more computers are being made available. Both Greek models did not have a computer system, although initiatives are being taken to improve this situation in connection with training for staff.

It must be acknowledged that communication technology is important in a job that has communication as its main feature. Thus, it is crucial to provide conditions where staff are able to spend enough time with users.

5   Conclusions

When looking at the working conditions of staff in the PROCARE models of integrated care, it becomes clear that many of the working conditions encountered are not only in line with working conditions in care of older people, but also in health care in general. However, some aspects of working conditions are especially pronounced for staff in integrated care.

Working conditions that were found here and correspond to those in care of older people in general are: low pay, no clear opportunities for career advancement, lack of systematic further education, a general lack of resources and time pressure among staff (Harris-Kojetin et al., 2004; Frerichs et al., 2004; Roche/Rankin, 2004).

Specificities of working conditions in integrated care (Wendt, 2001) are as follows. Firstly, there are a wide variety of different professions involved; staff from one profession may carry out different tasks and other times different professions will be carrying out very similar tasks. Secondly, we see that case managers have different professional backgrounds, mostly as a nurse or social worker, but in some cases as doctors. Despite the central role case managers play in integrated care, there does not appear to be specialist education for this role. Thirdly, while communication and teamwork is an important basis for all health and care work, it has a crucial meaning in integrated care. Successful communication and joint working is on the one hand an important outcome of integrated care, but at the same time a prerequisite for it, which is strongly connected to the satisfaction of staff and clients. Lastly, we find that staff members who are working closely together might be working for different employers, having different contracts, with implications on salaries and ultimately working relations.

In summary, those working conditions that foster integrated care are

- staff motivation and satisfaction,
- support by an open-minded positive management that involves staff in problem-solving,
- equality between employees and working as a team,
- regular open team meetings to discuss client cases,
- shared information,
- the interest of staff and the organisation in the well-being of clients,
- high level of staff education along with a favourable attitude towards training and education,
- accessibility of staff to each other (e.g. shared offices, phones).

Those that impede integrated care are:

- lack of resources: funding, personnel, time, training,
- physical, geographical distance (e.g. no personal communication),
- working for many different institutions and providers,
- structural differences (different wages, terms and conditions, employment contracts),
- lack of help with administration,
- lack of infrastructure.

As known from the area of care for older people (Zellhuber, 2003; Zimber et al., 2000), it becomes clear here again that this area of work has low extrinsic motivational factors (low pay, limited career opportunities, sometimes uncertain contracts) and high intrinsic motivational factors (work with older people, patients, feeling valued by them, finding pride in own work, high work autonomy). From this it follows that organisations need to balance the intrinsic and extrinsic rewards that workers get and make an extra effort to retain and reward workers.

It becomes clear that in integrated care there is such a wide variety of professional tasks as well as professions involved that the professional boundaries and tasks are not always clear. From this it follows that work at the interface of health and social provision requires an enormous amount of flexibility from the organisation as well as the staff. This is one of the great challenges for people working in this field. A prerequisite for this is a management approach that is open to change. Also, support by and cooperation through the management of involved institutions is a very important factor that supports the provision of integrated care.

Our research also showed the important role the care staff and case managers felt they had in achieving success. We saw how much informal initiatives, workers' motivation and 'sensibility' contributed to integrated care. In many cases, user and carer satisfaction were not only related to the service, but to single key workers. This put pressure on the workers themselves, but is also a message to services to keep staff turnover at bay and provide working conditions that promote satisfaction and motivation.

Also, it became clear that communication and mutual respect as well as good teamwork were very important to secure integrated care provision. In many cases a formal framework for teamwork existed. However, in other cases informal communication and personal initiatives of staff were still the basis for working together. Providers of integrated care should examine where more formal and systematic forms of communication are needed and make improvements accordingly.

A prominent issue that has the potential to create dissent among teams and integrated care services relates to the structural differences among staff. This includes different wages and employment contracts or different employers of staff who are working together. This can – but does not have to – be a factor that hampers integrated care provision. Thus, in integrated services it is very important to examine how to deal with differences that come about from staff having different contracts and / or employers.

Many of the problems connected with working conditions that have been elicited here are problems connected to implementing improvements into practice. Managed organisational change is the key to successful implementation and should be put on the policy agenda with respect to integrated care. An important task for integrated care providers is to balance the intrinsic and extrinsic rewards of their staff and to put an effort into retaining and rewarding workers, and developing specific inter-agency education and training to take integrated care forward.

Elements for Successful Integration Processes in Long-Term Care Services
Some Concluding Remarks

Jenny Billings, Kai Leichsenring, Nasrin Tabibian

1 General Recommendations

The efforts made in the selected countries to tackle evident problems at the interfaces between health and social care systems reveal much about the state of the art in developing long-term care systems. At the same time, these efforts – usually in the form of model projects – are dependent on the existing cultural, professional and social policy traditions in the respective country or even in the respective region only.

Our reflections thus have led to the conclusion that there cannot be a 'ranking' of the different models, neither can we provide general 'recipes' for integrating care services. The analysis, however, was able to supply what we have called 'elements for successful integration processes' in relation to some key features in long-term care provision that we would like to sum up in the following.

1.1 *General Framework Conditions and Financing*

First of all, it seems obvious that administrative and financial structures that are able to bring about change processes are needed to set up the general rules and the respective share of public resources that democratically governed societies decide to dedicate to long-term care. Should it be almost 3% of the GDP financed from general taxes as in Denmark, or would it be more sustainable to install a long-term care insurance financed by social insurance contributions? In the end, this political decision should consider that the closer health and social affairs are connected to the administrative level the easier it seems to start coordinating and integrating processes. As long as health reforms are made without considering the imminent developments in long-term care, we should abstain from speaking of coordination or integration. All the time that no real joint funding can be established, long-term care systems remain virtual and without a major impact on the sustainability of health and social security financing.

Most PROCARE model ways of working are projects depending on vulnerable funding sources. In some cases even positive evaluation studies did not help to turn model projects into mainstream services. The only 'consolidated direct service model' which was analysed demonstrates that, apart from positive framework conditions that invest in innovative approaches, long-term funding and organisational development are necessary to achieve a sustainable impact. The small Danish municipality of Skævinge has invested in its 'Health Centre Bauneparken' since 1984 and has achieved positive outcomes. Even though the number of older people has increased significantly over the past 20 years, the operational expenditures have decreased over the period due to the preventative focus of the integrated care scheme. There is no waiting time for apartments in the Health Centre or for domestic health and social care services; the preventative efforts have resulted in a surplus of capacity that has been used mainly to establish an intermediate care facility at the Health Centre in order to prevent unnecessary hospital admissions. Consequently, the number of days in hospitals has been reduced by 30-40% for all citizens in the municipality. Over the last 10 years no citizen from the municipality staying in a hospital has had to wait for discharge after having finished treatment, as those citizens are cared for either in the intermediate care facility at the Health Centre or in the citizens' own home. The municipality's use of and expenditure to national health insurance is below the average of all other municipalities in its county.

1.2 Defining Clear Objectives

It is suggested that a common understanding of integrated care between multi-professional staff is vital to prevent barriers to unification and quality of care. The PROCARE data provided a good opportunity to examine the extent of shared understandings across countries and to put forward an interpretation of what is meant by integrated care from a staff perspective. The data suggested that a common and interrelated European interpretation was possible across different contexts and environments, but that these definitions were somewhat idealised and moralistic. What was clear was that staff signalled challenges to its implementation that were inseparable from the rhetoric. The data suggested that a collective, morally strong understanding is unable to prevent barriers to integrated care and that tensions between services remain a prominent impediment, and this is reflected throughout the PROCARE analysis.

From the PROCARE model ways of working we were able to confirm however, that frontline staff are firmly connected towards client-orientation and towards a process of coordination and integration of different services, independently of welfare regimes and traditions. Successful coordination can thus be found by looking at the following indicators:

- A common understanding of what integrated care provision is there to achieve. It seems useful to involve different stakeholders from the very beginning in the definition of objectives, procedures, target groups and rules of working.
- In particular, the definition of 'client-orientation' and its meanings for daily work (e.g. seamless functioning of service provision, considering the client and his/her family as a resource) should be part of a constant exchange and adaptation.

Thinking in terms of quality management is useful in developing integrated care delivery. A clear statement concerning visions, objectives and strategies for their achievement foster a shared communication basis within the organisation, between organisations and between providers and users/clients. Working towards coordination and integration thus means also to work towards this common understanding among all stakeholders.

1.3 Regulating Access and Assessing Individual Needs

Needs assessment is one of the most crucial and initial steps in the provision of integrated care. Integrated care cannot be person-centred if demand follows only the given supply structure of services. PROCARE model ways of working assess clients' needs based on a commonly used method, using the same language to draft an individual care plan mutually agreed between all professionals, the client and his/her family.

Quality indicators for this procedure include the existence of a multi-professional and multi-dimensional needs assessment; multi-professional, so that the need to protect privileges and status of a professional group does not dominate and affect the outcome of needs assessment; multi-dimensional so that all life domains of the user are taken into consideration.

The gathering, using, sharing and storing of information are major issues in coordinating and integrating care service provision. The use of Information Technology (IT) and instruments such as individualised care plans can facilitate the flow and process of sharing information among professionals.

Users' knowledge of long-term care facilities is generally quite weak. Yet a paradox exists when information for users and their family carers is needed to be able to make the right choices in the complicated realm of long-term care, and to make sure they receive the right type of care suited to their specific needs throughout the care process. Single points of access with respective (independent) counselling are an important prerequisite to integrated care delivery.

Empowerment in this context means, however, to prevent users from becoming overwhelmed by the multitude of services and complexity of procedures and the data did reveal the disempowering nature of information neglect. A simple and manageable access procedure also paves the way for collaboration between different disciplines. In summary, access procedures should be *comprehensive* to cover the users' needs in various life domains, *understandable and negotiable* for the users and *manageable* for the professionals.

1.4 Promoting Joint Working

Joint working is the foundation of integrated care in practice yet harmony in this area continues to be fragile and sometimes elusive. Several barriers need to be overcome to make joint working a success among mixed professional groups, such as medical, socio-medical and social professionals. These barriers create cultural cleavages among professionals, but also structural (divisions among organisations), procedural (related to planning and information flow), and hierarchical divisions. Differences in the educational status and working conditions of various professional groups are impeding collaboration. In addition, different financing and policies in health and social care further interfere with cooperation. Despite these divides there are signs of improvement, with a strong desire to succeed running alongside a recognition of the difficulties. Elements of success in joint working evident within the PROCARE model ways of working can be summarised as follows:

- Where different staff groups share the same premises and are able to communicate informally, networks with clients develop and integral features of interdisciplinary working, such as 'shared cultures' and 'blurring of professional boundaries' are evident.
- Daily or weekly meetings or 'individual case conferences' foster better interpersonal relationships in a professional setting and can help staff acknowledge individual skills.
- Active management support for joint working and training, e.g. 'in-house' workshops helps overcome initial scepticism and increase the mutual 'belief' in the model and its goals.
- Allowing enough time for the 'integration process' to be managed is the key investment in the process of mutual understanding: shared meetings, travel, team development, contacts and jointly-agreed protocols and strategies are only some examples that, initially, take a lot of time but eventually will turn out as major asset in terms of job satisfaction and performance.
- A 'special group' in integrated care is represented by General Practitioners who have a potentially decisive role in guiding and supporting those in need of long-term care. However, their education, approach, cultural differences and working conditions usually do not allow them to act as 'case managers' or coordinators of care processes. Better communication and further incorporation of GPs in the care process could nevertheless be strengthened.

1.5 Making Use of Key Innovations

PROCARE model ways of working are applying a broad range of methods and instruments to improve networking, coordination and integration. These primarily aim at improving communication, joint working and quality management. Furthermore, organisational development approaches are gaining ground in many countries. Tools for use with the client are without doubt vital to promote individualised care and logical in order to identify needs, and are in widespread use. However, there is a long-standing problem attached to the user's true experience and understanding of the process. This may in part be due to the different levels of importance and expectation attached to the process from the professionals' viewpoint, and the inherent difficulties older people have in being able to engage in the process.

Organisational solutions for integrating care services include the creation of multi-professional teams for needs assessment and/or for the entire care process.

- To improve cooperation in teams it is necessary to organise regular meetings among professionals, to draft written procedures and forms (e.g. 'discharge forms'), to define roles and processes and thus to set up a quality management system in order to develop and monitor mutually agreed objectives, procedures and outcomes.
- Joint training sessions, seminars and conferences can improve inter- and intra-organisational learning and facilitate the exchange of experiences among the various groups of professionals.
- Another innovative solution is the already mentioned use of IT, in the form of a common database to ensure the flow and exchange of information and to improve communication among professionals, becoming established in Italy.

In some European countries, case management has emerged as one of the most important ways of coordinating health and social care services. Though case management in itself has many facets and is defined in different ways (e.g. in some countries: care manager), a common approach is to give a single professional the responsibility of managing the entire care process.

Those PROCARE model ways of working that applied case management have witnessed this method as being an impressive and effective tool for realising coordinated service delivery. Still, case management has only been applied as a mainstream service in a few countries. As the case manager covers a crucial professional role, the introduction of case management may be defined as a decisive step on the pathway towards integrated long-term care provision – respective education and training designs have to be defined to promote this new job profile and to develop skills of staff both in health care and in social care settings.

In this context it should be noted that innovations concerning monitoring and evaluation of outcomes at the client level are still scarce or, if existing at all, hardly used.

1.6   Considering the Role of Family as Caregiver

Even in the most developed welfare states, female family members mainly provide for the bulk of long-term care tasks. This dependency upon family members goes beyond what might be considered tradition, duty or moral obligation, as it would simply not be feasible to 'professionalise' all caring tasks in society. Cooperation between formal and informal caregivers is therefore a decisive factor in integrating care delivery:

- First of all, social, health and family policies are in place to acknowledge and remunerate the input of family carers on a national level.
- Secondly, responsible policy-makers at the regional and local levels should encourage and support the development of high-quality services and include informal carers.

At the interactive level, it is clear that the importance of information exchange about needs and services, and guidance in accessing these services remains paramount to meeting individual user and carer requirements. To this end, some of the PROCARE model ways of working have specialised in providing quick and comprehensive information based on pooled social and health care information supported by IT applications. Moreover, integrating family carers in PROCARE model ways of working goes beyond the access process and possible choices between providers and services. In particular, their involvement in the assessment of needs and the individual care planning is vital. All too often, however, there is a continued mismatch between the responsibilities and expectations of the family and state intervention at all levels and within a variety of contexts. What integrated care is there to achieve was not widely understood by individuals, and this was sometimes compounded by a professional 'distancing'. These factors appear to contribute towards an increased burden on informal carers. Satisfaction was expressed where time and money was invested to inform and understand users and family carers.

Without doubt, the findings from the data indicate that family care should remain an area of major attention in relation to the development of carers' rights and entitlements, counselling, choices and respite services. Non-governmental organisations (NGOs) and advocacy groups should be encouraged to take more responsibility for meeting some of these conditions.

1.7   Basing Decisions on User's Needs

The difficulties of involving people in their care are evident. What is also clear is that more effective ways of realising greater user and carer participation in the decision-making process of integrated care must be attained to truly meet the living needs of the client. In addition to this, a complex range of generational and cultural obstacles are to be overcome in order for aspirational workers to truly meet the professional quest of 'client-centredness', a term much referred to in this research.

Through a comparison of the life world and systems world perspectives, we can see that providers of services and clients are not always able to share the same aims. Though 'client-centredness' can be found in most service-charters in addition to the workers' own understanding, it remains difficult to reconcile the client's long-term care expectations with the organisational requirements of personal services, so as to always guarantee the same personal carer throughout the whole year. A comparison of the views of professionals and users/family carers on the issue of integrated care and of their opinion on its success shows differences in the way in which these two groups perceive the outcomes and success of care. While professionals predominantly concentrate on procedural and organisational aspects (system world perspective), the users and their informal carers judge the results more from a life world perspective. To ensure the quality of care as perceived by the users, policy-makers and practitioners should emphasise the continuity and flexibility of services and workers, personal attention and home visits, affordable services and attention to social as well as health needs. This latter point means that care should be organised in such a way as to ensure the continuation of social contacts with family members or friends and participation in activities in the local community.

While data was not plentiful, we were able to ascertain that what matters to users and carers is to receive the right type of care, to the right amount and at the right time. To make this possible, they need to be fully involved in the decision-making processes relating to needs assessment and choice of service provision.

Linked to this is the concept of empowerment of users and carers, which begs attention in both policy and practice of integrated care. This concept takes into account the changing status and position of the service users and carers and recommends the following aims: sustaining autonomy and functionality of the older people, maintaining or regaining their self-respect, providing sufficient and accessible information and economical options to regulate the service use. Service providers thus have to improve their communication skills and the ways in which they assess, monitor and evaluate their performance. Yet most model ways of working have shown difficulties with respect to these aspects of integrated care provision.

253

1.8 Elaborating on Specific Working Conditions in Long-Term Care

It is well-known that working conditions in long-term care are perhaps the most demanding yet at the same time less rewarding: jobs are often relatively badly paid, do not offer opportunities for career advancement; they are characterized by a lack of systematic further education, a general lack of resources and time pressure among staff. Notwithstanding the deficiencies in these extrinsic motivational factors, many of which are mirrored in the PROCARE model ways of working, professionals working in the models generally seem to be enthusiastic about their work: they are needed by and relied on by older people, they feel valued by them, find pride in their work and enjoy high work autonomy. These intrinsic motivational factors seem to have an impact on the way professionals view the shortcomings in their working conditions.

- To make integrated care work, managers need to take both extrinsic and intrinsic motivational factors into consideration and create conditions to satisfy both. Approaching different working cultures is not an easy task but forms a prerequisite for the process of integrated care.
- Joint training of different professionals within and between organisations appears to be an effective instrument in promoting communication, understanding and shared knowledge.

- Special attention should be placed on managing organisational change as the key to successful implementation of change processes to create more integrated care systems.
- Connected to this, the imminent labour shortages in long-term care call for a quick and effective upgrading of labour conditions in the whole sector. The dissemination of case management skills should be part of such a programme.
- Model ways of working have shown that a mix of different skills and a clear job definition are key. Rather than charging only health care staff with case management tasks, different professions should be trained to become case managers.

Any strategies to face challenges concerning labour shortages should be aware of the fact that integrating health and social care services does not only have a positive effect on clients but also helps raise the image, the content and the perseverance of staff in long-term care services.

2 Research Recommendations

We cannot stress enough the important role of the EU in supporting any research on ageing as realised in FP5. Unfortunately, in FP6 (2002-2006) research on ageing is almost absent. However, there still is a knowledge gap in the area of care of older people and therefore research in this area should be intensified, in particular as social policy priorities today are geared towards developing care systems for older people which safeguard the quality of life for this target group.

Research and development strategies are to support policies that tend to construct long-term care systems based on coordination, integration and user-orientation. In this area, and notwithstanding interesting results of cross-national research in FP5, social sciences are still far from having solutions for all features. This is mostly due to the fact that departmentalisation, specialisation and uncoordinated research strategies are simply a part of the problem as the social/health divide is reproduced in the existing social science system. Interdisciplinary research thus has to be developed to inform on the following issues related to the construction of integrated long-term care systems (see also Nies, 2004):

- instruments and strategies to overcome the 'social and health divide'

- to identify and present expenses, costs and potential future developments at the national, regional and local level
- to study the effects of decentralisation, privatisation and 'quasi-markets' on integrated care delivery
- to analyse issues concerning the integration of immigrants in integrated care systems both as professionals and as clients, and to analyse migration dynamics and participation of migrants in formal and informal care settings
- to develop strategies around how knowledge and evidence produced in model projects could be translated in mainstream policy-making
- to analyse different 'cultures of care', in particular the role of the family, in Europe
- to develop indicators for defining the target group for integrated care
- to do further research on groups with special needs in complex situations such as, for instance, people suffering from dementia
- to analyse 'learning organisations' in integrated care
- to identify the (social) costs of long-term care and potential gains by integrated care delivery
- to search for potentials of inter-regional coordination
- to overcome departmentalisation and specialisation
- to investigate labour force and qualifications needed in integrated care delivery
- to look for models of support for and empowerment of carers, e.g. concerning short- and long-term effects of different methods of support for family carers
- to look for partnerships and potential applications of new technologies in integrated care, in particular with respect to integrated information systems
- to further develop comparability in order to show financial evidence and outcome potentials of model ways of working
- to compare experiences trans-nationally (also by using knowledge produced in FP5 projects), e.g. by further exchange during seminars of similar projects within the Commission's Framework Programmes. Through the various projects (as, for example, OASIS, CARMEN, PROCARE, EUROFAMCARE) a stock of good practices has been developed and exchange of information should be enhanced to create synergies between research and policy-making.

255

Final Remark

In relation to the much more differentiated health system or other areas of social services, the development of long-term care systems is still at an early stage. However, the construction of legal regulations, services and institutions that cater for the special needs of older people suffering from chronic diseases, disabilities or other dependency problems is an ongoing process. Due to the rising demand of such services this process is speeding up, producing new visions and ideas for improvement.

Coordinating or even integrating the various services and stakeholders involved in long-term care delivery seems to be the most logical idea if one considers the complex needs in long-term care. Of course, a wealth of medical knowledge is now influencing the sector, but more and more specific knowledge in social gerontology, social work, psychology and a whole range of various therapeutic approaches are gaining ground. Apart from this important professional differentiation, we also witness a steady institutional change in long-term care with respect to the various forms in which help is provided. This includes organisational settings such as the increasing development of private commercial and non-profit providers that are complementing general public services. In this situation, future political debates and decisions will entail the crucial question who should coordinate with whom, with what means and based on whose rules. If we are to integrate different services towards a 'consolidated' long-term care provision it will be necessary to promote open dialogues on leadership in integrated services, on shared visions between providers and purchasers as well as on opportunities to involve users and carers in service development.

References

Adams, Robert (1996) *Social Work and Empowerment*. Basingstoke, Hampshire and London: Macmillan Press, Houndmills.

Alaszewski, A. / Billings, J. / Coxon, K. (2004) 'Integrated Health and Social Care for Older Persons: Theoretical and Conceptual Issues', pp. 53-94 in: Leichsenring, K. / Alaszewski, A. (eds.), *Providing Integrated Health and Social Care for Older Persons. A European Overview of Issues at Stake*. Aldershot: Ashgate.

Alber, J. (1995) 'A Framework for the Comparative Study of Social Services', *Journal of European Social Policy* 5 (2): 131-149.

Andersson, G. / Karlberg, I. (2000) 'Integrated Care for the Elderly. The Background and Effects of the Reform of Swedish Care of the Elderly', *International Journal of Integrated Care*, Vol. 0 / November (http: / / www.ijic.org).

Badelt, Ch. / Leichsenring, K. (1998) *Analyse und mögliche Neustrukturierung der Sozialausbildungen in Österreich*. Wien: Bundesministerium für Wissenschaft und Verkehr / Bundesministerium für Unterricht und kulturelle Angelegenheiten.

Badelt, C. / Holzmann, A. / Matul, C. / Österle, A. (1997) *Analyse der Auswirkungen des Pflegevorsorgesystems*. Wien: Bundesministerium für Arbeit, Gesundheit und Soziales.

Bahr, C. / Leichsenring, K. (1996) *"leben und pflegen" – Beratung und Koordination im Sozialsprengel. Evaluationsstudie*. Wien: European Centre.

Baldwin, S. (ed.) (1998) *Needs Assessment and Community Care: Clinical Practice and Policy Making*. London: Butterworth-Heinemann.

Baldwin, S. / Woods, P.A. (1995) 'Case Management and Needs Assessment: Some Issues of Concern for the Caring Professions', *Journal of Mental Health* 3: 311-322.

Ballew, J.R. / Mink, G. (1991) 'Was ist case management?', pp. 56-83 in: Wendt, W.R. (Hg.) *Unterstützung fallweise: Case management in der Sozialarbeit*. Freiburg im Breisgau: Lambertus.

Barr, O. (1996) 'A Consideration of the Nature of "Needs-Led Service" within Care Management in the UK', *Online Journal of Issues in Nursing* (http: / / www.nursingworld.org / ojin /).

Bartlett, Helen P. (1999) 'Primary Health Care for Older People: Progress towards an Integrated Strategy?', *Health & Social Care in the Community* 7 (5): 342-349.

Beresford, Peter (1997) 'Empowerment Must Be a Two-way Process', *Care Plan* 4 (2), December: 26-28.

Beresford, Peter / Croft, Suzy / Evans, Clare / Harding, Tessa (1997) 'Quality in Personal Social Services: The Developing Role of User Involvement in the UK', in: Evers, Adalbert / Haverinen, Riitta / Leichsenring, Kai / Wistow, Gerald (eds.), *Developing Quality in Personal Social Services. Concepts, Cases and Comments*. Aldershot: Ashgate.

Berger, Peter L./Luckmann, Thomas (1996) *Todellisuuden sosiaalinen rakentuminen* (The Social Construction of Reality). Helsinki: Gaudeamus.

Bertin, G. (a cura di) (2002) *Accreditamento e regolazione dei servizi sociali*. Padova: emme&erre libri.

Billings J./Alaszewski A.M./Coxon K. (2004) 'Integrated Health and Social Care for Older Persons: Theoretical and Conceptual Issues, in: Leichsenring, K./Alaszewski, A.M. (eds.), *Providing Integrated Health and Social Care for Older Persons. A European Overview of Issues at Stake*. Aldershot: Ashgate.

Billings, J./Coxon, K./Alaszewski, A.M. (2003) *Empirical Research Methodology for PROCARE Research Version 3*. Canterbury: Centre for Health Service Studies, University of Kent, UK.

Blinkert, B./Klie, Th. (2000) 'Pflegekulturelle Orientierungen und soziale Milieus. Ergebnisse einer Untersuchung über die sozialstrukturelle Verankerung der Solidarität', *Sozialer Fortschritt* 10: 237-245.

Block, S./Skrobacz, W. (2002) 'In Dialog treten: Dienstleistungen vernetzen. Hilfen effektiver und effizienter anbieten', *Häusliche Pflege* 3: 21-24.

Bloor, G./Dawson, P. (1994) 'Understanding Professional Culture in Organizational Context', *Organization Studies* 15 (2).

Boessenecker, K.-H./Trube, A./Wohlfahrt, N. (Hg.) (2000) *Privatisierung im Sozialsektor. Rahmenbedingungen, Verlaufsformen und Probleme der Ausgliederung sozialer Dienste*. Münster: Votum Verlag.

Broome, A. (1982) *Managing Change*. London: MacMillan Press (Essentials of Nursing Management).

Brown, Louise/Domokos, Teresa/Tucker, Christine (2003) 'Evaluating the Impact of Integrated Health and Social Care Teams on Older People Living in the Community', *Health and Social Care in the Community* 11 (2): 85-94.

Buijssen, H. (1996) *Die Beratung von pflegenden Angehörigen*. Weinheim: Beltz Psychologie Verlags Union.

Bundesministerium für Familie, Senioren, Frauen und Jugend (BMFSFJ) (2000) *Case Management – Erfahrungen aus neun Ländern: Materialband und Workshop-Diskussion*. Köln: Kohlhammer.

Bundesministerium für Familie, Senioren, Frauen und Jugend (BMFSFJ) (Ed.) (2002) *Fourth Report on the Situation of the Elderly Generation*. Berlin: BMFSFJ.

Burda, D. (1992) 'Seamless Delivery', *Modern Healthcare* 19: 38-42.

Burnside, I./Preski, S./Hertz, JE. (1998) 'Research Instrumentation and Elderly Subjects', *Image: Journal of Nursing Scholarship* 30 (2): 185-190.

Bytheway, B. (1995) *Ageism*. Buckingham: Open University Press.

Carpenter, GI./Field, Janet/Challis, DJ./Calnan, M./Swift, C. (2001) *Routine Use of a Standardised Assessment Instrument for Measuring the Outcome of Social Care*. Final report. CHSS/DoH.

Carpenter, John/Schneider, Justine/Brandon, Toby/Wooff, David (2003) 'Working in Multidisciplinary Community Mental Health Teams: The Impact on Social Workers and Health Professionals of Integrated Mental Health Care', *The British Journal of Social Work* 33 (8): 1081-1103.

Carpenter, John/Schneider, Justine/McNiven, Faye/Brandon, Toby/Stevens, Richard/Wooff, David (2004) 'Integration and Targeting of Community Care for People with Severe and Enduring Mental Health Problems: Users' Experiences of the Care Programme Approach and Care Management', *The British Journal of Social Work* 34 (3): 313-333.

Challis, D. et al. (eds.) (2002) *Care Management in Social and Primary Health Care: the Gateshead Community Care Scheme*. Aldershot: Ashgate.

Challis, D./Darton, R./Johnson, L./Stone, M./Traske, K. (1995) *Care Manangement and Health Care of Older People PSSRU*. University of Kent: Arena Publications.

Chevannes, M. (2002) 'Social Construction of the Managerialism of Needs Assessment by Health and Social Care Professionals', *Health & Social Care in the Community* 10 (3): 168-178.

Cichon, M./Jesse, A./Pal, K. (1998) 'Preparing for Ageing Societies? An Attempt to Evaluate Pension and Long-term Care Reforms in Europe', pp. 23-58 in: ISSA (ed.), *Social Security Documentation*. European Series, No. 26.

Colmorten, E. et al. (2003) *The Elderly Needs Help: Who Should Provide It?* Copenhagen: AKF-forlaget.

Colmorten, E./Clausen, T./Bengtsson, S. (2004) 'Providing Integrated Health and Social Care for Older Persons in Denmark', pp. 139-180 in: Leichsenring, K./Alaszewski, A. M. (eds.), *Providing Integrated Health and Social Care for Older Persons*. Aldershot: Ashgate.

Comas-Herrera, A./Wittenberg, R. (eds) (2003) *European Study of Long-Term Care Expenditure: Investigating the Sensitivity of Projections of Future Long-term Care Expenditure in Germany, Spain, Italy and the United Kingdom to Changes in Assumptions about Demography, Dependency, Informal Care, Formal Care and Unit Costs*. Report to the European Commission. Brussels: DG Employment and Social Affairs.

Commonwealth Fund (2004) *First Report and Recommendations of the Commonwealth Fund's International Working Group on Quality Indicators*. June 2004-08-31.

Congreskrant OL2000 (2002) *Denken en werken vanuit de burger*. Den Haag: Overheidsloket.

Cook, D./Brower, R./Cooper, J./Brochard, L./Vincent, J. (2002) 'Multicentre Clinical Research in Adult Critical Care', *Critical Care Medicine* 30 (7): 1636-1643.

Cornes, M.L./Clough, R. (1999) *"Trailblazers and Trouble shooters" – Report of External Evaluation of Four Intermediate Community Care Projects in Cumbria*. Lancaster University.

Coxon, K./Billings, J./Alaszewski, A. (2004) 'Providing Integrated Health and Social Care for Older Persons in the United Kingdom', pp. 455-498 in: Leichsenring, K./Alaszewski, A. M. (eds.), *Providing Integrated Health and Social Care for Older Persons*. Aldershot: Ashgate.

Daatland, S.O./Herlofson, K. (eds.) (2001) *Ageing, Intergenerational Relations, Care Systems and Quality of Life – An Introduction to the OASIS Project*. Oslo: NOVA.

Davies, B. (1992) *Care Management, Equity and Efficiency: The International Experience*. Kent: University of Kent at Canterbury/PSSRU.

Davies, Bleddyn (1993) 'Caring for the Frail Elderly: An International Perspective', *Generations*, Winter.

Davies, B.P./Fernandez, J.L./Nomer, B. (2000) *Equity and Efficiency Policy in Community Care: Needs, Service Productivities, Efficiencies and Their Implications*. Aldershot: Ashgate.

Davies, Brian/Knapp, Martin (1981) *Old Peoples´s Homes and the Production of Welfare*. London: Routledge & Keagan.

de Klerk, M.Y. (ed.) (2000) *Rapportage gehandicapten 2000*. Den Haag: Sociaal en Cultureel Planbureau.

Deacon, A. (2002) *Perspectives on Welfare. Ideas, Ideologies and Policy Debates*. Buckingham: Open University Press.

Delnoij, D./Klazinga, N./Glasgow, I.K. (2002) 'Integrated Care in an International Perspective: EUPHA Proceedings December 2001', *International Journal of Integrated Care* 2 (http://www.ijic.org/cgi-bin/pw.cgi/2002-3/000122/article_content.htm).

Denton, M. (1997) 'The Linkages between Informal and Formal Care of the Elderly', *Canadian Journal on Aging* 16: 30-50.

Department of Health (2000) *The NHS Plan: A Plan for Investment. A Plan for Reform*. London: Department of Health.

Department of Health (2001a) *Older People: National Service Framework of Older People*. London: Department of Health.

Diözesan-Caritasverband für das Erzbistum Köln e.V. (Hg.) (2003) *Zur Lebenslage pflegender Angehöriger psychisch kranker alter Menschen*. Münster: Lit-Verlag.

Ditch, J./Bradshaw, J./Eardley, T. (1994) 'Care and Family Obligations', in: European Observatory on National Family Policies (ed.), *Developments in National Family Policies*. York: University of York/Social Policy Research Unit.

Donabedian, A. (1980) *The Definition of Quality and Approaches to Its Assessment*. Ann Arbor, MI: Health Administration Press.

Dutheil, N. (2001) 'Les aides et les aidants des personnes âgées', *Etudes et résultats* 142.

Dwyer, Peter (2000) *Welfare Rights and Responsibilities*. Bristol: Polity Press.

Economic Policy Committee (2001) Budgetary Challenges Posed by Ageing Population. Retrieved from http://europa.eu.int/comm/economy_finance/publications/european_economy/reportsandstudies0401_en.htm.

Emke-Poulopoulou, I. (1999) *Greek Old Citizens, Past, Present and Future*. Athens: Ellin.

Eng, C./Pedulla, J./Eleazer, G. P./McCann, R./Fox, N. (1997) Program of All-inclusive Care for the Elderly (PACE): An Innovative Model of Integrated Geriatric Care and Financing, *Journal of the American Geriatrics Society* 45 (2) Feb: 223-232.

Esping-Andersen, G. (1990) *The Three Worlds of Welfare Capitalism*. New York: Polity Press.

EUROFAMCARE: www.uke.uni-hamburg.de/institute/medizinsoziologie/ims2/gerontologie/eurofamcare/

European Commission (DG for Economic and Financial Affairs) / Economic Policy Committee (2001) *Budgetary Challenges Posed by Ageing Populations* (EPC/ECFIN/655/01-EN final).

European Commission (DG for Employment and Social Affairs) (2003) *The Social Situation in the European Union*. Brussels: DG Employment and Social Affairs.

EUROSTAT (2001) *Population and Social Conditions*. Luxembourg: EUROSTAT.

Evers, A. (1997) 'Quality Development – Part of a Changing Culture of Care in Personal Social Services', pp. 9-24 in: Evers, A./Haverinen, R./Leichsenring, K./Wistow, G. (eds.), *Developing Quality in Personal Social Services. Concepts, Cases and Comments*. Aldershot: Ashgate.

Evers, A./Ungerson, C. (eds.) (1994) *Payments for Care. A European Overview*. Aldershot: Ashgate.

Evers, A./Olk, T. (1996) 'Von der pflegerischen Versorgung zu hilfreichen Arrangements. Strategien der Herstellung optimaler Beziehungen zwischen formellem und informellen Hilfesystem im Bereich der Pflege älterer Meschen', pp. 347-372 in: Evers, A./Olk, T. (Hg.) *Wohlfahrtspluralismus*. Opladen: Westdeutscher Verlag.

Evers, A./Haverinen, R./Leichsenring, K./Wistow. G. (eds.) (1997) *Developing Quality in Personal Social Services. Concepts, Cases and Comments*. Aldershot: Ashgate.

Ewers, M./Schaeffer, D. (Hg.) (2000) *Case Management in Theorie und Praxis*. Bern: Huber.

Ex, C./Gorter, K./Janssen, U. (2004) 'Providing Integrated Health and Social Care for Older Persons in the Netherlands', pp. 415-454 in: Leichsenring, K./Alaszewski, A.M. (eds.), *Providing Integrated Health and Social Care for Older Persons: A European Overview of Issues at Stake*. Aldershot: Ashgate.

Fakiri, F./Sixma, H.J./Weide, M.G. (2000) *Kwaliteit van huisartsenzorg vanuit migrantenperspectief: ontwikkeling van een meetinstrument*. Utrecht: Nivel.

Flick, U (1998) *An Introduction to Qualitative Research*. London: Sage Publications.

Flora, P. (ed.) (1986) *Growth to Limits: The Western Welfare States Since World War II*. Berlin, New York: de Gruyter.

Flynn, N (2002) *Public Sector Management* (4th Edition). Harlow, Essex: Pearson Education Ltd.

Fontana, A./Frey, J.H. (2003) 'The Interview: From Structured Questions to Negotiated Text', pp. 47-60 in: Denzin, N.K./Lincoln, Y.S. (eds.), *Collecting and Interpreting Qualitative Materials*. Thousand Oaks, CA: Sage Publications.

Fountain, J./Griffiths. P./Hartnell, R. (2000) 'Qualitative Research on Drug Use in the European Union', pp. 301-308 in: Greenwood, G./Robertson, K. (eds.), *Understanding and Responding to Drug Use: the Role of Qualitative Research*. Luxembourg: EMCDDA (EMCDDA Scientific Monograph Series 4).

Freeman, R. (2000) *The Politics of Health in Europe*. Manchester: Manchester University Press.

Frerichs, F./Freundlieb, A./Krämer, K./Sporket, M./Wienold, K. (2004) *Personalstrukturen, Arbeitsbedingungen und Arbeitszufriedenheit in der stationären Altenpflege*. Dortmund: Forschungsgesellschaft für Gerontologie e.V.

Frossard, M./Genin, N./Guisset, M .J./Villez, A. (2004) 'Providing Integrated Health and Social Care for Older Persons in France – An Old Idea with a Great Future', pp. 229-268 in: Leichsenring, K./Alaszewski, A. M. (eds.), *Providing Integrated Health and Social Care for Older Persons*. Aldershot: Ashgate.

Giddens, Anthony (1998) *The Third Way: The Renewal of Social Democracy*. Cambridge: Polity Press.

Glendinning, C. (2003) 'Breaking Down Barriers: Integrating Health and Care Services for Older People in England', *Health Policy* 65 (2): 139-151.

Glendinning, C./Rummery, K./Clarke, R. (1998) 'From Collaboration to Commissioning: Developing Relationships between Primary Health and Social Services', *British Medical Journal* 317: 122-125.

Godfrey, M./Hardy, B/Wistow, G (2003) 'The Situation in England', in: van Raak et al. (eds.), *Integrated Care in Europe. Description and Comparison of Integrated Care in Six EU Countries*. Maarsen: Elsevier Gezondheitszorg.

Godfrey, Mary/Randall, Tracy/Long, Andrew/Grant, Maria (2000) *Reviews of Effectiveness and Outcomes of Home Care*. Exeter: Centre for Evidence-Based Social Services.

Goodwin, R./Kozlova, A./Kwaikowska, A. et al. (2003) *Social Science and Medicine*.

Goodwin, R./Kozlova, A./Kwaikowska, A./Anh Nguyen Luu, L./Nizharadze, G./Realo, A./Kulvet, A./Rammer, A. (2003) 'Social representations of HIV/AIDS in Central and Eastern Europe', *Social Science and Medicine* 56 (7): 1373-1384.

Grand, A./Grand-Filaire, A./Clément, S./Bocquet, H. (1999) 'Caregiver Stress: A Failed Negotiation. A Qualitative Study in South-West France', *The International Journal of Aging and Human Development* 49 (3).

Gräßel, E. (1998a) 'Häusliche Pflege dementiell und nicht dementiell Erkrankter, Teil I. Inanspruchnahme professioneller Pflegehilfe', *Zeitschrift für Gerontologie und Geriatrie* 31: 52-56.

Gräßel, E. (1998b) *Belastung und gesundheitliche Situation der Pflegenden. Querschnittsuntersuchung zur häuslichen Pflege bei chronischem Hilfs- oder Pflegebedarf im Alter*. Egelsbach, Frankfurt, a.M., Washington: Verlag Dr. Hänsel-Hohenhausen.

Greenwood, G./Robertson, K. (eds.) (2000) *Understanding and Responding to Drug Use: The Role of Qualitative Research*. EMCDDA Scientific Monograph Series 4; Luxembourg: EMCDDA.

Grilz-Wolf, M./Leichsenring, K./Strümpel, Ch./Komp, K. (2004) 'Providing Integrated health and Social Care for Older Persons in Austria', pp. 97-138 in: Leichsenring, K./Alaszewski, A.M. (eds.), *Providing Integrated Health and Social Care for Older Persons: A European Overview of Issues at Stake*. Aldershot: Ashgate.

Gröne, O./Garcia-Barbero, M. (2001) 'Integrated Care: A Position Paper of the WHO European Office for Integrated Health Care Services', *International Journal of Integrated Care* 3 (http://www.ijic.org/cgi-bin/pw.cgi/2001-6/000076/article_print.html).

Grundböck, A. et al. (1997) 'Das Krankenhaus daheim', *ProSenectute* 3: 13-15.

Grundböck, A. et al. (1998) 'Ganzheitliche Hauskrankenpflege – ein Modellprojekt des Wiener Roten Kreuzes', S. 91-112 in: Pelikan, J.M. et al. (Hg.), *Virtuelles Krankenhaus zu Hause – Entwicklung von Qualität und Ganzheitlicher Hauskrankenpflege*. Wien: Facultas.

Grunow, D./Wollmann, H. (Hg.) (1998) *Lokale Verwaltungsreform in Aktion: Fortschritte und Fallstricke*. Basel/Boston/Berlin: Birkhäuser.

Guisset, M.J. (2004a) 'Comment accompagner la personne malade et ses proches', pp. 26-32 in: Fondation Médéric Alzheimer (ed.), *Accompagner les personnes atteintes de la maladie d'alzheimer et de troubles apparentés*. Paris: Fondation Médéric Alzheimer.

Guisset, M.J. (2004b) 'Les espaces relais: accueil de jour, de nuit, temporaire, familial, équipe mobile de répit', pp. 48-58 in Fondation Médéric Alzheimer (ed.), *Accompagner les personnes atteintes de la maladie d'alzheimer et de troubles apparentés*. Paris: Fondation Médéric Alzheimer.

Guisset, M.J. et al. (2003) 'Les groupes de parole pour les aidants familiaux', *CLEIRPPA* 9, janvier: 7-26.

Habermas, Jürgen (1981) *Theorie des kommunikativen Handels*. Augsburg: Suhrkamp Verlag.

Halsig, N. (1998) 'Die psychische und soziale Situation pflegender Angehöriger', in: Kruse, A. (Hg.), *Psychosoziale Gerontologie, Bd. 2: Intervention*. Göttingen: Hogrefe.

Ham, C./Alberti, K.G. (2002) 'The Medical Profession, the Public and the Government', *British Medical Journal* 324: 838-842.

Hamalainen, P.M./Perala, M.L./Poussa, T./Pelkonen, M. (2002) 'Patient Participation in Decision-making on the Introduction of Home Respiratory Care: Who Does Not Participate?', *Health Expectations* 6: 118-127.

Harding, Tessa/Beresford, Peter (eds.) (1996) *Standards We Expect: What Service Users and Carers Want from Social Services*. London: Contact Publications, National Institute for Social Work.

Hardy, Brian/Wistow, Gerald (1997) 'Quality Assured or Quality Compromised? Developing Domiciliary Care Markets in Britain', in: Evers, A./Haverinen, R./Leichsenring, K./Wistow, G. (eds.), *Developing Quality in Personal Social Services*. Ashgate: Aldershot.

Harris-Kojetin, L./Lipson, D./Fielding, J./Kiefer, K./Stone, R.I. (2004) *Recent Findings on Frontline Long-term Care Workers. A Research Synthesis 1999-2003*. U.S. Department of Health and Human Services.

Haubrock, M./Hagmann, H./Nerlinger, T. (2000) *Managed Care. Integrierte Versorgungsformen*. Bern: Hans Huber.

Hébert, R./Durand, P.J./Dubuc, N./Tourigny, A. (2003) 'PRISMA: A New Model of Integrated Service Delivery for the Frail Older People in Canada', *International Journal of Integrated Care*, 18 March 2003 – www.ijic.org

Hennessy, P. (1995) *Social Protection for Dependent Elderly People: Perspectives from a Review of OECD Countries* (Labour Market and Social Policy, Occasional Papers No. 16). Paris: OECD.

HID/INSEE (1998-1999) *Enquête Handicaps, Incapacités, Dépendance*. INSEE.

Hiscock, J./Pearson, M. (1999) 'Looking Inwards, Looking Outwards: Dismantling the "Berlin Wall" between Health and Social Services?', *Social Policy and Administration* 33 (2): 150-163.

Holtom, M. (2001) 'The Partnership Imperative: Joint Working between Social Services and Health', *Journal of Management in Medicine* 15 (6): 430-445.

Hudson, B. (2002) 'Interprofessionality in Health and Social Care: The Achilles' Heel of Partnership?', *Journal of Interprofessional Care* 16 (1): 8-17.

Hudson, B./Henwood, M. (2002) 'The NHS and Social Care: the Final Countdown?', *Policy and Politics* 30 (2): 153-166.

Hudson, B./Hardy, B./Henwood, B./Wistow, G. (1997) 'Working Across Professional Boundaries: Primary Health Care and Social Care', *Public Money and Management* 17 (4): 25-30.

Hultberg, E.-L./Lönnroth, K./Allebeck, P. (2002) 'Evaluation of the Effect of Co-financing on Collaboration between Health Care, Social Services and Social Insurance in Sweden', *International Journal of Integrated Care* 2/October (www.ijic.org).

Huntington, J.A. (1997) 'Health Care in Chaos: Will We Ever See Real Managed Care?', *Online Journal of Issues in Nursing* (http://www.nursingworld.org/ojin/tpc2/tpc2_7.htm).

Irvine, D. (2001) *Patients and Doctors: All Change?* Newcastle upon Tyne: University of Northumbria.

Jacobzone, S. (1999) *Ageing and Care for Frail Elderly Persons: An Overview of International Perspectives.* Paris: OECD (Labour Market and Social Policy Occasional Papers, No. 38).

Jedeloo, S./De Witte, L.P./Schrijvers, A.J.P. (2001) 'Quality of Regional Individual Assessment Agencies Regulating Access to Long-term Care Services: A Client Perspective', *International Journal of Integrated Care* 2/June (www.ijic.org).

Johri, M./Beland, F./Bergman, H. (2003) 'International Experiments in Integrated Care for the Elderly: A Synthesis of the Evidence', *International Journal of Geriatric Psychiatry* 18 (3): 222-235.

Kanavos, Panos/Mossialos, Elias (1996) *The Methodology in International Comparisons of Health Care Expenditures: Any Lessons for Health Care Policy?* London: LSE Health (Discussion Paper, No. 3).

Kautto, M. (2002) 'Investing in Services in West-European Welfare States', *Journal of European Social Policy* 12 (1): 53-65.

Keen, J./Packwood, T. (2000) 'Using Case Studies in Health Services and Policy Research', pp. 50-58 in: Pope, C./Mays, N. (eds.), *Qualitative Research in Health Care.* London: BMJ Books.

King, N./Ross, A. (2003) 'Professional Identities and Interprofessional Relations: Evaluation of Collaborative Community Schemes', *Social Work and Health Care* 38 (2):51-72.

Knapp, Martin (1988) 'Searching for Efficiency in Long-Term-Care: De-institutionalisation and Privatisation', pp. 149-171 in: Davies, B./Knapp, M. (eds.), *The Production of Welfare Approach: Evidence and Argument from the PSRU.* Oxford: University Printing House (The British Journal of Social Work, Vol. 18, Supplement).

Kodner, Dennis, L. (2000) 'Fully Integrated Care for Frail Elderly: Two American Models', *International Journal of Integrated Care* 1/November.

Kodner, Dennis L. (2003) 'Consumer-directed Services: Lessons and Implications for Integrated Systems of Care', *International Journal of Integrated Care* 3/June (www.ijic.org).

Kodner, Dennis L./Kyriakou, Corinne Kay (2000) 'Fully Integrated Care for Frail Elderly: Two American Models', *International Journal of Integrated Care* 2/November (www.ijic.org).

Kodner, D.L./Spreeuwenberg, C. (2002) 'Integrated Care: Meaning, Logic, Applications, and Implications: A Discussion Paper', *International Journal of Integrated Care* 2/November (www.ijic.org)

Komp, K./Strümpel, Ch./Grilz-Wolf, M. (2002) *The Understanding of Integrated Care in An International Perspective and in Austria.* Vienna: European Centre (PROCARE Working Paper, nr. 1).

Kopiec, K. (2002) *The Work Experiences of Certified Nursing Assistants in New Hampshire.* Concord, NH: The New Hampshire Community Loan Fund.

Lamura, G. et al. (2004) Usage of Services Supporting Family Carers in Europe. Paper presented at the 7th International Long Term Care Conference in Torun, 21-23 September 2004.

Leichsenring, K./Alaszewski, A.M. (eds.) (2004) *Providing Integrated Health and Social Care for Older Persons. A European Overview of Issues at Stake.* Aldershot: Ashgate.

Leichsenring, K. (2004a) 'Providing Integrated Health and Social Care for Older Persons: A European Overview', pp. 9-52 in: Leichsenring, K./Alaszewski, A.M. (eds.), *Providing Integrated Health and Social Care for Older Persons: A European Overview of Issues at Stake.* Aldershot: Ashgate.

Leichsenring, K. (2004b) 'Developing Integrated Health and Social Care Services for Older Persons in Europe', *International Journal of Integrated Care* 5/September (www.ijic.org).

Lesemann, Fr./Martin, C. (eds.) (1993) *Home-based Care, the Elderly, the Family and the Welfare State: An International Comparison.* Ottawa: University of Ottawa Press.

Leutz, W. N. (1999) 'Five Laws for Integrating Medical and Social Services: Lessons from the United States and the United Kingdom?', *The Milbank Quarterly* 77 (1): 77-110.

Linehan, M (2001) 'Key Issues in the Senior Female International Career Move: A Qualitative Study in a European Context', *British Journal of Management* 12 (1): 85-96.

Lock, K. (1996) 'The Changing Organisation of Health Care: Setting the Scene', in: Twinn, S./Roberts, B./Andrews, S. (eds.), *Community Health Care Nursing: Principles for Practice.* Oxford: Butterworth-Heinemann.

Mäkinen, E./Niinistö, L./Salminen, P./Karjalainen, P. (eds.) (1998) *Kotihoito* (Home Care). Porvoo: WSOY.

Martin, C. (ed.) (2003) *La Dépendance des personnes âgées. Quelles politiques en Europe?* Rennes: Presses Universitaires de Rennes.

Mätzke, N./Wacker, E. (2000) 'Beratung und Fallmanagement: Information und Hilfeplanung für ältere Menschen und ihre Angehörigen', *Blätter der Wohlfahrtspflege* 9/10: 220-222.

Messina, Patrizia (a cura di) (2003) *Sistemi locali e spazio europeo.* Roma: Carocci.

Meyer, M. (2004) EUROFAMCARE. National Background Report for Germany. Retrieved from http://www.uke.uni-hamburg.de/extern/eurofamcare/documents/nabare_germany_rc1_a5.pdf.

Miles, M.B./Huberman, A.M. (1994) *Qualitative Data Analysis: An Expanded Sourcebook* (2nd edition). Thousand Oaks, CA: Sage Publications.

Ministry of Health and Welfare (1999) *Health Care in Greece.* Athens: Ministry of Health and Welfare.

Ministry of Social Affairs and Health (1999a) *Policy on Ageing.* Helsinki: Brochures of the Ministry of Social Affairs and Health 1999:4eng.

Ministry of Social Affairs and Health (2002) *Sosiaali- ja terveyskertomus 2002* (Report on Social Affairs and Health 2002). Helsinki: Publications of the Ministry of Social Affairs and Health 2002:11.

Mintzberg, H. (1989) *Mintzberg on Management.* New York: The Free Press, Macmillan Inc.

MISSOC (Mutual Information System on Social Protection in the EU Member States and the EEA) *Social Protection in the Member States in the EU Member States.*

Morgan, D. (1997) *Focus Groups as Qualitative Research* (2nd edition). Thousand Oaks: Sage Publications.

Morgan, G. (1997) *Images of Organisation*. London: Sage Publications.

Motel-Klingebiel, A./Tesch-Roemer, C./von Kondratowitz, H.-J. (2002) 'The Role of the Family for Quality of Life in Old Age – A Comparative Perspective', in: Bengtson, V./Lowenstein, A. (eds.), *International Perspectives on Families, Aging, and Social Support*. New York: de Gruyter.

Motel-Klingebiel, A./von Kondratowitz, H.J./Tesch-Römer, C. (2001) 'Unterstützung und Lebensqualität im Alter', pp. 201-227 in: Motel-Klingebiel, A./von Kondratowitz, H.-J./Tesch-Römer, C. (Hg.), *Lebensqualität im Alter*. Opladen: Leske + Budrich.

Mur-Veeman. I./Hardy, B./Steenbergen, M./Wistow, G. (2003) 'Development of Integrated Care in England and the Netherlands: Managing across Public-private Boundaries', *Health Policy* 65 (3): 227-241.

Mutschler, R. (1998) 'Kooperation ist eine Aufgabe Sozialer Arbeit: Zusammenarbeit und Vernetzung als professionelle Verpflichtung – Regionale Arbeitsgruppen als Standard beruflicher Sozialarbeit', *Blätter der Wohlfahrtspflege* 3/4: 49-52.

Nemeth, C./Pochobradsky, E. (2002) *Pilotprojekt: Qualitätssicherung in der Pflege*. Wien: Bundesministerium für soziale Sicherheit und Generationen.

Nesti, G./Campostrini, S./Garbin, S./Piva, P./Di Santo, P./Tunzi, F. (2004) 'Providing Integrated Health and Social Care for Older Persons in Italy', pp. 371-414 in: Leichsenring, K./Alaszewski, A. M. (eds.), *Providing Integrated Health and Social Care for Older Persons*. Aldershot: Ashgate.

Nies, H. (2004) A European Research Agenda on Integrated Care for Older People. Dublin: EHMA (http://www.ehma.org/_fileupload/publications/EuropeanResearchAgenda. pdf).

Nies, H./Berman, P.C. (eds.) (2004) *Integrating Services for Older People: A Resource Book for Managers*. Dublin: European Health Management Association.

Niskanen, J. (2002) 'Finnish Care Integrated?', *International Journal of Integrated Care* 2/June (www.ijic.org).

Nocon, A./Qureshi, H./Thornton, P. (1997) *The Perspectives of Users' and Carers' Organisations*. York: University of York.

Oates, M.R./Cox, J.L./Neema, S./Asten, P. et al. (2004) 'Postnatal Depression across Countries and Cultures: A Qualitative Study', *British Journal of Psychiatry* 184 (supplement 46): 10-16.

Observatory for the Development of Social Services in Europe (ed.) (2003) *Indicators and Quality of Social Services in a European Context*. Frankfurt/M.: ODSSE (http://www.sozialedienste-in-europa.de).

OECD (ed.) (1999) *A Caring World. The New Social Policy Agenda*. Paris: OECD.

OECD (2004) *Health Data*. Paris: OECD.

OECD (2005) *Long-Term Care for Older People*. Paris: OECD.

Ovretveit, John (1992) *Health Service Quality*. Oxford: Blackwell Scientific Press.

Ovretveit, John (1998) *Evaluating Health Interventions. An Introduction to Evaluation of Health Treatments, Services, Policies and Organisational Interventions*. Buckingham, Philadelphia: Open University Press.

Pacolet, J./Bouten, R./Lanoye, H./Versieck, K. (1999) *Social Protection for Dependency in Old Age in the 15 EU Member States and Norway*. Leuven: HIVA.

Patmore, Charles (2001) 'Improving Home Care Quality: Individual-centred Approach', *Quality in Ageing* 2 (3): 15-24.

Patmore, Charles (2002) 'Morale and Quality of Life among Frail Older Users of Community Care: Key Issues for Success of Community Care', *Quality in Ageing* 3 (2).

Patmore, Charles (2004) 'Quality in Home Care for Older People: Factors to Pay Head to', *Quality in Ageing* 5 (1).

Pearlin, L.I./Pioloi, M.F./McLaughlin, A.E. (2001) 'Caregiving by Adult Children: Involvement, Role Disruption, and Health', in: Binsock, R.H./George, L.K. (eds.), *Handbook of Aging and the Social Sciences*. New York: Academic Press.

Peck, Edward/Towell, David/Gulliver, Pauline (2001) 'The Meanings of "Culture" in Health and Social Care: A Case Study of the Combined Trust in Somerset', *Journal of Interprofessional Care* 15 (4): 319-327.

Penning, M.J. (2002) 'Hydra Revisited. Substituting Formal for Self- and Informal in Home Care among Older Adults with Disabilities', *The Gerontologist* 42: 4-16.

Philp, I. (ed.) (2001) *Family Care of Older People in Europe*. Amsterdam et al.: IOS Press.

Pieper, R. (2004) 'Integrated Organisational Structures', in: Nies, H.S./Berman, P. (eds.) *Integrating Services for Older People: A Resource Book for Managers*. Dublin: EHMA, ISBN 90-5957-283-1 http://www.ehma.org/

Pierson, Peter (ed.) (2001) *The New Politics of the Welfare State*. Oxford: Oxford University.

Piva, P. (1998) *Vita normale. Guida ai servizi per le persone non autosufficienti*. Roma: Spi-Cgil/Fnp-Cisl/Uilp-Uil.

Pollitt, C. (1997) 'Business and Professional Approaches to Quality Improvement: A Comparison of their Suitability for the Personal Social Services', pp. 25-48 in: Evers, A./Haverinen, R./Leichsenring, K./Wistow, G. (eds.), *Developing Quality in Personal Social Services. Concepts, Cases and Comments*. Aldershot: Ashgate.

Ponzetti, J.J. (ed.) (2003) *International Encyclopaedia Marriage and Family* (2nd edition). New York: Macmillan/Gale Group.

Pope, C./Mays, N. (2000) 'Qualitative Methods in Health Research', pp. 1-10 in: Pope, C./Mays, N. (eds.), *Qualitative Research in Health Care*. London: BMJ Books Chapter 1.

Qureshi, Hazel/Patmore, Charles/Grinor, Nicholas/Bamford, Claire (1998) *Outcomes in Community Care Practice. Number Five. Overview: Outcomes of Social Care for Older People and Carers*. York: The University of York (SPRU).

Ranade, W./Hudson, B. (2003) 'Conceptual Issues in Inter-Agency Collaboration', *Local Government Studies* 29 (3) (Autumn 2003: Partnerships between Health and Local Government): 33-50.

Ranta, H. (ed.) (2001) *Sosiaali- ja terveydenhuoltolainsäädäntö 2001* (Statutory Social Welfare and Health Care Services 2001). Helsinki: Kauppakaari; Talentum Media Oy.

Reilly, S./Challis, D./Burns, A./Hughes, J. (2003) 'Does Integration Really Make A Difference? A Comparison of Old Age Psychiatry Services in England and Northern Ireland', *International Journal of Geriatric Psychiatry* 18 (10): 887-893.

Reis, C./Schulze-Böing, M. (Hg.) (2000) *Planung und Produktion sozialer Dienstleistungen. Die Herausforderung neuer Steuerungsmodelle*. Berlin: ed. Sigma.

Robson, C. (1993) *Real World Research*. Oxford: Blackwell Science.

Roche, D./Rankin, J. (2004) *Who Cares? Building the Social Care Workforce*. London: Institute for Public Policy Research.

Rosenmayr, L./Majce, G. (1998) *Was können Generationen einander bieten? Zweifel und Hoffnungen für das kommende Jahrhundert*. Wien: Bundesministerium für Umwelt, Jugend und Familie.

Rossi, Peter (1997) 'Program Outcomes: Conceptual and Measurement Issues', pp. 20-43 in: Mullen, Edward J./Magnabosco, Jennifer L. (eds.), *Outcomes Measurement in the Human Services. Cross-Cutting Issues and Methods*. Washington DC: National Association of Social Workers Press.

Roth, G./Reichert, M. (2004) 'Providing Integrated Health and Social Care for Older Persons in Germany', pp. 296-328 in: Leichsenring, K./Alaszewski, A.M. (eds.), *Providing Integrated Health and Social Care for Older Persons: A European Overview of Issues at Stake.* Aldershot: Ashgate.

Rushner, R./Pallis, G. (2002) 'Inter-Professional Working: The Wisdom of Integrated Working and The Disaster of Blurred Boundaries', *Public Money & Management* 23 (1): 59-66.

Salonen, P./Haverinen, R. (2004) 'Providing Integrated Health and Social Care for Older People in Finland', pp. 181-228 in: Leichsenring, K./Alaszewski, A.M. (eds.), *Providing Integrated Health and Social Care for Older People: A European Overview of Issues at Stake.* Aldershot: Ashgate.

Schneekloth, U./Leven, I. (2003) *Hilfe- und Pflegebedürftige in Privathaushalten in Deutschland 2002.* Schnellbericht. Erste Ergebnisse der Repräsentativerhebung im Rahmen des Forschungsprojektes „Möglichkeiten und Grenzen einer selbständigen Lebensführung hilfe- und pflegebedürftiger Menschen in Privathaushalten. München: Infratest Sozialforschung.

Schnetzler, R. (2000) 'Die Case-Managerin/der Case-Manager: ein neuer Beruf', *Managed Care* 8: 20-23.

Schubert, H.-J./Zink, K. J. (1997) *Qualitätsmanagement in sozialen Dienstleistungsunternehmen.* Neuwied usw.: Luchterhand.

Schulz, C. (2001) 'Wege aus dem Labyrinth der Demenz. Beratung, Unterstützung und vernetzte Hilfe für Angehörige von Demenzkranken durch die Alzheimer Beratungsstelle Bochum', pp. 230-240 in: Tackenberg, P./Abt-Zegelin, A. (Hg.), *Demenz und Pflege: eine interdisziplinäre Betrachtung.* Frankfurt/M.: Mabuse Verlag.

Schwab, T.C./Leung, K.M./Gelb, E./Meng, Y.Y./Cohn, J. (2003) 'Home-and Community-based Alternatives to Nursing Homes: Services and Costs to Maintain Nursing Home Eligible Individuals at Home', *Journal for Aging Health* 15 (2): 353-370.

Seng, T. (1997) 'Managed Care – Instrumente und institutionelle Grundlagen', *Sozialer Fortschritt* 12: 289-293.

Sheffield Institute of Studies on Ageing (2003) http://www.prw.le.ac.uk/intcare/

Shonk, J. H. (1994) *Tiimipohjaiset organisaatiot* (Team-based Organisations) Helsinki: Oy Rastor Ab.

Sissouras, A. et al. (2003) *National Report: Informal Care for the Elderly.* Athens: EKKE.

Sissouras, A./Ketsetzopoulou, M./Bouzas, N./Fagadaki, E./Papaliou, O./Fakoura, A. (2004) 'Providing Integrated Health and Social Care for Older Persons in Greece', pp. 329-370 in: Leichsenring, K./Alaszewski, A.M. (eds.), *Providing Integrated Health and Social Care for Older Persons: A European Overview of Issues at Stake.* Aldershot: Ashgate.

Steiner, A. (1997) *Intermediate Care: A Conceptual Framework and Review of the Literature.* London: King's Fund.

Steiner-Hummel, I. (1991) 'Case Management in der Altenhilfe', pp. 162-180 in: Wendt, W.R. (Hg.), *Unterstützung fallweise: Case Management in der Sozialarbeit.* Freiburg i.B.: Lambertus.

Stewart, A./Petch, A./Curtice, L. (2003) 'Moving towards Integrated Working in Health and Social Care in Scotland: From Maze to Matrix', *Journal for Interprofessional Care* 17 (4): 335-350.

Stricker, S./Krückel, T./Kusej, A. (2002) *Entlassungsmanagement im Hartmannspital.* Wien: Hartmannspital/Wiener Rotes Kreuz.

Sullivan, H./Skelcher, C. (2002) *Working across Boundaries – Collaboration in Public Services.* Basingstoke: Palgrave Macmillan.

Tamsma, Nicole (2004) Advancing Integrated Care for Older People through EU Policy, Working Paper. Dublin: European Health Management Association.

Taylor-Gooby, Peter (2001) *European Welfare States under Pressure*. London: Sage.

Teperoglou, A. (1990) *Evaluation of the Contribution of the Open Care Centres for The Elderly*. Athens: National Centre for Social Research / Ministry of Health and Welfare.

Teperoglou, A. (1993) 'The Institution of Open Care for the Elderly: Stagnation or Evolution?', pp. 293-300 in: Kyriopoulos, J. / Georgoussi, E. / Skoutelis, G. (eds.), *Health, Social Protection for Third Age*. Athens: Centre for Health and Social Sciences.

Teperoglou, A. (1996) *KAPI Centres. A "Home" Open to the Elderly for Support and Social Integration*. Athens: EKKE.

Teperoglou, A. (2003) 'Family in Greece', in: Ponzetti, J.J. (ed.), *International Encyclopaedia Marriage and Family* (2nd edition). New York: Macmillan / Gale Group.

The Commonwealth Fund (2000) First Report and Recommendations of the Commonwealth Fund's International Working Group on Quality Indicators.

Timmermans, J.M. (red.) (2003) Mantelzorg: *Over de hulp van en aan mantelzorgers*. Den Haag: Sociaal en Cultureel Planbureau.

Tinker, A. (1995) 'Elderly People, Discrimination and Some Implications for Interprofessional Work', *Journal of Interprofessional Care* 8 (2): 193-207.

Trice, H.M. (1993) *Occupational Subcultures in the Workplace*. New York: ILR Press.

Truman, Corrine / Triska, Olive H. (2001) 'Modelling Success: Articulating Program Impact Theory', *The Canadian Journal of Program Evaluation/La Revue canadienne d'evaluation de programme* 16 (2): 101-112.

Vaarama, M. (1995) *Vanhusten hoivapalvelujen tuloksellisuus hyvinvoinnin tuotanto – näkökulmasta* (Performance In The Care Of Elderly A Production Of Welfare - Analysis Of The Public Care System In The Finnish Municipalities). Helsinki: Stakes, Tutkimuksia 1995:55.

van Raak, Arno / Mur-Veeman, Ingrid / Hardy, Brian / Steenbergen, Marike / Paulus, Aggie (2003) *Integrated Care in Europe. Description and Comparison of Integrated Care in Six European Countries*. Maarssen: Elsevier gezondheitsorg.

Villez, A. (2005) 'Aider les aidants', pp. 19-35 in: Villez, A. (ed.), *Adapter les établissements pour personnes âgées. Besoins, réglementation, tarification*. Paris: Dunod.

Ware, John E. (1997) 'Health Care Outcomes from the Patients´ Point of View', in: Mullen, Edward J. / Magnabosco, Jennifer L. (eds.), *Outcomes Measurement in the Human Services. Cross-Cutting Issues and Methods*. Washington DC: NASW Press.

Watt, Susan / Browne, Gina / Gafni, Amiram / Roberts, Jacqueline / Byrne, Carolyn (1999) 'Community Care for People with Chronic Conditions: An Analysis of Nine Studies of Health and Social Service Utilization in Ontario', *The Milbank Quarterly* 77 (3): 363-392.

Wendt, W.R. (1991) 'Die Handhabung der sozialen Unterstützung. Eine Einführung in das Case Management', pp. 11-55 in: Wendt, W.R. (Hg.), *Unterstützung fallweise: Case Management in der Sozialarbeit*. Freiburg i.B.: Lambertus.

Wendt, W.R. (2001) *Case Management im Sozial- und Gesundheitswesen. Eine Einführung*. Freiburg im Breisgau: Lambertus.

Wendt, W.R. (2002) 'Case Management – Stand und Positionen in der Bundesrepublik', pp. 13-36 in: Löcherbach, P. et al. (Hg.), *Case Management: Fall- und Unterstützungssysteme in Theorie und Praxis*. Neuwied: Luchterhand.

Whitten, P. / Kailis, E. (1999) *Statistics in Focus, Population and Social Conditions*. Luxembourg: EUROSTAT.

Wistow, G. / Hardy, B. (1991) 'Joint Management in Community Care', *Journal of Management in Medicine* 5 (4): 40-48.

Wistow, G. / Waddington, E. / Lai Fong Chiu (2002) *Intermediate Care: Balancing the System*. Leeds: Nuffield Institute for Health.

Witz, A. (1990) 'Patriarchy and Professions: The Gendered Politics of Occupational Closure', *Sociology* 24 (4).

Yin, R.K. (2003) *Applications of Case Study Research* (2nd Edition). London: Sage Publications.

Zarit, S.H. / Reever, K.E. / Bach-Peterson, J. (1980) 'Relatives of Impaired Elderly: Correlates of Feelings of Burden', *The Gerontologist* 20: 649-655.

Zawadski, R.T. (1983) 'The Long-term Care Demonstration Projects: What They Are and Why They Came into Being', *Home Health Care Services Quarterly* 3 (4): 3-19.

Zellhuber, B. (2003) Altenpflege – ein Beruf in der Krise? Dissertation. Dortmund: Universität Dortmund.

Zimber, A. / Albrecht, A. / Weyerer, D. (2000) 'Die Beanspruchungssituation in der stationären Altenpflege', *Pflege aktuell* 5: 272-275.

ZonMw (2002) *Over vraagsturing in de gezondheidszorg en toerusting van de zorggebruiker*. Verslag van het congres op 26 september, Congrescentrum de Reehorst, Ede. The Hague: ZonMw (Netherlands Organisation for Health Research and Development).

Interview and Documentation Forms

Appendix 1a *Organisational Data*

Section 1. Service Purpose and Structure
- Please describe the service that this organisation provides to older people (e.g. home care, home adaptations, nursing care, personal care, carer support).
- How long has this service (model/organisation) been operating? (minimum 6 months – study criteria)
- How many staff are employed by the service? (minimum 15 – study criteria)
- How many users/carers/clients does the service have? (minimum 15 – study criteria)
- How does this service integrate health and social care provision for older people?
- In what ways is this service innovative, compared to existing services?

Section 2. Service Development
- Was it designed for a specific purpose/need?
- How was this need/purpose identified?
- Was it a response to an existing (government) policy? Or new legislation? If this is the case, please describe which policy/legislation led to this service being developed.
- How does this service meet the aims of the policy/legislation?
- Was it a collaborative venture? If so, which agencies or organisations or government departments or professional groups were involved?

- How does this service manage the integration of health and social care?
  - Ask for details, such as number of organisations, number of separate professions, other involved agencies (voluntary, lay, religious, political groups).
- How is this service financed?
  - If this information is freely available, check whether it can be divulged if there are sensitive commercial interests.
  - If there are a number of finance sources, ask about the percentages contributed from each source.
- Where does this service fit into the existing framework of service provision? Is it a project or a mainstream service? Will it exist in the medium/long term, or is it a pilot service? Does it replace or compete with existing services?
- Which of the following does the service have:
  - Written quality management policies (e.g. procedures and protocols).
  - Policies/protocols for managing collaboration between health and social care organisations (or their professional representatives) – *for example managing shared records, deciding which is the 'lead' professional, identifying who is accountable for the clients' care.*
  - Statistics about service uptake (*are these published?*).
  - Statistics about services allocated to clients.
  - Statistics about clients excluded from services/referred to other agencies.
  - A written complaints procedure for users.
  - A format for regular user/carer feedback (*i.e. not just feedback arising from complaints*).
  - A written flow chart/care pathway.
  - Written care plan (*where is this kept? Is it paper or computer based? Does the user/carer have access to it or input into it?*).
- How is the service being evaluated? (Is there ongoing research? Is this conducted by external bodies, or is it conducted by the organisation? Is it evaluation conducted by audit, or more in-depth methods?)

Appendix 1.1   Organisational Data Checklist

The following table lists the minimum data items to be addressed within organisations. Its purpose is to offer a checklist for baseline organisational data.

Date:	
Researcher name:	
Researcher centre:	
1. Study entry criteria	
Name of model:	
Contact person(s):	
Contact details:	
Phone no, email etc:	
Source(s) of data:	
Date model commenced providing service:	
Number of staff employed by service:	
Number of users/carers/clients:	
How health and social care are integrated by this model:	
Describe how service is innovative, compared to (pre-)existing services:	
2. Organisational Data	
Organisations involved:	
Professions involved (include numbers for each):	
Goals of model:	
Service(s) provided:	
Annual budget (EUR):	
Sources of funding: (show % if known)	
Length of time funding secured over:	
Methods of audit/evaluation:	
Methods of user/carer feedback:	
Complaints procedure available?	
Written organisational policies available?	
Written care plans for users?	
Written care pathway available to clients?	
Discharge procedure available (to staff/users)?	
3. Other Information	

Appendix 1.2   Health Profile Data

1.   Date:

2.   Name (or linked anonymous code) of respondent:

3.   Respondent is a (tick as appropriate):
☐ Service User
☐ Informal (family) carer for a service user
☐ Formal carer (e.g. care manager, nurse, therapist, home carer)

4.   Health Profile data (must relate to service user not carer!!)
4a. Age: _____
4b. Gender: M/F
4c. Main health and social problems (user perspective ideally, carer
    perspective if service used is unable to take part):

5.   Level of 'Formal Care' (Tick as appropriate)
☐ Client receiving 24 hour medical care in hospital/acute unit
☐ Client receiving 24 hour nursing care (but not medical care) in nurs-
    ing ward or nursing home
☐ Client receiving 24 hour social care in residential home/unit
☐ Client receives the following formal care in own home (complete
    for a typical week):

	Personal Care*	(no of visits)	Social Care*	(no of visits)	Social Support*	Other	Notes
Example	Yes	3	Yes	1	30 min – chat	GP visit	fall
Monday							
Tuesday							
Wednesday							
Thursday							
Friday							
Saturday							
Sunday							

Other types of formal care received at (or from) home over a typical week*:

	Nursing Care*	Therapy* (specify)	Therapy (specify)	Hospital Outpatient*	Day-care*	Notes
Monday						
Tuesday						
Wednesday						
Thursday						
Friday						
Saturday						
Sunday						

OR
❏ Client receives no formal care

6. Level of Informal Care
Definition: 'Informal Care' is care provided by spouse, family, friends or neighbours on a voluntary, unpaid basis.
   It can be really difficult for carers to know how much time they spend giving personal care, social care (help with shopping, cooking etc) and social support. One simple approach is to gather the following data:
- How may informal carers provide care to this person?
- What sort of care do they provide?
- How much time in total (estimate) do they spend giving this care?

E.g. for a man whose wife tends to him 24 hours a day, 7 days a week (i.e. he would need 24-hour care if his wife was not there), and whose son does shopping and pays bills for his parents, and also visits on Sundays:
- 2 informal carers (wife and son).
- Personal care, IADL care and social support provided by wife 24/7 (148 hours per week).
- IADL care and social support provided by son (8 hours per week).
- = 168 hours per week informal care.

Alternatively, a chart could be completed, e.g.
Informal Care Dependency: Client receives the following informal care:

	Personal Care (hours per week)	Social Care (hours per week)	Social Support (hours per week)	TOTAL
Main Informal Carer e.g. wife				168 (with client 24/7)
Informal Carer 2 e.g. son	0	2 (does shopping/finances)	6 (spends Sundays with parents)	8
Informal Carer 3	N/A			
Total				176

<u>OR</u>

❑   Client receives no informal care

Appendix 1.3   Client Interview Schedule

Suggested introduction to interview: We would like to find out something about your experiences of (*selected innovatory service). Thinking about your most recent experience of this service, we would like to take you through step-by-step and ask some questions about this.

QA1. Services Received
- What services do you receive from (model studied)?
- How long have you been receiving this service/these services for?
- How often do you receive it/them? (e.g. how many times a week, or a day)

For day care or resident care:
- How long have you been attending (centre)?
- How often do you go to (day centre)?
- What sorts of services do you get at (day centre or residential centre)? (E.g. advice, personal care, physiotherapy, meals etc)

QA2. Initial Contact
Describe how you contacted (or were put in touch with) this service.
- What were the events leading up to this?
- Was it a self-referral, or did a professional or family caregiver make the referral? Were you in hospital at the time or at home?
- Who was the initial contact with?
- How did you feel about the initial contact?
- What (if any) were your expectations of this service?
- Did you feel you needed this service?
- Was it the right thing to do?

QA3. Needs Assessment
- Did (the professional) ask you questions about your health and social care needs? If so, can you describe this experience to me?
- Were you aware of any assessment (of your needs) taking place?
- If so, was there just one assessment, or more than one?
- Were you provided with a written care plan? (or similar). If so, where was this document kept? Do you know why it was written?
- Was there a waiting list to receive any part of the service?
- Did you get the care you needed (from this service) when you needed it?

277

QA4. Evidence of Person-centred Care

- Did you feel that you were involved in any decisions taken about your situation? Could you have a say in what happened? (please give examples)
- Did you get what you wanted?
- Were your wishes respected?
- Were your needs respected?
- Did a relative (or spouse etc) arrange for you to receive this service? If so, did you feel confident that your relative knew/understood what you needed?
- What sort of information was provided by the service? Was this the right sort of information for you? Was it presented in a way you could understand?

QA5. Evidence of Joint Working/Seamless Care

- Did the staff keep you informed about your *case? (or *request or *assessment or*enquiry)
- If so, how did they keep you up to date with your progress?
- How many different services do you receive?
- How many staff members are involved with your care?

If more than one, ask:

- Do different staff members know what they are each doing for you?
- Are different staff members aware of how you manage?
- Did you/do you know which worker is in charge of your case?
- Who would you get in touch with if you had any questions or concerns about your *case?
- If there are any changes in your condition, do you think that (they) would be aware of this? If so, how?

QA6a. Experience of Service

(Based on responses to Q5 above, try to discover the clients' experience of each of the model's integrated services.) Countries will need to formulate this question in relation to the service they are investigating, e.g.

- Could you describe your experience of receiving personal care from (service) carers?
- OR Could you describe your experience of home adaptations by (service)?
- OR Could you describe your experience of day care by (service)?

- OR Could you describe your experience of being assessed by (service)?
- Would you say that the service has met your needs?
- Could you describe how this service has changed things for you?
- Could you arrange to attend clinics OR to have adaptations made at a time that suited you? (Or your relative/carer if they also needed to be present.)

QA6b. Experience of Personal Care
(OPTIONAL – only use this question if personal care is part of the service provided.)
- What is your experience of personal care given to you by paid carers?
- Was enough time allocated to you?
- Could you request a caregiver with whom you felt at ease? (E.g. Male carer for male client)
- Could you ask for carers to come at a time convenient to you?
- Was the service reliable? i.e. did carers turn up when you expected them? Did you know which carer was coming, and why they were coming? Were you told about carer's holidays in advance, and was there cover available? What about if a carer was unwell?
- If a new carer was coming, did they know about your needs/ how to care for you?
- How did your carers manage sensitive issues such as dignity, privacy or confidentiality?
- Could you talk about your worries or feelings with your carer?

QA7. Discharge Issues
(OPTIONAL – use only if:
- the model being investigated has a documented discharge process, and
- the client has some experience of being discharged by the service,
to discover how client is discharged from the service and what follow-up measures and integrated communication measures exist. This does NOT relate to hospital discharges or previous discharges from other services, although the client may of course make comparisons.)

- Could you describe your experience of the discharge process from this service?
  - Did you have any problems when the service ended?
  - After the service ended, did anyone get in touch with you to find out how you are getting on?
  - Do you think you were discharged (from this service) at the right time?
  - What was the reason for discharging you from this service?
  - Would you say that the service had met your needs?
  - Did you feel that you were ready to be independent of the service?
  - What, if any, support did you have when the service ended? (This could be support from family or friends, or support from the service prior to discharge, e.g. information about discharge, other agencies that might help.)
  - If a new service started, did they know about your needs?
  - Were there any arrangements for getting in touch if you needed the service again?
  - What, if anything, could be done to improve discharge from this service?

QA8. Overall Experience of This Service
- Could you describe your overall experience of (model)?
  - What, if anything, could be done to improve this service?
  - What was the best thing about this service?
  - What was the worst thing about this service?
  - Do you have any comments about the cost of this service? (Did you get any financial help? Was it enough to allow you to pay for the service?)

Appendix 1.4   Carer Interview Schedule

We would like to find out something about your experiences of (selected model) from your perspective as a carer. Thinking about your most recent experience of this service, we will take you through step-by-step and ask some questions about this.

QB1. Services Received
- What services does your relative receive from (model studied)?
  - How long have they been receiving this service/these services for?
  - How often do they receive it/them? (e.g. how many times a week, or a day)

Or, for day care or resident care:
  - How long has your relative been attending (centre)?
  - How often do they go to (day centre)?
  - What sorts of services do you get at (day centre or residential centre)? (E.g. advice, personal care, physiotherapy, meals etc)

281

QB2. Initial Contact
- How did you/your relative come to be in contact with this service?
- Why did you contact with this service?
  - What were the events leading up to this?
  - Were you providing care to your relative before the service became involved?
  - If so, could you describe what sort of care you were providing?
  - Are you still providing care to your relative?
  - Did you make the referral, or did a professional make the referral?
  - Was your relative in hospital at the time or at home?
  - Who was the initial contact with?
  - How did you feel about the initial contact?
- What (if any) were your expectations of this service?
  - Did you feel you/your relative needed this service?
  - Was it the right thing to do?

QB3. Needs Assessment

- Did (the professional) ask you questions about your relative's health and social care needs? If so, can you describe this experience to me?
  - Were you aware of any assessment (of your relative's needs) taking place?
  - If so, was there just one assessment, or more than one?
  - Were you (or your relative) provided with a written care plan? (or similar). If so, where was this document kept? Do you know why it was written?
  - Was there a waiting list to receive any part of the service?
  - Did you get the care you needed (from this service) when you needed it?

QB4. Evidence of Person-centred Care

- Did you feel that you were involved in any decisions taken about your relative's situation? Could you have a say in what happened? (please give examples)
  - Did you get what you wanted?
  - Did your relative get what he/she wanted?
  - Were your wishes/needs respected?
  - Were your relative's wishes/needs respected?
  - Did you feel confident that you knew/understood what your relative needed?
  - Did you feel confident that the services staff knew what your relative needed?
  - What sort of information was provided by the service? Was this the right sort of information for you? Was it presented in a way you could understand?

QB5. Evidence of Joint Working/Seamless Care

- Did the staff keep you informed about your relative's case? (or request or assessment or enquiry)
- If so, how did they keep you up to date with their progress?
- How many different services does your relative receive?
- How many staff members are involved with your relative's care?

If more than one, ask:

- Do different staff members know what they are each doing for your relative?

- Are different staff members aware of how much your relative can manage?
- Did you/do you know which worker is in charge of your relative's case?
- Who would you get in touch with if you had any questions or concerns about your relative's case?
- If there are any changes in your relative's situation, do you think that (all the agencies involved) would be aware of this? If so, how?

QB6a Experience of Service

(Based on responses to Q5 above, try to discover the carer's experience of each of the model's integrated services.) Countries will need to formulate this question in relation to the model they are investigating, e.g:

- Could you describe your relative's experience of receiving personal care from (service) carers?
- OR Could you describe your relative's experience of home adaptations by (service)?
- OR Could you describe your relative's experience of day care by (service)?
- OR Could you describe your relative's experience of being assessed by (service)?
- OR Country variation
- Would you say that the service has met your relative's needs?
- Could you describe how this service has changed things for you/your relative?
- Could you arrange for your relative to attend clinics OR to have adaptations made at a time that suited you?(if carer needed to be present)

QB6b. Experience of Personal Care

(OPTIONAL – only use this question if personal care is part of the service provided.)

- What is your experience of personal care given to your relative by paid carers?
  - Was enough time allocated to your relative?
  - Could you request a caregiver with whom you and your relative felt at ease? (E.g. Male carer for male client)
  - Could you ask for carers to come at a time convenient to you?

- Was the service reliable? i.e. did carers turn up when you expected them? Did you know which carer was coming, and why they were coming? Were you told about carer's holidays in advance, and was there cover available? What about if a carer was unwell?
- If a new carer was coming, did they know about your relative's needs/ how to care for your relative?
- How did your carers manage sensitive issues such as dignity, privacy or confidentiality?
- Could you talk about your worries or feelings (about your relative) with your relative's carer?

QB7. Discharge Issues
(OPTIONAL – use only if:
- the model being investigated has a documented discharge process, and
- the carer has some experience of their relative being discharged by the service,

to discover how client is discharged from the service and what follow-up measures and integrated communication measures exist. This does NOT relate to hospital discharges or previous discharges from other services, although the carer may of course make comparisons.)
- Could you describe your relative's experience of the discharge process from this service?
  - Did you or your relative have any problems when the service ended?
  - After the service ended, did anyone get in touch with you to find out how you are managing?
  - Do you think your relative was discharged (from this service) at the right time?
  - What was the reason for discharging your relative from this service?
  - Would you say that the service had met your relative's needs?
  - Did you feel that your relative was ready to be independent of the service?
  - What, if any, support did you have when the service ended? (This could be support from family or friends, or support from the service prior to discharge, e.g. information about discharge, other agencies that might help.)

- If a new service started, did they know about your relative's needs?
- Were there any arrangements for getting in touch if you needed the service again?
- What, if anything, could be done to improve this service?

QB8. Overall Experience of This Service

- Could you describe your overall experience of (model)?
- Could you describe your relative's overall experience of (model)?
- What, if anything, could be done to improve this service?
- What was the best thing about this service?
- What was the worst thing about this service?
- Do you have any comments about the cost of this service? (Did you / your relative get any financial help? Was it enough to allow you to pay for the service?)

Appendix 1.5   Key Worker Individual Interview Schedule

QC1a. Key Worker's Individual Role

- I'd like to talk to you about the job that you do ... Could you describe a typical working day?
  - What sort of things do you do?
  - Do you enjoy your work?
  - What is good about your job? Can you give examples?
  - What is bad about your job? Can you give examples?

QC1b. (Pay, Hours, Conditions, Job Security, Job Satisfaction)

- Do you enjoy your job?
- Are you satisfied with your working conditions (hours worked, breaks, environment)?
- Is your pay reasonable for the job that you do?
- Do you get paid holidays?
- Do you get increased pay for unsocial hours? (nights, weekends, evenings)
- Do you feel that your job is secure?
- Are you ever asked to do things that you don't feel trained (or ready) to do?

(This may be a sensitive subject. In some cases it may not be possible to ask direct questions about salary and terms and conditions. The following questions are suggestions if a more general approach is needed.)

- How are your hours (duties) organised?
- Do you have any say in how your work is organised?
- Do you feel secure in your job? Can you tell me why? (Or why not)
- What are the working conditions like? (please provide examples)
- Do you feel valued? (by your organisation, by your managers, by your team, by your clients)
- Do you feel supported? (by your manager, by your team)
- Do you think that you are paid well enough for the job that you do?
- What opportunities are there for training/education?

QC2. Integrated Care/Evidence of Joint Working/Seamless Care

- Does your job involve 'integrated working' (**seamless care or coordinated care**) between health and social care?

- Could you tell me what 'joint working' (**or seamless care or coordinated care**) means to you?
- Would you say that all the professionals/agencies involved in your client's care are able to collaborate and work together for the client?
- Do you know the other professionals/workers who are involved with your clients?
- Are you able to contact these individuals if the need arises to discuss a case?
  - Can you plan any changes to care alongside other professionals?
  - To what extent are you able to work together with other health and social care professionals (or workers)?
  - How does 'joint working' affect your working practice on a day-to-day level?
  - How do you communicate with other professionals/agencies involved in your client's *case?
  - Is a 'lead professional' identified? (i.e. between health and social care, not within a group of the same profession) Could you describe how the lead professional is chosen, and how this is communicated to the client?
  - What advantages/disadvantages exist for you as a member of a 'joint working' service?
  - Compare your role now with other jobs that haven't been about joint working. What do you do differently now? (this question is intended for employees of new 'schemes' which have been set up for joint working, and who have previously worked in different settings)
- Does your organisation support you in 'joint working'?
- Have you experienced conflict with other professional groups? Are you able to give some examples of this?
- Have you experienced collaboration with other professional groups? Are you able to give some examples of this?
- If there has been conflict, does your organisation help you to find solutions to these problems?
- Do you have time to coordinate meetings with other people who provide care/assistance to your clients? Are you able to share data about clients?

QC3. Access to Service

- Does your job involve helping clients obtain this service?
- If so, please describe how clients access the service you provide ...
- Can individuals self-refer, or do they need to contact you through another professional, e.g. doctor or community nurse?
- Do you think that potential clients are able to access this service if they need it?
- Do you gather information about individuals who may contact your service but do not receive the service for any reason? E.g. clients who decline to receive services, or who do not fit any criteria for suitability that may exist.

QC4. Needs Assessment

- Does your job involve assessing whether or not a client needs a service?
- If so, can you describe the process of assessing a client's needs within this service?
  - Is there usually one assessment, or do several professionals make their own assessments?
  - Who actually conducts the assessment?
  - How do you communicate the outcome of any assessment to clients/their carers?
  - Is there a written plan of care (or similar) for each client? If so, is this shared with other agencies involved? How is the plan of care reviewed/evaluated?
  - Is this service able to provide care/support/intervention to all clients that fit into the service criteria? I.e. are there times when assessed needs can't be met due to lack of resources?
  - Is there a waiting list for any part of this service? If so, how long would a client have to wait (on average) before receiving assessment/service?

QC5. Purchasing Care

- Is your client charged for the service you provide?
- If so, please describe how (this service) organises and supplies care or interventions or adaptations for clients ...
- In your view, is the service provided to your clients reliable?
- Are your clients able to afford this service?

- Could you describe how this service has changed things for your client or their family carers?
- Is there a waiting list for any of the services you provide, including assessment?
- Could your client (or their carer) arrange to attend clinics OR to have adaptations made at a time that suited them? (or you, if you needed to be present too)

QC6. Person-centred Care (or 'Holistic' Care)
- How do you see 'person-centred' care?
- How do you involve clients and/or their carers in decisions about their cases within this service?
- Are you able to discuss each case with the clients involved? (assuming that the client is cognitively able to do this)
- To what extent are family carers involved in decisions?
- Does the client have a say in the outcome of his/her case?
- Are there any arrangements in place to get 'feedback' from users about the service? If so, how is this information used within the organisation?

QC7. Discharge Issues
(OPTIONAL – use only if:
- the model being investigated has a documented discharge process, and
- the key worker is involved in client discharge from the service,

to discover how a client is discharged from the service and what follow-up measures and integrated communication measures exist. This does NOT relate to hospital discharges or previous discharges from other services, although the key worker may of course make comparisons.)
- Does your job involve planning discharge from the service with your clients?
- If so, could you describe how discharge is planned within this service?
- How do you assess whether a client is ready for discharge? What are the discharge criteria?
- Are all other health or social care professionals involved with the client informed of an impending discharge?
- Is there any follow-up of clients after the service has ended?
- Can clients or their carers self-refer if they require the service again?

QC8. Overall Experience of Service

- Could you describe how you see this (model)?
- What, if anything, could be done to improve this service?
- Are you able to compare this service with other similar services you have been involved with?
- What do you think is the best thing about your service?
- What do you think is the worst thing about your service?

Appendix 1.6   Organisation Focus Group Schedule

Section 1 – Joint Working/Seamless Care

(Purpose of questions: to discover the organisation's definition of integrated care, and how/whether the organisation's **structure** supports integrated working between health and social care.)

QD1a. What is your understanding of 'joint working' [*seamless care/*coordinated care/*integrated working/*transmural care] between health and social care?

- Which other professionals (or professional groups) do you regularly (at least weekly) have contact with?

(The term 'workers' or 'persons' may be more appropriate than 'professionals' where the integration is with unqualified workers from a different agency, BUT this question does not refer to unpaid family carers.)

- To what extent are you able to work together with other professionals, agencies, workers?

QD1b. How does 'joint working' affect your working practice on a day-to-day level?

- What arrangements exist to help your organisation/staff communicate with other professionals/agencies involved in your clients *case(s)?

QD1c. Compare your roles now with other jobs that haven't been about joint working.

- What do you do differently now?
- Is there clarity about where professional roles begin and end?
- How does this service fit in alongside other services for the same client group?
- Are policies and protocols clear? (I.e. are these written down, easy to find, often used by workers?)

Section 2 – Process (How the Service Is Provided)

(Purpose of section: to identify the process of coordinated and collaborative service provision, from the organisational perspective, along the continuum from needs assessment to user feedback).

QD2a. Describe how clients access the service you provide ...

- Do you think that potential clients are able to access this service if they need it?
- Can individuals self-refer, or do they need to contact you through another professional, e.g. doctor or community nurse?
- Are clients assessed before entry to the service, to see whether they are suitable?
- Can this service provide care/support/intervention to all clients that require it/fit the entry criteria?
- Would you consider that this service is 'demand-led', i.e. services are supplied to all clients that meet criteria, or is it 'supply-led', i.e. services are in short supply, and perhaps targeted at the most at-risk or vulnerable clients?
- Can the service help everyone who fits the criteria? Is there ever a shortfall between supply and demand?
- Is there a waiting list for any part of the service?
- Do you gather information about individuals who may contact your service but not receive the service for any reason? E.g. clients who decline to receive services, or who do not fit any criteria for suitability that may exist.

QD2b. Could you explain how client's needs are identified within your service?

- Is a holistic assessment of need conducted? (i.e. 'single assessment')
- Is there usually one assessment, or do several professionals make their own assessments?
- Which of the following areas would the assessment(s) cover?
  - Physical health/well-being
  - Functional health/well-being (ability to do PADL's or IADL's)
  - Mental health (e.g. emotions, safety, support, isolation)

- Cognitive health (e.g. independence, decision-making, presence of cognitive impairment such as dementia or side-effect from stroke (CVA)
- Current family and formal support (include voluntary provision)
- Housing issues (e.g. appropriate housing for dependency, availability of 'aids')
- Financial issues (ability to pay/savings/insurance)

- Is a written care plan drawn up to document assessment, needs and care or interventions? If so, is this given to users? Is it accessible to other professionals who are involved with the client?

QD2c. Is it your experience that the (model you work for) can provide person-centred care?

- How are clients and/or their carers involved in decisions about their individual cases within this service?
- What steps are taken to involve clients and carers in the audit of this service? – Are there client or user feedback groups within the service structure?
- What do you think your clients get from your service? Are you able to give examples?

QD2d. How is discharge from this service organised?
(OPTIONAL – use only if the model being investigated has a documented discharge process, to discover how a client is discharged from the service and what follow-up measures and integrated communication measures exist. This does NOT relate to hospital discharges or previous discharges from other services, although the organisational staff may of course make comparisons.)

- How are other professionals involved in a client's care included in discharge planning?
- What sorts of criteria exist for deciding to discharge a client?
- How are clients and carers involved in the discharge planning process?
- What sort of follow-up/aftercare arrangements exist?
- How do clients access the service if their needs change again after discharge?

Section 3. Overall perspectives of integrated working within this model

(Purpose of question: to identify evidence of solutions to joint working problems within the organisation.)

- What could be done to improve this service?
- What are the best examples of improved joint working that (this model) offers? (ask for details/examples)
- What are the main continuing problems with joint working experienced by (this model) (ask for details/examples)
- Is (this model) under any sort of threat? (e.g. funding, competition)
- Is this model likely to be adopted, or to expand in your country/area?
- What would you do differently after experiencing joint working or what might you do differently to promote joint working between health and social care?

Model Ways of Working

Overview: Model Ways of Working Analysed in the 9 PROCARE Countries

Country	Code	Name/Place
Austria	A1	Integrated Social and Health Care District in Hartberg (Styria)
	A2	Discharge management at the Hartmann Hospital (Vienna)
Denmark	DK1	Rehabilitation upon discharge from hospital in Søllerød
	DK2	Integrated care in Skævinge: the Health Centre 'Bauneparken'
Finland	FIN1	Integrated home care for older people living at home (Municipality of Helsinki)
	FIN2	Integrated home care for older people living at home (City of Espoo)
France	F1	Local Information and Gerontological Coordination Centre (CLIC) in Chalûs
	F2	Local Information and Gerontological Coordination Centre (CLIC) in Phalempin
Germany	D1	Home Care Nürnberg (HCN) – Praxisnetz Nürnberg (PNN)
	D2	Geronto-psychiatric-geriatric association in Oberspreewald-Lausitz (GPGV OSL)
Greece	EL1	Open Care Centres for Older People (KAPI) in Alimos, Marousi, Ilioupoli and Nea Philadelphia
	EL2	Help at home for elderly persons in Kifissia, Nikaia and Nea Ionia
Italy	I1	Working Unit of Continuous Care (WUCC) in the Province of Vicenza
	I2	Single Point of Access to Home Care in Empoli (Tuscany)
The Netherlands	NL1	Home care facility "Zijloever" in Leiden
	NL2	Chain of care for older people in Kerkrade, Landgraaf and Simpelveld
United Kingdom	UK1	Limes Livingstone Integrated Care Project (LLICP), Dartford (Kent) (Inpatient rehabilitation care)
	UK2	Shepway Community Assessment and Rehabilitation Team (CART) (Community based rehabilitation care)

A1

Integrated Social and Health Care District in Hartberg

The district of Hartberg (Styria) has 67,778 inhabitants of which 20% are over 60 years of age. 96.7% of the older population live in private households, about 50% of them with their families. Daily care activities are mainly covered by family members (wife, daughter, daughter-in-law).

In 2003, the Integrated Social and Health Care District (ISGS) directly served 1,619 elderly, with a staff of 51 persons (managers, home nurses, home carers, home helpers) plus volunteers. In 2002, staff worked a total of 48,319 hours . 28,696 hours were spent for hands-on care and 2,536 hours for case management. The yearly budget of the district is 1.3 million Euro.

General description and organisational context

The ISGS in Hartberg, established in 1989, is a regional organisation for coordination and cooperation of health and social care organisations. It is run by the Red Cross, involving also other non-profit home care providers (Caritas and Volkshilfe), GPs and old-age and nursing homes in the district. Since 2000, the ISGS also cooperates with the district hospital to promote more integrated care delivery. The ISGS Hartberg is a specific model way of working in Styria, a South-Eastern province of Austria.

Type of integration/coordination

Horizontal integration of social and health care professionals, intermediate care (the hospital-community care interface).

Objectives

*   To offer patients in need of care the possibility to stay at home by means of integrated care arrangements (with the help of a case manager).
*   To improve the offer of health and social care organisations in the district.
*   To help patients and their families to find the appropriate organisation according to their needs.
*   To start and develop support and training programmes for family carers.

Methods
- Needs analysis on the district level.
- Information centre for clients and their families.
- Integrated provision of home nursing, family care, meals on wheels, visiting services and health prevention (contracts between different providers).
- Regular communication with GPs.
- Regular visits at the hospital and discharge management.
- Case management.

Results (strengths and weaknesses)
- The ISGS Hartberg is an example of how to start more integrated care delivery at the provincial level by coordinating hospital care and various providers of home care in the community.

  "We all work together and we are all integrated in the model way of working; the clients do not know if we are from the Red Cross, the Caritas or the Volks- hilfe. That is really not important for the clients." (key worker)

- The ISGS is heavily dependent on the cooperation of family carers

  "I take care of my mother and the home nurses care helps me a lot. If my mother would need more help I would have to give up my own little coffee shop." (carer)

Address
Österreichisches Rotes Kreuz, Bezirksstelle Hartberg, Rotkreuzplatz 1, A-8230 Hartberg

A2

Discharge Management at the Hartmann Hospital (Vienna)

In 1997 the financing structure of hospitals in Austria and thus in Vienna was changed. Since then, the average length of a patient's stay in hospital has decreased, but the rate of admissions has increased. Patients are discharged in a state worse than before and more help and care is needed at home. This was the background and one of the main reasons for the Viennese Red Cross to initiate a hospital discharge programme that is located in several Viennese hospitals. The Viennese Red Cross analysed the problem that the interaction between hospitals and home help and care services was lacking.

> "As an extramural service, we soon saw the classical problem, that there was no interface between intra- and extramural services. For example, that many hospitals discharge their patients on Friday at 10 o'clock and then they do not receive appropriate provisions during the weekend. Our staff was very unsatisfied with this situation. We asked our research institute to develop ideas, how to implement a project on "Interface-management." (Director, Viennese Red Cross)

Objectives
- To foster cooperation between hospital and home care service providers to guarantee the continuity of provision for older people in need of care.
- To offer individual services in the hospital (before discharge) for elderly in need of care at home.
- To limit the length of stay in hospital.

Type of integration
Vertical integration at the interface between hospital and community care, focusing on discharge management.

Methods
The discharge management takes place in different hospital wards as the heads of wards refer the patients to the discharge manager. Hospital staff delegates the responsibility for organising and coordinating the provision of home care for the patients while they are still in hospital to the discharge manager.

In 2002 389 patients were consulted concerning their discharge from the hospital, on average about 32 per month.

One staff member is responsible for discharge management in the hospital and there is a colleague at the Viennese Red Cross that substitutes her in case of absence. This colleague also works in other hospitals that cooperate with the Viennese Red Cross' discharge management programme.

Results (strengths and weaknesses)

- The patients and their families receive 'made-to-measure' help from the discharge manager with organising their care at home.
- The discharge manager works in cooperation with patients, families, the hospital and social care services. The personal confidence between discharge manager, patients and their families helps to reduce the fear and the insecurity caused by the new personal situation of elderly in need of care and their families at home.
- The cooperation between hospital and discharge managers demonstrates the limits and possibilities of mobile social care services and promotes the bilateral understanding of hospital and social care services.
- The discharge managers relieve the hospital employees in their work and the duration of the patients' hospital stay gets shorter. While in 2000 the average length of stay had been 7,82 days per patient, this value was reduced to 6,56 days per patient in 2002 (in the ward for internal medicine, it was reduced from 13,31 to 9,34 days per patient).
- The social care service receives detailed information from the discharge manager on the need for care. Thus, the social service providers have enough time to prepare special services for older people in need of care at home.
- Discharge management has a high standard: discharge managers need to have knowledge about the medical sector, the mobile care services and have to organise the network between different systems and persons (hospital employees, social care employees, elderly in need of care and their families). The high standard of the cooperation agreement between hospital, discharge manager and social care system is a prerequisite for an effective network.

299

- High satisfaction of the patients and their families.
- Enough time for the social care organisation to prepare the care at home.

Address

- Hartmannspital, Nikolsdorfergasse 26-36, A-1050 Wien
- Forschungsinstitut des Wiener Roten Kreuzes, Nottendorfer Gasse 21, A-1030 Wien

DK1

Rehabilitation upon Discharge from Hospital in Søllerød

In the municipality of Søllerød, situated in Copenhagen County, the rehabilitation facility (the departments of occupational therapy and physiotherapy) is situated at the nursing home Hegnsgården. 12 therapists are employed at the departments and in 2002 they serviced 198 outpatients. 90 persons were admitted for intermediate care whilst undergoing their rehabilitation programme. Persons admitted for intermediate care during their rehabilitation programme are serviced at the nursing home by the regular staff and the costs of the rehabilitative services are thus difficult to single out from the overall costs of running the nursing home.

On a more general note, the municipality of Søllerød has roughly 31,500 inhabitants and of these about 5,500 are aged 67 or more. Of these approximately 1,100 persons receive personal and/or social care and/or nursing in their own homes and a further 124 persons below 67 also receive such services that are available 24 hours a day. The bulk of the domestic care services delivered pertain to personal services. The staffs in the domestic primary health and social/personal care services roughly count 50 nurses and 150 social-and-health assistants and social-and-health helpers (FTE).

General description and organisational context

The focus of the model is on rehabilitation of older persons upon discharge from hospital. As the older person is discharged from hospital the needs for further rehabilitation in the municipal rehabilitation facility are assessed. Rehabilitation is deployed in order to enhance the capacity of the citizen to return to his/her own home with the required support from the domestic primary health and social/personal long-term care services. At the end of the rehabilitation programme it is assessed whether the individual can return to his/her own home or whether some form of sheltered housing might be more appropriate.

Rehabilitation of older persons upon discharge from hospital requires a coordinated effort from care providers (counties and municipalities) located at different levels of government. In order to establish an integrated care-pathway from hospital via intermediate care facilities to older people's own home the municipality of Søllerød has introduced a discharge management scheme that is maintained by two nurses that coordinate the discharge process of individual elderly patients. Furthermore, an elaborate assessment tool has been developed and deployed for the assessment of rehabilitation needs of the individual elderly and his/her needs for primary health and social/personal long-term care services after the rehabilitation programme has been completed.

The following long-term care services – subject to needs assessment – are on offer in the municipality of Søllerød:

- Nursing homes (including specialised facilities for persons with dementia).
- Adapted dwellings.
- Day-care facilities.
- Intermediate care facilities and rehabilitation.
- 24 hour domestic care services (social care, personal care and home nursing).
- Meals-on-wheels and transportation.
- Adaptations to housing.
- Aides and alarm services.
- Preventative home visits and contact visits to other groups in potential need.
- Coordination of the work of voluntary associations.

Types of integration/coordination
- Coordination between the hospital and the rehabilitation facility or the domestic primary health and social/personal care services as provided by the coordinating nurse exemplifies an instance of vertical integration
- Coordination between the rehabilitation facility and the domestic primary health and social/personal care services exemplifies an instance of horizontal integration

Objectives
To establish an integrated care-pathway for elderly persons in need of rehabilitation who are discharged from hospital. The emphasis of the model is on the process of providing the necessary types of expertise and care for specific individuals with specific needs at the right moments in the integrated care-pathway in order to lay the foundations for the individual to lead a life on terms deemed 'as-normal-as-possible'.

"It is in the interest of the municipality to ensure that the citizens [who are discharged from hospital] obtain as good a rehabilitation and adequate domestic care as possible. The alternative is a lot of frail elderly in need of massive amounts of domestic services, day-care facilities and meals-on-wheels. And finally you end up with a lot of citizens requiring care in nursing homes." (key worker)

Methods

- Case management/discharge management.
- Assessment tools are deployed before and after the intervention of rehabilitation in order to assess needs for rehabilitation, to gauge the progress made and to assess the ability of older citizens to return to his/her own home and the amount and types of long-term care services required to make such a living arrangement viable.
- Written rehabilitation plans.
- Written care plans.
- Multi-disciplinary discharge conferences with participation of the rehabilitation facility and representatives of the primary health and social/personal care services.

303

Results (strengths and weaknesses)

- The introduction of case management/discharge management has improved collaboration between the county and the municipality of Søllerød on discharge of frail elderly persons.
- The introduction of formal assessment tools has – according to the management – enhanced the capacity of the rehabilitation facility to provide uniform needs assessments across the user group.
- Users appear to experience a smooth passage through an integrated care-pathway.
- Although the day-to-day collaboration between the discharging hospitals and the municipality of Søllerød has improved from the discharge management scheme, not all problems are solved in the relation of vertical integration.
- The practising therapists at the rehabilitation facility find that the work with the formal assessment tools has added a bureaucratic dimension to their duties without adding to the quality of the assessment carried out.

More information

www.sollerod.dk

DK2

Integrated Care in Skævinge: The Health Centre 'Bauneparken'

The municipality of Skævinge is situated in the county of Frederiksborg in Northern Zealand in a largely rural area. Elderly care services in Skævinge are publicly provided by the municipality through the Health Centre 'Bauneparken'.

In 2003 the municipality of Skævinge had roughly 5,600 inhabitants of which 10% (560) were above the age of 67 (170 were 80+). Also the needs of 191 persons below the age of 67, who had retired due to disability, are covered by the Health Centre 'Bauneparken'. Of this group of potential users, 55 persons were residing in the apartments in the Health Centre, 192 persons received domestic care, 104 persons received training and re-habilitation and 141 persons were attached to the regular day care facility at the Health Centre (roughly 90 external residents and the 55 residents at the Health Centre). About 10 persons used the 'Garden Room', which is the day-care facility for persons with dementia, and 4-5 persons used the 'Small Garden Room' which is a day-care facility for persons with severe dementia. Finally, 522 persons had received aids or adaptations to housing at the time of investigation.

The Health Centre 'Bauneparken' has an annual budget of 5,2 million Euros and income of around 1,3 million Euros. The remainder of the budget is covered through general taxation. At the time of investigation a total of 136 persons from 13 different professional groups were employed in the elderly care sector in Skævinge (FTE/PTE).

General description and organisational context

The project of providing integrated health and social/personal care for older persons in the municipality of Skævinge was launched in 1984. The aim of the project was to provide integrated health and social/personal care on a 24-hour basis irrespective of the housing status of the citizen – i.e. if the citizens in need live in their own homes or in apartments in the Health Centre 'Bauneparken'.

The municipality of Skævinge provides a series of different services that are brought into play according to the specific needs of the individual elderly citizen. All the services that are listed in the flow-chart are provided

Flow-chart of the access to care services provided at the Health Centre 'Bauneparken' in the municipality of Skaevinge

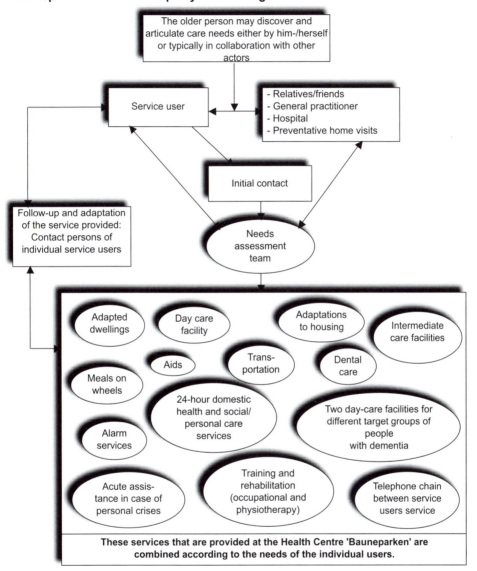

by the Health Centre 'Bauneparken'. Furthermore, the physical proximity between the key workers of different professions enhances communication, coordination and integration of services around the needs of the individual. Recipients of care or other services are assigned to two designated contact persons (usually the regular carer and a nurse) who can be addressed in case the older person has a request regarding the contents or planning of the service(s) provided.

> "I see integrated care as a process of creating a unified 'package' that corresponds with the needs and wishes of the individual. Accordingly, the challenge is to provide individually adapted services that respect the integrity of the citizens and to make the 'system' behind the services invisible for the citizen." (key worker)

Type of integration/coordination
The services provided at the Health Centre 'Bauneparken' exemplify instances of horizontal integration of health and social/personal care, i.e. processes of horizontal integration are predominant in this model.

The Health Centre 'Bauneparken' also cooperates with the local county in relation to the discharge of its elderly citizens from hospital. This hospital-community interface exemplifies an instance of vertical integration.

Objectives
*   To integrate the traditional health and social/personal care sectors and bring them together in one common organisation in the Health Centre 'Bauneparken' in order to obtain a better and more flexible utilization of the pooled resources.
*   To separate housing status from access to health and social/personal care and introduce 24-hours integrated health and social/personal care. According to their needs, elderly persons living in their own homes have access to health and social/personal care as persons living in the nursing home facility in 'Bauneparken'.
*   To provide preventative and individualised care in order to obtain better health and to prevent hospital admissions amongst elderly persons in the municipality.
*   To promote a common professional understanding between the health- and social/personal care workers by applying the concept of self-care as a basis for the provision of prevention-oriented health and social/personal care.

Methods

- Person-centred integration of cure, care and social inclusion of elderly citizens in the municipality.
- The Health Centre 'Bauneparken' constitutes a single point of contact for potential users of health and social/personal care in the municipality.
- The contact persons of individual elderly service users provide case-management.
- The application of the concept of self-care informs the staff on the basic value of the care services provided by the Health Centre 'Bauneparken'.

Results

Surveys conducted in Skævinge in 1985 and again in 1997 indicate that the subjective well-being among older persons has improved subsequent to the introduction of the integrated care scheme.

Even though the number of older persons has increased significantly over the past 20 years the operational expenditures have decreased over the same period. This is to a large extent held to stem from the preventative focus of the integrated care scheme.

There is no waiting time for apartments in the Health Centre or for domestic health and social care services.

The preventative efforts have entailed a surplus of capacity that has been used mainly to establish an intermediate care facility at the Health Centre in order to prevent unnecessary hospital admissions. Consequently, the number of days at hospitals has been reduced by 30-40% for all citizens in the municipality.

Over the last 10 years no citizen from the municipality of Skævinge staying in a hospital had to wait for discharge after having finished treatment as the municipality has been able to take those citizens 'home' and care for them either in the intermediate care facility at the Health Centre or in the citizens' own home.

The municipality of Skævinge's use of and expenditure to national health insurance is below the average of all other municipalities in the county of Frederiksborg.

Address

Health Centre Bauneparken, Harløsevej 24, DK-3320 Skævinge

307

FIN1

Integrated Home Care for Older People Living at Home

The City of Helsinki is divided into seven geographical areas, called great regions. Every great region has its own social centre and health centre, and these centres work together in home care, including discharge. Home care means care and services, arranged by multi-professional teams and includes care, cure and help in daily tasks.

In Finland home care is funded by municipal taxation and by customer fees (dependent on the monthly household income). The political purpose behind integrated home care is that older people who need daily help will increasingly live at home with the help received from municipal home care.

Type of integration

Home help and home nursing have formed a team to cooperate in the care of older people. Most often an old person becomes a client following a hospital stay. A common case is that the doctor and/or discharge nurse agrees on a first visit with the chief home-care officer. The service that the client needs is provided by a multi-professional team. A team consists of 6 to 10 practical nurses and/or home helpers, a home-care nurse and a chief home care officer. Each client has a defined carer.

Elements of the model

- A first visit: The chief home care officer and home nurse or practical nurse together carry out the first needs assessment visit at the home of the older person, where preferably also the family members and other relevant people for the older person are present.
- The care and service plan: This plan should include the assessment of the old person's abilities, medications and illnesses, the content of the home care services to be provided, their frequency (days and tasks), and the rehabilitation plan. The plan should be drawn up together with the client who also keeps her/his own copy. A regular evaluation of the plan is foreseen.
- A defined carer: Each client has his/her "own" carer, i.e. a professional who visits her/him regularly and thus has the best knowledge of her/him and her/his needs.

- Regular team meetings, documentation and informal communication.
- Common space for formal and informal meetings.
- Continuous assesment of the care process and provided services by all workers.
- The chief home-care officer as a case manager.

Strengths and weaknesses
- Shared objectives.
- Shared understanding of the client's needs and common information.
- Autonomy.
- Cost effectiveness.
- Good atmosphere.
- Care and service plan as a commitment.
- Some old persons had too few visits of homecare.
- Shortcomings in working conditions; the haste.
- Social care risks to lose its value as against health care.
- Medicalisation.

309

FIN2

Integrated Home Care for Older People Living at Home

The City of Espoo is divided into five districts of which two have been analysed. In these two districts 713 elderly received nursing home care, home help or integrated home care, 37% of whom received integrated home care (36% received only nursing home care, and 27% only home help). All home care clients live in their own homes.

Number of staff involved (chief home care officers, home nurses, home carers, home helpers):

- District Kanta-Leppävaara: 18 workers per 100 clients over 65 years of age.
- District Kanta-Viherlaakso: 12 workers per 80 clients over 65 years of age and 40 day care clients.

Annual budget (2002): € 4,800,000.

General description and organizational context

Integrated home care has been mainstream care for older persons in the city of Espoo since 1993. The city is divided into five regional administrative social and health care districts. Thus, staff is able to use regional knowledge about local living conditions and population structures. The intra- and extramural social and health care services have been integrated into one organization. This means that all social and health care services are integrated horizontally and coordinated by a chief home care officer, who is managing the entire service net and the work of different care providers. Home care is a municipal responsibility funded by taxation and small customer fees (dependent on the monthly household income). The political rationale for providing integrated home care is to provide adequate services in the municipality for the increasing number of older people in need of care.

Definition and aims

Integrated home care means providing home help and home nursing for older people living at home. Integrated home care is available on every weekday (from 7 a.m. to 4 p.m.) but also evening services (4-11 p.m.) and night services (11 p.m. till 7 a.m.) as well as services during weekends (7 a.m. till 11 p.m.) are offered. Municipal home care teams work daily from 7 a.m. to 11 p.m. and during weekends, night services are provided by a semi-private organization. Integrated home care is provided by home nurses and home helpers/practical nurses who work in functional cooperation in multiprofessional teams called homecare-teams. The aims of integrated home care are

- to give support and care to the old person living at home so that s/he can live independently at home as long as possible,
- to support independent living of the old person at home by means of rehabilitative home care.

Integrated home care is directed by the chief officer of home care in coopera-tion with the local GP who directs home nursing. The target groups are clients whose daily living functions (ability to move, walking, washing, getting up and down to/from bed, dressing, ability to go to the toilet and eating) has decreased noticeably, according to an assessment method (RAI) carried out by the chief home care officer and a home nurse. Additionally, integrated home care is available to those clients who are cared for by a family member, who need professional medical or social help in daily living at home, and/or if the caring family member is at risk of burn-out. Integrated home care is also offered to clients whose care in institutions is not appropriate.

311

Type of integration

Horizontal integration (integrated assessment, care planning and provi-sion/evaluation; case management) with partly vertical integration (the hospital-home care interface).

Process

The initiative to integrated home care can come from various sources: from the old person her/himself, her/his family members, a social worker or physician while discharged from hospital, the GP in a health care centre, or from a neighbour. The initiative is always recorded and assessed.

The chief home care officer and a home nurse visit the older person at home for a first needs assessment, preferably with family members and other relevant people for the old person being present. The chief home care officer and the home nurse make an interview and study all available medical records. When back in the office they calculate the RAI-index for the old person: with a RAI-index of at least 1.8 the older person qualifies for integrated home care services.

Once admitted, the chief home care officer and the home nurse will design the care and service plan for the client in the presence of important relatives or informal carers. The care and service plan should include the assessment of the client's functional, social and psychological abilities, medications and illnesses, the frequency and content of care, and the rehabilitation plan. The care plan, a copy of which stays with the client, should be evaluated regularly.

Key workers (home nurses, home helpers, home carers) assess the overall well-being of the old person during every visit. Whenever needed, the content and extent of care is adapted.

Key workers have one regular meeting per week to share all information about the clients' situations. Additionally, key workers check the daily situation of staff and consequently, the daily organisation of the given care, every morning as changes might happen frequently (for example, hospitalisation of a client). Other mediums for information exchange are a computer-based client system and home care records.

In case of hospital discharge, care needs are assessed before discharge so that the necessary care services can be provided immediately.

312

The chief officer of integrated home care is the coordinator of the whole services net of the old person living at home, including support services, day care services, meals-on-wheels, shopping service, cleaning service, and care at night times.

F1

Local Information and Gerontological Coordination Centre (CLIC)
in Chalûs

In 2000 the Ministry for Employment and Solidarity launched a 5-year programme for the creation of 1,000 Local Information and Gerontological Coordination Centres (CLICs) with financial support from the state. The objective is to set up a geographically based network with three levels of competencies: Level 1 – welcoming, informing, advising and supporting; level 2 – assessing needs, compiling personalised care plans; level 3 – implementing, monitoring and adapting those care plans. A certification process allows the actions carried out by each CLIC to be qualified for each of these levels.

The CLIC Chalûs is situated in a rural and small area: 2,400 inhabitants 60+, a limited number of professionals. It is run by the Association for the Coordination of Actions in Favour of the Elderly (ACAFPA). The association manages itself some services (mandatory service for local employment and relationship support service) that were created to fill a local gap.

313

Aims
- Welcoming, informing, advising and supporting.
- Assessing needs, compiling personalised care plans.
- Implementing, monitoring and adapting those care plans.

Strengths and weaknesses
- Each professional knows everybody.
- A common gerontological culture.
- Key workers are involved.
- Central role played by the president (local GP) and the coordinator.
- Individual knowledge of each case in the local area: old people and their families feel trust.
- From the users' point of view, coordination is 'invisible'; only the services received are 'visible'.
- From the professionals' point of view, coordination is joint working.

F2

CLIC in Phalempin

- A large area: many old people and many professionals.
- Coordination is not very well identified by old people and key workers.
- Coordination is focused on the link between hospital and home.
- Coordination promotes a common gerontological culture at the organisational level.
- The coordinator is only one actor among others.

D1

Home Care Nürnberg (HCN) – Praxisnetz Nürnberg Nord (PNN)

In the District Nürnberg North (120,000 inhabitants) HCN, established in 2000, is a regional organisation for coordination and cooperation of health and social care organisations. It is run by the PNN, involving 180 practitioners (generalists and specialists), one hospital under contract and others in cooperation.

Case management includes the cooperation of all regional health care providers, which are needed to optimise the quality of health care. HCN is the first physician-induced and reimbursed case-management system in Germany.

Type of integration/coordination
Sector bridging, interdisciplinary, integrative system of case management: individual and structural integration of medical, care, social and private services including administrative support.

315

Objectives
The Practitioners Network Nürnberg focuses at patient orientation, a holistic approach and the voluntary integration of health care.

On the individual level, HCN's case management is focusing on information, advocacy, empowerment and social support.

HCN's case management on the structural level is focusing on gatekeeping, bridging structural gaps between medicine, care, social care and administration, and network management.

The aims are
- to offer clients in need of care the possibility to stay at home by means of integrated care arrangements (with the help of a case manager),
- to improve and guarantee the offer of health and social care organisations in the district,
- to help clients and their families to find the appropriate organisation according to their needs,
- to start and develop support and training programmes for family carers.

Methods
- PNN – health passport.
- Prolonged opening hours on weekends and evenings.
- Guidelines (blood pressure, diabetes, cold, depression).
- Coordination with hospitals.
- Use of external clinical pathways.
- Coordination and quality management systems within the net.

HCN:
- Needs analysis on the district level.
- Information centre for clients and their relatives.
- Integrated provision of home nursing, family care, meals-on-wheels, visiting services and health prevention (contracts between different providers).
- Regular communication with GPs.
- Regular visits at the hospital and discharge management.
- Case management (Resident Assessment Instrument, own screening and assessment instruments, electronic data evaluation, data-based information broker).

Results (strengths and weaknesses)
- The HCN is the first overall health care integrative project in Germany, which has succeeded to overcome the project status and to continue as a reimbursed service within the PNN.
- The future of HCN is dependent on its ability to demonstrate its effects on the clients' quality of life and on the efficiency within the PNN but until now no tools are existing with which these effects can be measured.

Address
Home Care Nürnberg, Vogelsgarten 1, D-90402 Nürnberg

D2

*Geronto-Psychiatric-Geriatric Association in Oberspreewald-Lausitz
(GPGV OSL)*

The district Oberspreewald-Lausitz (Land Brandenburg) has 139,062 in-habitants, 27.6% of them are over 60; there are about 1,600 people suffering from dementia.

Members of the 'GPGV OSL' include a hospital with a geriatric and psychiatric section and psychotherapy, a hospital with a psychiatric section and psychotherapy, 9 out-patient services, 7 old-age and nursing homes, 2 advisory and mediation offices, and, in an advisory capacity, the district administration, especially the health department and social department, the health insurance (AOK) and the medical service of the health insurances. Yearly budget: around € 25.000.

General description

The 'GPGV OSL' has developed from a project of the Alzheimer Society Brandenburg, ('Alzheimer Gesellschaft Brandenburg e.V.') in cooperation with the Polytechnique Lausitz/Department of Sociology (Fachhochschule Lausitz). The project started in 2000 and ended 2003. It was sponsored by the Federal Ministry of Family, Senior Citizens, Women and Youth (Bunde-sministerium für Familie, Senioren, Frauen und Jugend). Since May 2003 it is financed by its members and sponsored by the administrative district (Landkreis). The organisation aims to improve the local provision of infor-mation, advice, treatment and care for older people in need of care as well as for their families.

Objectives
- Providing information and transparency for users of services as well as for all facilities being involved in the care process.
- Improving cooperation in favour of the user (overcoming problems at the interfaces in Public Health).
- Elaborating on cooperation structures.
- Establishing a knowledge basis and activities concerning advice, treat-ment, care and welfare services by professional personnel, based on the latest findings in research on dementia and related diseases.

- Developing a forum in order to follow changes in the need situation and to encourage innovative care provision for people suffering from dementia.

Type of integration / coordination

- Integration of out-patient, partially in-patient and in-patient services.
- The association employs a coordinator (19,25 h / week) whose task is, among others, to prepare, coordinate and present the quarterly conferences of the association in which a representative of each member of the GPGV takes part. The coordinator is supported by three spokesmen ('Verbundsprecher'): one representative of the in-patient services, the out-patient services and the hospitals, respectively. They are elected by the associations' members for one year and represent the 'GPGV OSL' in public.

Methods

- Evaluation of the local support structures and living conditions of older people.
- Documentation and provision of important information to the association, older people and their families.
- Establishment and maintenance of the local association structure.
- Conferences of the association (quarterly) and subject-related working groups.
- Offers for further education for members of the association and family carers.
- Transition sheet.
- Case conferences.
- Quality management.
- Public relations.
- Case management.

Results

- The cooperation between the different services / facilities is much better than before, especially due to the mutually-agreed and developed transition sheet ('Pflegeüberleitungsbogen'). The transition sheet is used in an increasing manner in order to submit basic patient information as well as special data concerning geronto-psychiatric diseases beyond the medical treatment levels. It aims to facilitate a smooth transition between the different treatment levels. Apart from the utilisation of the transition sheet, the employees of the discharging and the receiving facilities get into personal contact or contact by phone in order to guarantee a continuous medical treatment.

- Every member of the association is well informed about other services / facilities in the care sector (a handbook of existing provisions was disseminated); this way, they can give advice according to the individual needs of their clients.
- Many professionals (e.g. nurses) but also many informal carers attended further training.
- Many people in the district – especially older people and their families – are reached by the public relations activities. They regularly receive information about gerontopsychiatric and geriatric diseases, local services / facilities. The association also represents the interests of older people suffering from dementia and their families in public discussions.

319

Address
GPGV OSL, Kirchstr. 8, D-03205 Calau

EL1

Open Care Centres for Older People (KAPI) in Alimos, Marousi, Ilioupoli and Nea Philadelphia

The Local Authorities (Municipal Social Services) of Alimos, Marousi, Ilioupoli and Nea Philadelphia (all situated in the larger Athens area) are characterised by the following demographic aspects (2001):

Municipality	total inhabitants	inhabitants +60 years (%)	Men +60 years (%)	Women +60 years (%)
Alimos	38,047	7,837 (20.59%)	3,391 (18.91%)	4,443 (22.08%)
Marousi	69,470	14,319 (20.61%)	6,301 (19.51%)	8,018 (21.56%)
Ilioupoli	75,904	15,569 (20.51%)	6,759 (18.61%)	8,810 (22.25%)
Nea Philadelphia	24,112	5,131 (21.27%)	2,136 (18.69%)	2,995 (23.61%)

Source: www.statistics.gr

Structural features of the KAPIs

Municipality	staff	no. of registered users	yearly budget
KAPI Alimos	1 social worker, 1 health visitor, 1 physiotherapist, 1 ergotherapist, 1 family assistant and 2 GPs on contract basis	550	140,000 €
KAPI Marousi	2 social workers, 3 nurses , 1 physiotherapist, 1 administrative employee, 4 family assistants	3,500	368,828 €
KAPI Ilioupoli	1 social worker, 1 nurse, 2 health visitors, 1 physiotherapist, 2 family assistants	2,500	710,000 €
KAPI Nea Philadelphia	1 social worker, 2 health visitors, 2 physiotherapists and 4 family assistants	3,150	250,000 €

320

General description and organisational context

In 1979 the Directorate for the Protection of Elderly Persons of the Ministry of Health and Welfare, in cooperation with the Association of Volunteer Workers set up a pilot Open Care Centre for Elderly Persons (hereafter referred to as 'KAPI' following the Greek abbreviation and the scheme of care for older people). A year later, these centres were institutionalised and by the end of 1981, eight relevant programmes were operating with the contribution of volunteer organisations, the Greek Red Cross (GRC) and the Christian Youth Organisation (CYO). With Law N. 1416/84, article 68, the state transferred the responsibility of their management and operation to the local authorities. Currently they are spread all over the country with a total number of 607 centres.

KAPI are Public Legal Entities managed by a 7-member Board of Directors. They are funded by the municipality to which they belong and they have their own budget. They operate in proper houses of the Municipalities. Elderly users are involved in programme planning and implementation via their representative in the KAPI governing board. The 'Unified Organization of KAPI' operates in each municipality and there are different sub-centres in accordance with the needs of the older population and budgetary constraints.

Type of integration/coordination

The most essential service of the KAPI centres is the integration of older people into the community: KAPIs are considered as areas of social intervention. The model emphasises the neighborhood and its social capital in re-building social solidarity. KAPIs might be more social (preventative) than medical. There is a "one stop shop" approach (all personnel can be found in the same facilities) that ensures better use of available resources and improved care of older people. KAPIs as a kind of horizontal integration (provider mix) have been partly implemented.

Objectives

- To facilitate care at home and improve the quality of life of older people.
- To provide care to older persons helping them to maintain their independence and their physical and psychological condition to the greatest possible extent.
- To reduce residential care demand.

- To support family carers.
- To raise the awareness of the neighbourhood and of society in general to promote support of older people and development of voluntary services at municipal level.

Methods
- Social participation actions, through which the team tries to alleviate the feeling of loneliness of older people by providing them with opportunities to discuss, communicate, develop various hobbies and feel useful and necessary for their families and society.
- Preventive medicine, divided into primary (vaccinations, advice relating to healthy eating habits, etc) and secondary (performance of medical tests aiming at early diagnosis in order to avoid frequently lengthy treatments).
- Active participation of older people through the creation of activity teams corresponding to their interests (theatre, choir, traditional dances, and gymnastics).
- Staging of cultural and recreational activities (excursions, camping, attending various events, etc).
- Turning their skills and experience to advantage.
- Promoting awareness of the community and solidarity between generations. Creation of links and cooperation with other bodies (Popular Education Committees, schools, cultural associations) in order to jointly organise activities and bridge the generation gap.

Results (strengths and weaknesses)
- Responsible for the development and implementation of this institution are local authorities, which have first-hand knowledge of the needs and particularities of older people living in their area.
- The network of KAPI covers most of Greece. Older people have expressed positive opinions and welcomed the creation of KAPI.
- There is significant participation of older people in recreational and cultural activities.
- KAPI are linked to the 'IKA' (Public Insurance Fund) in order to cover their members' needs, no matter which insurance fund they originally belong to.

- Lack of cooperation and integration between the KAPI and other organizations. Integrated services are partly implemented, depending upon informal networks.
- Lack of a mechanism of study, recording and permanent follow-up of the elderly population, in order to identify their needs and accordingly complete or modify the services provided.
- Insufficient staffing with scientific personnel.
- The lack of a central administrative structure ('Computerized Records'), in order to input all the data and facilitate structure evaluation and redesigning.
- Problems related to the buildings used (difficult access, inappropriate buildings).
- Limited financial resources impacting on the quality of available programmes, number of employees and opening hours.

Addresses

KAPI Alimos, Elefteriou Venizelou Street 37, EL-17456 Alimos

KAPI Marousi, Perikleous Street 22

KAPI Ilioupoli, Pantazh and Hvis Street

KAPI Nea Philadelphia, Dekelias Avenue 120, EL-14341 Nea Philadelphia

323

EL2

Help at home for elderly persons in Kifissia, Nikaia and Nea Ionia

From a considerable number of Help at Home Programmes in Greece, those of Kifissia, Nikaia and Nea Ionia in the larger Athens area have been chosen for analysis. The selection was underpinned by an effort to ensure a certain degree of balanced geographical and socio-economic distribution. The Municipality of Kifissia serves the northern suburbs of Athens, that of Nea Ionia the western suburbs, while Nikaia serves the southern suburbs of Pireus.

Statistical information on the municipalities

Municipality	total inhabitants	inhabitants +60 years (%)	Men +60 years (%)	Women +60 years (%)
Kifissia	43,929	10,060 (22.90%)	4,540 (22.06%)	5,520 (23.63%)
Nikaia	93,086	19,478 (20.92%)	8,302 (18.56%)	11,176 (23.11%)
Nea Ionia	66,017	13,024 (19.72%)	5,489 (17.33%)	7,535 (21.93%)

Source: www.statistics.gr

Structural features

Municipality	staff	no. of users/ informal carers	yearly budget*)
Help at Home Municipality of Kifissia	1 social worker, 2 nurses, 1 family assistant, 1 administrative employee, 1 GP and 1 driver on contract basis	43 users and 20 informal carers	n.a.
Help at Home Municipality of Nikaia	1 social worker, 2 nurses, 3 family assistants	55 users and 39 informal carers	81,936.90 €
Help at Home Municipality of Nea Ionia	1 social worker, 1 nurse, 2 family assistants	70 users and 10-15 informal carers	approx. for salaries 3,000 €

Note: Funded by the State and European Community Funds (3rd Common Support Framework).

General description and organisational context
'Help at Home' was institutionalised by Law N. 2082/92 and is implemented by the Ministry of Health in cooperation with Local Authorities, the Church and Non-Governmental/Voluntary Organisations. Help at Home Programmes are closely linked to the Open Care Centres for Older People of each municipality, while the programme as a whole is coordinated and evaluated by a Monitoring Committee. Today, there are 284 'Help at Home' programmes in 253 municipalities in operation. The services provided are free of charge.

Objectives
The aim of the programme is to promote, maximise and restore, to the greatest possible extent, the independence of elderly persons, providing them with support and help so as to avoid physical disability, exclusion from social participation and confinement.

In the framework of primary care, the services provided by the programme aim at supporting elderly persons and their families so they can cope with the increased needs of their condition, temporarily or permanently, and continue to be together with their families and remain part of their social environment.

Methods
- Social services (consulting and psychosocial support, information concerning rights of older people and contacts with health, welfare and insurance organisations).
- Health care services (medical and nursing care, health education and prevention, medication prescription, physiotherapy at home, accompaniment to see the physician).
- Family assistance (home and personal care, feeding, chores, keeping of company, etc.)
- The person-centredness of the programme: The team providing services to the older people operates as a coordinated team fully aware of the users' condition.

Results (strengths and weaknesses)
- The major advantage of the service is the fact that the user remains at home and does not change his/her daily habits. He/she stays near his/her family and friends and does not get isolated.

- Team communication, informal communication processes.
- Good relationship between clients and employees: Open communication channels between clients and staff.
- The scheme is an interesting experiment of public policy and public cooperation. It unites in a 'tripartite model' the Ministry of Health and Welfare, the Ministry of the Interior and the Municipalities as the third actor responsible for organising and providing services.
- The programme does not foresee a formal joint working/seamless care process. The staff operates on an informal, voluntary and non-institutionalized basis.
- Inability to cover all requests and needs due to lack of time and personnel: Time pressure, shortage of resources and personnel.
- There is no centralised information system.
- Personnel works on contract basis and does not enjoy job security.
- No specialised training.

Addresses:
- Help at Home Municipality of Kifissia, Dionusou 58 and Spartis, EL-14261 Kifissia
- Help at Home Municipality of Nikaia, P. Tsaldari Street 10, EL-18353 Nikaia
- Help at Home Municipality of Nea Ionia, Hroon Kalogrezas Street 51-53, EL-14234 Kalogreza

I1

Working Unit of Continuous Care (WUCC) in the Province of Vicenza

The Local Health Unit 4 gathers several municipalities in the Province of Vicenza with 176,609 inhabitants, 41,807 (23,7%) of whom are over 60 years of age (2003). From its foundation (in June 2000) till September 2003, WUCC provided care services to 1,740 older people.

Staff involved: the director of the geriatric department, the social worker of the hospital, a professional nurse (responsible for data collection and nursing assessment). During the patient's needs assessment a physiotherapist and the nurse of the unit where the older person was cared for are also involved.

Half of the patients are discharged after less than 9 days.

Yearly budget: € 91,000 (estimate, because the budget of WUCC is a part of the overall budget of the geriatric unit).

327

General description and organisational context
The service, established in 2000, is, in fact, a Geriatric Assessment Unit, composed by health and social workers but is organised within the hospitals of Thiene and Schio (Province of Vicenza), rather than by the Health District. The WUCC has the duty to overlook an older person's hospital discharge, by organising and providing continuous and integrated health and social care follow-up. The social worker, uncommon within Italian hospitals, represents the interface between the hospital and the outside. Her fundamental role is to keep in touch with caregivers and with the municipal social worker in order to plan and prepare an older person's discharge from hospital.

Type of integration/coordination
Vertical integration of social and health care professionals

Objectives
* To guarantee the well-being of a patient with chronic diseases, answering in a coherent and effective way to the client's real needs.
* To develop and maintain patients' residual capabilities, guaranteeing their dignity and autonomy.

- To take charge of the subject (creating virtual circles and conducting him/her along this pathway).
- To reduce avoidable admissions to the hospital.
- To rationalise resource exploitation (using the best resource with less costs).

Methods

- Use of instruments and forms readable by professionals at every level (nurses, doctors, social worker, ...).
- Communication of the multi-dimensional assessment results to the municipality (local district and general practitioner).
- Team meetings to define an individual project in short time.
- Second assessment to evaluate the results of the project.
- Motto: 'Always a solution before discharge'.
- Professionals' kindness and patience.

Results (strengths and weaknesses)

- The care plan is the result of an interdisciplinary effort and represents a real project as it takes into account all resources actually available in the area, rather than drawing on an ideal but unrealistic solution.

  "The WUCC is a circuit way of working where the start coincides with the end. When a user is intercepted, he/she enters the circuit and he/she is guided through it until he/she finds a solution to his/her problem"(key worker)

- The service adopts a multi-dimensional and multi-professional approach to seamless care, techniques of project management, written procedures and forms.

  "The WUCC realizes integration using multi-dimensional assessment instruments usable by everyone, validated at the international level, filled by single professionals and then discussed to define a common goal."(key worker)

- The WUCC is not evident: users and almost all carers do not recognize it as a service, their satisfaction is not related to the WUCC but to single key workers.

  "Nobody has explained the service, nor was I told about the specific function of it. I had never heard about it, I got in touch with doctor G. (the geriatric primary division) by chance, when my mother was staying overnight." (carer)

- The WUCC is strongly identified with its promoter (the geriatrician) and depends on the cooperation and collaboration among different professionals.

  "The main weakness is doctors' lack of humility, It could also fail because of a low level of professionalism as the WUCC requires professionalism at every level."(key worker)

Address

Unità Operativa di Continuità Assistenziale (UOCA), Azienda ULSS 4 Alto Vicentino, Via Camillo De Lellis 1, I-36015 Schio

I2

Single Point of Access to Home Care in Empoli (Tuscany)

The Local Health Agency no. 11 in Empoli District (Tuscany) covers 221,787 inhabitants, 45,000 (20%) of which are over 65 years of age (2002). The professionals involved in the Single Point of Access are 4 district doctors (one doctor is also the coordinator of the service), 9 physiotherapists, 54 nurses full-time and 2 nurses part-time, 1 nurse coordinator, 15 social assistants, and 8 socio-medical assistants (*OSS=operatori socio-sanitari*).

The target group are all persons with health and social care needs. From January till September 2003 the total number of users was 703 of which there were 435 users with a low level of problems, 179 users with a medium level of problems, and 89 users with a high level of problems. Furthermore, 587 persons used the Single Point of Access for general information or particular matters, e.g. needing medical aids without further care services.

General description and organisational context
In 1998, in order to facilitate the collaboration between the professionals involved in home care services, the Local Health Agency (LHA) 11 of Empoli developed a protocol of protected discharge from hospital. To facilitate the access to home care, the LHA has activated, as an experiment, a Single Point of Access situated in the Empoli District, to which the requests for integrated home care (IHC) are addressed, including the requests from hospital departments. Last but not least, in order to create an efficient collaboration between the operators, a unified information system has been introduced for all provisions in the territory.

Type of integration/coordination
Horizontal and vertical integration of social and health care.

Objectives
- To restrict hospitalisation to the acute phase.
- To decrease the average hospitalisation period for pathologies that can also – or better – be treated at home.
- To increase the survival rate.
- To increase the efficiency and effectiveness of home care.
- To increase the satisfaction of the client / patient.

- Furthermore , the Single Point of Access gathers all requests for home care in one single information desk, thus facilitating the immediate activation of interventions. In the future two new information desks will be opened and citizens will have the possibility to address their needs directly (front office, person-to-person).
- In addition, the centralised information system traces every citizen that is being assisted by either the GP, social and health services, a hospital, or by rehabilitation services through one unique users' archive that is constantly updated. In the future it will be possible to access a database, also by mobile phones or palm-top computers.

Methods
- Protocols, agreements (unique way of working, defined processes).
- Single Point of Access (one-stop window).
- Needs analysis on the district level.
- Territorial Assessment Unit (TAU) to define the individualised programme of interventions (multidimensional and multiprofessional needs assessment).
- Unified information system: computer net of software and hardware able to manage all the activities carried out on the territory.
- Multiprofessional team.

Results (strengths and weaknesses)
- Integration and coordination of provisions.
- Procedural simplification of taking the patient in charge.
- Facilitation of patients' return back home after discharge from hospital.
- Simplification of the relationship between hospitals and territorial (community care) services.

The success of this system is defined by the agreements between the Local Health Agency that is in charge of the health services and the municipalities that are in charge of the social services (delegated management for the Empolese-Valdelsa area; protocol to manage the social and health services for older persons in need of care in the Valdarno area).

However, it is difficult to coordinate the interventions maintaining 'the centrality of the person' due to limited resources (money, workers) and few incentives for staff delivering home care compared to people working in hospitals or private care facilities.

331

As a corollary, cooperation between the municipality and the hospital as well as the relationship between doctors and non-medical workers should be improved.

The strengths of the centralised information system:

- The database is available on the net for all professionals involved in health and social services: thus collaboration is facilitated and the information passages between the offices are reduced.
- Administration and bureaucracy are simplified.
- The data of citizens are gathered and entered only once.
- Both territorial and hospital services are put on-line.

A weakness of the system is that it necessitates a specific software that, in this case, is provided by one particular company only. Furthermore, there is still resistance from professionals both concerning the integration of working methods and the use of computer systems to communicate.

Address

Distretto Socio-Sanitario di Empoli, Azienda USL 11 Empoli (FI), Via Rozzalupi, 57, I-50053 Empoli (FI)

NL1

Home Care Facility 'Zijloever' in Leiden

Zijloever was established in 1990 as an innovative project in the care provision for elderly citizens in Leiden, a city with almost 120,000 inhabitants, 11% of which are over 65 years of age. It offers a comprehensive package of services to its clients (including 24-hour care), comparable with care in residential homes for older people, but clients continue living in their own homes.

Zijloever is a rather small organisation, with approximately 135 clients and 80 staff members (50 FTE), and a yearly budget of 2.15 million Euro.

Type of integration/coordination
Horizontal integration of social care provision, including services for well-being, and partial coordination with health care providers (GP's and hospitals).

Objective
- To offer around-the-clock care to older people that are entitled for intramural care, aiming at reinforcement of their independent living at home.

Methods
- Provision of information and needs analysis for new clients.
- Integrated provision of personal care and domiciliary care.
- Cooperation with other service providers (services for well-being, home nursing, pharmaceutical services, physiotherapists).
- Communication with general practitioners, hospitals and nursing homes.

Results (strengths and weaknesses)
- Care provision is well-coordinated, flexible and tuned to the needs of the clients.
- The whole chain of care is made accessible to the clients, permitting them to stay in their own homes.
- Information exchange with medical service providers (general practitioners and hospitals) is often inadequate.

Address
Julianastraat 74, NL-2316 NZ Leiden

NL2

Chain of Care for Older People in Kerkrade, Landgraaf and Simpelveld

This model consists of three components: the assessment agency (RIO), the Bureau for Care Allocation and Referral (BCAR) and the organisations that provide care. The bureau for care allocation is the main focus of our study but its function has to be seen in relation to and in collaboration with the other two components. Together they provide integrated care for older people in the region Kerkrade, Landgraaf and Simpelveld (three cities in the southern province of Limburg), the KLS-region. The unique character of this model lies in the fact that many organisations work together to provide the necessary care for older people from the moment the need arises to the moment a client receives care. It is a comprehensive model in which medical and social care are combined with activities to enhance the well-being not only of older people but also of their carers. It has been created in order to streamline the care process for older people from beginning to end, striving to provide a client-oriented service.

Type of integration/coordination
Horizontal and vertical integration of social and health care with well-being.

Objectives
- To offer patients one location for care requests from the moment a need arises to the moment when care is given.
- To assist older people and their families with information and decision-making on the choice of care.
- To streamline the process and provision of care, cure and well-being services.
- To provide substitute care and diminish waiting lists for care services.

Methods
- Integration of cure, care and well-being for older people.
- One contact point for requests for needs assessment, allocation and provision of care, cure and well-being.

- BCAR as link between the needs assessment agency and providers of services and products in care, cure and well-being.
- Informing and supporting clients and their families in their choice of services and products.
- Case management per component.

Results (strengths and weaknesses)
- BCAR and the providers of services and products have succeeded in coordinating their efforts to provide care, cure and well-being.
- Older people and their informal carers are generally positive about the care they receive.
- Vertical integration between care assessment agency and BCAR is not successful.

Address
Zorgtoewijzingsbureau Kerkrade, Landgraaf en Simpelveld, Sintpieterstraat 143, NL-6463 CS, Kerkrade

UK1

Limes Livingstone Integrated Care Project (LLICP), Dartford, Kent

The LLICP is situated in Dartford, a town which is about 18 miles southeast of London. It is part of Dartford, Gravesham and Swanley Primary Care Trust (DGSPCT). This is a local health care organisation, which serves a population of 240,000, of whom 20% (approximately 48,000) are over retirement age. The Primary Care Trust works closely with the local NHS acute hospital and Kent Social Services to provide seamless, integrated care for older people in the area.

The LLICP has about 90 staff (WTE). They provide 24-hour nursing, rehabilitation and social care at Limes recuperative care centre (26 beds) and Livingstone hospital (38 beds).

The combined annual budget is in the region of 2.48 million EUR (£1.6million). The Primary Care Trust (health sector) funds Livingstone hospital, and Limes recuperative care centre is funded by Kent Social Services. They have some jointly funded posts.

General description and organisational context
The Limes Livingstone Integrated Care Project (LLICP) is a partnership project, initiated by DGSPCT and Kent Social Services. The project developed because there was pressure on beds at the acute hospital, whilst the Livingstone community hospital beds were under-used. The Livingstone hospital is on the same site as the Limes recuperative care centre, which provides short-term (up to 6 weeks) intensive rehabilitation programmes for older people who wish to return home to independent living. Senior managers developed a strategy for an integrated or 'partnership' project, to involve both Limes centre and Livingstone hospital working together for older people.

Type of integration/coordination
Both Limes and Livingstone provide 'intermediate care'. This is multidisciplinary rehabilitation care, which is geared towards assisting older people regain their independence and return to living in their own homes.

The strategic integration is both horizontal (across social services, acute health services and the primary care sector) and vertical (involving the strategic health authority, the local council, the acute and community hospital and a number of agencies that provide ongoing care to older people).

Objectives

- To provide rehabilitation (nursing support, occupational therapy, physiotherapy, medical oversight, social support and 24-hour care) to older people who are recovering from surgery or acute health problems (falls, illness, stroke) so that they become able to return home to independent or supported living.
- To reduce pressure on acute hospital beds and reduce the uptake of residential/nursing care beds (long-term placement in an institutionalised setting).
- To help patients manage at home safely (preventing re-admission to hospital) and provide the optimum level of support to patients and their immediate family carers.

Methods of care integration

- Each client is assessed by the multi-disciplinary team, and an individualised programme of rehabilitation therapy is developed and implemented.
- At the Limes centre, therapy is provided every weekday morning.
- At the Livingstone hospital, nursing care is provided continuously and therapists visit several times a week.
- A 'care manager' works for both centres. This role includes liaison with individual clients, their families and the teams at the centres. Discharges are carefully planned, with home visits for safety assessment, and equipment or adaptations put in place before the client returns home.
- The LLICP receives medical support from local GPs and hospital consultants.
- The project has developed the role of 'generic rehabilitation worker'. These support workers are trained to help clients with their physiotherapy, occupational therapy and nursing programmes of care.
- Livingstone nurses provide nursing care to clients at the Limes.

Results (strengths and weaknesses)

- LLICP staff are able to deliver effective rehabilitation assessment and care to older people.

- Staff reported high levels of work satisfaction, because of the variety of work, and because they could see their clients getting better and going home:

  "It's nice to be in a setting where you can see them progress, where you can see them getting on, and that they are actually going home."

  "The best thing about working (here) is helping someone to get back home when they really want to."

- Role of generic worker is well developed, with good training provision. This enhances the level of rehabilitation care at LLICP.
- Innovative nursing role has emerged, with ward nurses providing community nursing to Limes clients.
- Service users feel well cared for and are pleased with the progress that they make:

  "I can't find words to explain. It just seems out of this world that there's a place like this that exists to help me walk again."

- The service achieves a high rate of discharge home to independent living (however the long-term outcomes for clients have not been evaluated).
- LLICP is under pressure to accept admissions from the acute sector, and this means that patients who are too heavily dependent (on nursing or social care) to benefit from rehabilitation are admitted there.
- Staff identified weaknesses of resource provision. They felt that there was not enough physiotherapy input at the centre. Service users also noted this.
- Continuing problems of financial and contractual differences between the health and social care organisations involved meant that the goal of true integration (joint funding, recruitment and shared staff) had not yet been achieved. The negotiation process continues however.
- Some service users reported feeling isolated at home after receiving 24-hour care and support during their stays at LLICP.

Address

Limes Livingstone Integrated Care Project, c/o Dartford, Gravesham and Swanley Primary Care Trust

UK2

Shepway Community Assessment and Rehabilitation Team (CART)

The population of Shepway is approximately 102,000 with about 10% aged 75 or over. The area has a number of towns including Folkestone and Hythe, as well as coastal and rural villages on the Romney Marsh.

Whilst the South-East of England is relatively well off in financial terms compared to other areas of the UK, some areas within the Shepway PCT (e.g. Folkestone and Hythe) have high levels of deprivation (www.odpm. gov.uk/indices). Part of the local strategy for meeting the needs of older people is the provision of high-quality integrated services to older people in the community, and the local health and social care agencies have been particularly supportive of community-based initiatives such as CART and Rapid Response nursing.

The CART team was established in 1999. There are approximately 18 staff (WTE) who provide the service for up to 50 clients at a time. The CART team budget is about € 769,000 (£519,000) per annum, and the source of funding is the health sector, although social services fund the care management post.

General description and organisational context

In the UK, the 'CART' model is an established type of integrated care, with some teams being formed as long as 20 years ago. CART means 'Community Assessment and Rehabilitation Team'. These teams often operate from the health sector, and are usually housed within hospitals. The teams are made up of multi-disciplinary professionals including physiotherapists, nurses, occupational therapists and rehabilitation support workers. There is usually a Social Services care manager attached to the team. CART team members visit clients in the community following referral, and provide rehabilitation input in the client's own home, usually on a short-term basis (approximately 4 weeks).

Shepway CART was established in 1999, and is a particularly well-developed example of a community team for older people. The aims of CART team intervention are to maximise the older person's independence at home, and prevent hospital admission – for example, if an older person is becoming less mobile or prone to falls, then the CART team can offer rehabilitation support. The CART team also becomes involved with some older people to speed up discharge from hospital, and help people become safe and independent at home.

A parallel development in the Shepway area has been the formation of a 'Rapid Response' team. This team also attends older people at home, but is designed to offer short-term (up to 2 weeks) nursing and care support to older people who become unwell (but not acutely ill) at home. The rapid response team can provide care for up to 24 hours a day, and can help older people with dementia, or who have a carer crisis. CART and Rapid Response work closely together, providing a range of specialist nursing, medical and rehabilitation care to older people in their own homes.

Type of integration/coordination

The Shepway CART team is an 'intermediate care' initiative, designed to provide rehabilitation care to older people in the community and prevent hospital admission or hasten hospital discharge.

Integration is mainly horizontal. The core team is multi-disciplinary, and liaises closely with the acute health sector (consultant-led hospitals) and the primary care team (GPs and district nurses). There is also integration with Social Services care managers and family carers, and the services liaise with a wide range of voluntary sector organisations.

Objectives

- To assist clients to reach maximum levels of independence.
- To prevent hospital admission (or re-admission).
- To help older people get home from hospital quickly by providing holistic rehabilitation care.
- To extend access to specialist services for older people at home and in rural areas.
- To foster the integration of voluntary organisations (the 'voluntary sector') in the community care of older people.
- To facilitate integration of older people's health and social care providers.
- To support and train community rehabilitation assistants, and develop the role of multi-disciplinary professionals working in the community.

Methods

- Each client is given a comprehensive general assessment. The multi-disciplinary team worker whose skills are most relevant to their case also carries out a specialist assessment.
- The professional key worker then designs an individualised plan of care for the client.
- Professionals or support workers visit the client daily, to help the client with his/her activities and implement the rehabilitation exercises. Visits take between 30 minutes and 2 hours.
- CART team members have the support of a consultant physician and can arrange rapid access to outpatient clinics or even home visits by the consultant if medical assessment is required.
- The CART team meets weekly with Social Services care management and plans ongoing care, arranges home aids or equipment, and manages client discharge.

Results

- The Shepway CART team had developed a strong model of integrated care, and the opportunity to work along side both the hospital and the rapid response team made the service very comprehensive:

  "We are an integrated network of professional people, in a small environment, serving a large environment. We've become an epicentre for communication of information for not only ourselves as a team but for our patients."

- The team members reported high levels of job satisfaction, because they were able to deliver effective rehabilitation care and help their clients to remain independent:

  "It's about their quality of life – we had a lady who needed someone to feed her. We made her independent again."

- The CART team also felt they were able to offer 'person-centred' care:

  "Once the clients have got to know us, they might say to a rehab worker, 'well, I'd really like to do that ...' and then we can refocus our goals to facilitate that. I think that's a really good part of our service."

- Service users also reported that the CART team had made a difference to them:

  "To me it was a lifesaver. I've got nothing but praise for what they did for me. They made me feel that I wanted to go on a bit longer."

- Staff from the CART team identified that the differences between professions had been ironed out over time:

  "Part of our success is how people have learned how to negotiate the way they work ...we are truly inter-professional, not multi-professional, because of the way we negotiate the care that we provide for clients."

  "In this setting there is a blurring of our roles. If a crisis or problem does arise, I've got to address those issues, but I will seek the advice of a nurse or a physiotherapist if the issue involves their area."

- The CART team is able to offer continuity of care, because a named professional manages care, and the same team members go to visit clients every day.

- The CART team felt that good communication was central to their success:

  "Within the team, we have good communication skills, and with the rapid response as well – we can link in with other people."

- Having enough time to spend with people was also seen as being important:

  "We have got time to sit and discuss things with patients that you don't get on the ward and that makes a difference."

- The main weakness identified by staff was that the service was limited to 4-6 weeks:

  "We're only going in there for four to six weeks and there are some things you can't achieve in that time. You can't rush people."

- Service users also found that this could be a problem:

  "They stopped coming in directly he'd finished respite. There's no follow up, nothing."

- There was concern that some older people might not be offered the CART service, if their GPs were not aware of the service or of how to make a referral.

- Funding for the service was uncertain, because of national policy changes to the structure of health care provision

- There was a shortage of physiotherapists and occupational therapists, and this made recruitment difficult. The team is small so there are few opportunities for career progression, which meant that experienced staff might leave to achieve promotion.

Address

Shepway CART, Royal Victoria Hospital, Radnor Park Avenue, Folkestone CT19 5BN

List of Contributors

Natalia Alba, Researcher at emmeerre S.p.A., Padua

Sirpa Andersson, Researcher at the National Research and Development Centre for Welfare and Health (STAKES), Helsinki

Dominique Argoud, Sociologist, Professor in Educational Sciences at the University of Paris XII

Steen Bengtsson, Sociologist, Senior Researcher at the Danish National Institute of Social Research

Jenny Billings, Research Fellow at the Centre for Health Service Studies at the University of Kent in Canterbury

Francesca Ceruzzi, Sociologist, Senior Researcher and Consultant at Studio Come s.r.l., Rome

Cécile Chartreau, Researcher at the "Union nationale interfédérale des œuvres et organismes privés sanitaires et sociaux" (UNIOPSS), Paris

Thomas Clausen, Political Scientist, Researcher at the Danish National Institute of Social Research, Copenhagen

Kirstie Coxon, Research Associate at the Centre for Health Service Studies at the University of Kent in Canterbury

Klaas Gorter, Social Psychologist, Researcher at Verwey-Jonker Institute, Institute for Research into Social Issues, Utrecht

Margit Grilz-Wolf, Researcher at the European Centre for Social Welfare Policy and Research, Vienna

Marie-Jo Guisset, Gerontologist, Consultant for the "Union nationale inter-fédérale des oeuvres et organismes privés sanitaires et sociaux" (UNIOPSS) and at the "Fondation Médéric Alzheimer", Paris

Riitta Haverinen, Development Manager, Head of the Evaluation of Social Services Group at the National Research and Development Centre for Welfare and Health (STAKES), Helsinki

Andrea Kuhlmann, Gerontologist, Researcher at the Institute of Gerontology at the University of Dortmund, "Forschungsgesellschaft für Gerontologie e.V."

Kai Leichsenring, Political Scientist and Consultant in Organisational Development, Research Associate at the European Centre for Social Welfare Policy and Research

Maili Malin, Medical Sociologist, working with the National Research and Development Centre for Welfare and Health (STAKES), Helsinki

Laura Maratou-Alipranti, Sociologist, Senior Researcher at the National Centre for Social Research (EKKE), Athens

Giorgia Nesti, Political Scientist, Researcher at emmeerre S.p.A., Padua

Monika Reichert, Psychologist, Professor at the Institute of Gerontology at the University of Dortmund, "Forschungsgesellschaft für Gerontologie e.V."

Günter Roth, Chair in Social Management at the University of Applied Science of the German Red Cross, Göttingen, "Forschungsgesellschaft für Gerontologie e.V.", Institute of Gerontology at the University of Dortmund

Aris Sissouras, Professor of Operational Research at the University of Patras

Charlotte Strümpel, Psychologist, Senior Researcher at the European Centre for Social Welfare Policy and Research, Vienna

Nasrin Tabibian, Educational Scientist, Senior Researcher at the Verwey-Jonker Institute, Utrecht

Aphrodite Teperoglou, Political Scientist, Director of Research at the Institute of Social Policy of the National Center of Social Research (EKKE), Athens

Eftichia Teperoglou, Political Scientist, Junior Researcher at the National Centre for Social Research (EKKE) and other institutions, Athens

Alain Villez, Technical Advisor concerning services and policies for older persons at the "Union nationale interfédérale des oeuvres et organismes privés sanitaires et sociaux" (UNIOPSS), Paris

Wohlfahrtspolitik und Sozialforschung
Herausgegeben vom Europäischen Zentrum Wien
mit dem Campus Verlag, Frankfurt am Main/New York

Campus Verlag, Postfach 90 02 63, D-60442 Frankfurt am Main
Tel: (069) 97 65 16-0; Fax: (069) 97 65 16
www.campus.de, info@campus.de, vertrieb@campus.de

Wohlfahrtspolitik und Sozialforschung
Herausgegeben vom Europäischen Zentrum Wien
mit dem Campus Verlag, Frankfurt am Main/New York

Band 9.1: DAVY, U. (Hg.) (2001)
Die Integration von Einwanderern.
Rechtliche Regelungen im europäischen Vergleich
1056 S., EUR 69,-

Band 9.2: WALDRAUCH, H. (2001)
Die Integration von Einwanderern.
Ein Index der rechtlichen Diskriminierung
582 S., EUR 51,-

Band 10: MARIN, B. (2000)
Antisemitismus ohne Antisemiten.
Autoritäre Vorurteile und Feindbilder
880 S., EUR 51,-

Band 11: KRÄNZL-NAGL, R., MIERENDORFF, J.,
OLK, Th. (Hg.) (2003)
Kindheit im Wohlfahrtsstaat.
Gesellschaftliche und politische Herausforderungen
474 S., EUR 34,90

Band 12: OECD (2003)
**Behindertenpolitik zwischen
Beschäftigung und Versorgung.**
Ein internationaler Vergleich
408 S., EUR 34,90

Band 13: ZARTLER, U., WILK, L.,
KRÄNZL-NAGL, R. (Hg.) (2004)
Wenn Eltern sich trennen.
Wie Kinder, Frauen und Männer Scheidung erleben
500 S., EUR 45,-

Band 14: WALDRAUCH, H., SOHLER, K. (2004)
Migrantenorganisationen in der Großstadt.
Entstehung, Strukturen und Aktivitäten am Beispiel Wien
708 S., EUR 59,90

Campus Verlag, Postfach 90 02 63, D-60442 Frankfurt am Main
Tel: (069) 97 65 16-0; Fax: (069) 97 65 16
www.campus.de, info@campus.de, vertrieb@campus.de

Public Policy and Social Welfare
A Series Edited by the European Centre Vienna
vols. 1-10 with Campus Verlag/Westview Press, Frankfurt am Main/Boulder, Co.

Publications Officer, European Centre, Berggasse 17, A-1090 Wien
Tel: (01) 319 45 05-27; Fax: (01) 319 45 05-19
www.euro.centre.org, stamatiou@euro.centre.org

Public Policy and Social Welfare
A Series Edited by the European Centre Vienna with
Ashgate, Aldershot, Brookfield USA, Singapore, Sydney

www.ashgate.com

Public Policy and Social Welfare
A Series Edited by the European Centre Vienna with Ashgate, Aldershot, Brookfield USA, Singapore, Sydney

www.ashgate.com